Praise for Turning Silver into Gold

"*Turning Silver into Gold* is a 'must read' for all those entrepreneurs who are considering entering the senior market. Through the great examples in a wide variety of business opportunities, Mary Furlong stimulates us to develop our own business ideas.

—*Jeannette de Noord, Senior Director at Philips Consumer Healthcare Solutions*

"Mary is an evangelist who has been selling the dream of the boomer/senior market for over twenty-five years. She understands the customer segment better than anyone, and this book reflects her insight."

—*Guy Kawasaki, Managing Director, Garage Technology Ventures and author of* The Art of the Start

"Dr. Mary Furlong is a true visionary. Her insights and market intelligence are consistently spot on and her notions about what to do and how to do it demand serious attention from start up entrepreneurs to Fortune 500 executives. In *Turning Silver into Gold* she has done a masterful job of revealing a broad range of timely and actionable paths to success. I heartily recommend this book to anyone interested in gaining a better understanding, and meeting the myriad needs, of a maturing population."

—*Ken Dychtwald, Ph.D., President of Age Wave, Author of* The Age Wave, Age Power, and The Power Years

"Mary Furlong's book has a social heart as well as a business sense. She is trying to assist people who are in business, but not simply for the sake of exploiting a market. Adding value to life is as important to her as it is to us at AARP."

—*From the Foreword by Bill Novelli, Chief Executive Officer, AARP*

"Mary Furlong is an expert on the Baby Boomer demographic as an academic, entrepreneur, and marketer. She has lots to teach about how to successfully reach and impact this enormous market."

—*Myrna Blyth, Founding Editor,* More Magazine

"Furlong displays a genuine grasp of boomer sensibilities, especially those of decency and happiness and the common good; when she speaks of value added, it is not just the markup but how the product or service adds to the pleasure of living right and well."

—**Kirkus Business & Personal Finance Report**

TURNING
SILVER
into GOLD

FINANCIAL TIMES

In an increasingly competitive world, it is quality
of thinking that gives an edge—an idea that opens new
doors, a technique that solves a problem, or an insight
that simply helps make sense of it all.

We work with leading authors in the various arenas
of business and finance to bring cutting-edge thinking
and best-learning practices to a global market.

It is our goal to create world-class print publications
and electronic products that give readers
knowledge and understanding that can then be
applied, whether studying or at work.

To find out more about our business
products, you can visit us at www.ftpress.com.

TURNING SILVER
into GOLD

HOW to PROFIT
in the new
BOOMER MARKETPLACE

MARY FURLONG

FT Press
FINANCIAL TIMES

Vice President and Editor-in-Chief: Tim Moore
Executive Editor/Acquisitions Editor: Jim Boyd
Editorial Assistant: Pamala Boland
Development Editor: Russ Hall
Associate Editor-in-Chief and Director of Marketing: Amy Neidlinger
Publicist: Amy Fandrei
Marketing Specialist: Megan Colvin
Cover Designer: Chuti Prasertsith
Managing Editor: Gina Kanouse
Project Editor: Michael Thurston
Copy Editor: Deadline-Driven Publishing
Indexer: Erika Millen
Compositor: Carlisle Publishing Services
Manufacturing Buyer: Dan Uhrig

© 2007 by Mary Furlong
Publishing as FT Press
Upper Saddle River, New Jersey 07458

FT Press offers excellent discounts on this book when ordered in quantity for bulk purchases or special sales. For more information, please contact U.S. Corporate and Government Sales, 1-800-382-3419, corpsales@pearsontechgroup.com. For sales outside the U.S., please contact International Sales at international@pearsontechgroup.com.

Company and product names mentioned herein are the trademarks or registered trademarks of their respective owners.

Printed in the United States of America

Second Printing, March 2007

ISBN: 0-13-185698-7

Pearson Education LTD.
Pearson Education Australia PTY, Limited.
Pearson Education Singapore, Pte. Ltd.
Pearson Education North Asia, Ltd.
Pearson Education Canada, Ltd.
Pearson Educatión de Mexico, S.A. de C.V.
Pearson Education—Japan
Pearson Education Malaysia, Pte. Ltd.

Library of Congress Cataloging-in-Publication Data

Furlong, Mary S.
Turning silver into gold : business and investment opportunities in the boomer marketplace/Mary Furlong.
    p. cm.
    ISBN 0-13-185698-7 (hardback : alk. paper) 1. Target marketing—United States.
2. Baby boom generation—United States. 3. Older consumers—United States. 4.
Consumer behavior—United States. 5. Investments—United States. I. Title.
    HF5415.127.F87 2006
    658.8—dc22

                            2006022287

With love and gratitude to Fred, Daniel,
Michael, and Mom.

CONTENTS

FOREWORD

For years, I have talked about the importance of the "longevity bonus," the wonderful possibilities and opportunities available to us resulting from our ability to live longer, more productive lives. So I was convinced when I picked up Mary Furlong's *Turning Silver into Gold*—and discovered early in the book the phrase "bonus round"— that I was in the presence of a soul mate. Reading on through the end of this impressive book, I became even more convinced.

After more than 20 years of studying aging and, more important-ly, *listening* to older men and women, there is little in this field that Mary Furlong has not encountered, thought about, or sought to solve. She is keenly aware of the importance of having fun as we age and the value we put on staying fit and productive. She understands that older people are as complex and diverse as any other group and will not fit neatly into a box—especially the boomers. She knows that work is a necessity for many older people and, as she puts it, "a kick start" for many others, including those who must work to make ends meet. And she wisely notes that older people are becoming a domi-nant force, not just a "demographic," in our society.

Mary's aim is to guide those who want to market to older people and to encourage those who might not have contemplated doing so to give it serious thought. This is not always an obvious or intuitive undertaking. But in Mary's hands, this process does not seem daunt-ing because she keeps things simple. There are really just five basic ideas or trends to keep in mind, she notes, and the reader will find them recurring throughout the book, whether the topic is real estate, sex, work, or investment.

The first of these ideas she calls "global markets," because aging is a worldwide phenomenon. China and Italy, for example, are gray-ing faster than the United States. The second is longevity which, among many other things, implies that we will be spending nearly as much time after retirement as we spent working, and that providing the means to stay healthy and active will be critical to the well-being of individuals as well as their governments. The third she calls "lifestage transitions." This important idea flies in the face of the stereotypical notion that older people are set in their ways. Surprise: They change jobs, divorce, remarry, care for older parents, and face the death of their friends, among many other lifestage transitions. The fourth is technology—specifically, how it can be used to make life better for us as we grow older. And the fifth, which speaks eloquently for itself, is spirituality combined with giving back to our communities, family, and nation.

But Mary Furlong's book has a social heart as well as a business sense. She assists people who are in business, but not simply for the sake of exploiting a market. Adding value to life is as important to her as it is to us at AARP. And that brings me to a point that I think is very important.

While there is no question that *Turning Silver into Gold* will hold a special interest for entrepreneurs and investors, I think it will find an equally eager and appreciative audience among boomers (and their parents and their children) for its insights into aging and the possibilities that a long life offers all of us. For example, Furlong notes that people in their 60s are the greatest buyers of wine (entrepreneur alert!), and then adds that anyone can set up a wine-tasting club (DIY alert!). Or this gem: "Love for the baby boom generation is not about the first time any more—it's about making love *feel* like it did the first time."

Turning Silver into Gold is filled with nuggets like these. And Mary Furlong, drawing upon her years of experience and vast expertise, does an admirable job of spinning them into gold.

William D. Novelli,
Chief Executive Officer, AARP

ABOUT THE AUTHOR

With more than 20 years of experience, Mary Furlong, Ed.D., is the leading authority on baby boomers as they reach their 50s and beyond. She founded Mary Furlong & Associates (MFA) in 2003 to help socially responsible, consumer-conscious companies understand the real needs of this explosive market.

She is executive professor of Entrepreneurship and Women in Leadership at the Leavey School of Business at Santa Clara University in California.

Dr. Furlong founded the nonprofit organization SeniorNet in 1986. SeniorNet was one of the first social networks and online communities. SeniorNet's mission was to create an organization that would bring the wisdom of older adults into the information age. It accomplished this through its vibrant online community, SeniorNet.org, and its learning centers. During her tenure, SeniorNet grew to over 100 learning centers and served over 500,000 older adults. Much of her time was spent in the field at the learning centers (there are now 250 centers) to understand issues related to technology, community and older adults. SeniorNet was funded by the Markle Foundation, IBM, and many of the telecommunication companies.

In 1996, Dr. Furlong founded ThirdAge Media with a group of private and corporate investors. ThirdAge was a media and marketing company that focused on the baby boomers (1946-1964). ThirdAge.com created content, commerce, community, and context in a variety of channels to serve the boomer interests. ThirdAge Media reached two million members and did pioneering work in advertising and community challenges to serve the boomers. As a result of this, Mary won the AdTech top leadership award. ThirdAge is a durable online community and continues to serve the boomer market. Through the work of SeniorNet, ThirdAge, and MFA, Mary has raised over $120 million in venture capital funds, corporate sponsorships, and foundation grants.

Dr. Furlong has guided the online and offline marketing strategies for major U. S. corporations for their 45+ age markets for more than two decades. Her client list has included such notables as IBM, Johnson & Johnson, Merrill Lynch, Viacom (CBS), Advance Publications, Procter & Gamble, Pfizer, Microsoft, AT&T, and AARP. She also advises start-up companies such as Posit Science and emerging nonprofits such as Women Sage.org.

Dr. Furlong has appeared on CBS, PBS, NPR, and NBC's *Today* show to discuss trends in aging and technology. Her expertise has been recognized in *The New York Times*, *USA Today*, *Business Week*, *Fortune*, *People*, and *Fast Company*, among other publications. *Time Magazine* honored her in 1999 as one of its "Digital 50." In 2001, *Fortune Small Business* named Dr. Furlong one of its "Top 25 Women Entrepreneurs" and *Interactive Age* has included her among its "Twenty-Five Unsung Heroes on the Web." She also received the New Choices Award from *Readers Digest*, joining the ranks of fellow recipients Jimmy Carter and Lena Horne. Dr. Furlong served as a White House Commissioner on Libraries and Information Science during the Clinton administration, and she has conducted hearings on aging and technology for the U.S. Senate. Dr. Furlong has also authored several books including *Grown-Up's Guide to Computing*, published by Microsoft Press.

MFA co-produces the successful "What's Next Boomer Business Summit" with the American Society on Aging (ASA), and the annual Boomer Business Plan Competition and Silicon Valley Boomer Venture Summit with the Leavey School of Business. Dr. Furlong is a member of the ASA's Business Forum on Aging, the Leadership Council of the National Council on Aging, and the AARP Women in Leadership group. She also serves on several corporate advisory boards. More information about Dr. Furlong and MFA is available at www.maryfurlong.com.

ACKNOWLEDGMENTS

For the past 25 years, I have had the privilege of working with amazing thought leaders in the fields of aging and business. The trends, insights, stories, and data points in *Turning Silver into Gold* are based on stirring conversations and projects with these clients and team members.

They sowed the seeds that have flowered into this book's message: that the key to a sustainable future is the boomer marketplace. As the boomers enter the third act of their lives, new solutions, products, and services will be required. These entrepreneurs and change agents care enough to create products and services that address the issues of a rapidly aging society and have inspired the success stories profiled here. I honor their contributions in helping create a blueprint to shape this new boomer revolution.

This book has been a spirited venture from day one when Jim Boyd, our publisher at Financial Times Press, called to suggest that it be written. I wish to thank him and his team—most notably editor Russ Hall—for their belief in this project and for their guidance and tenacity in shaping the manuscript.

I am especially grateful for the support of my colleagues at Santa Clara University, in particular Dean Barry Posner of the Leavey School of Business. He provided support and space for the Silicon Valley Boomer Business Plan competitions and annual summits that led to connections with entrepreneurs profiled here. All involved in the competition provided inspiration and insight, especially my exemplary Santa Clara students, Women in Leadership. I deeply appreciate how you keep us in the loop regarding business trends.

It is humbling to share the talented list of thought leaders who provided the insight and direction needed to compose this manuscript. Here are some of the valuable contributors:

Beth Witrogen McLeod, who guided the project, managed the team, shaped and edited the manuscript, and brought her sensibility and writing into the process. Collaborating with her was a joy and an inspiration; her experience on topics on aging from caregiving to spirituality was invaluable.

Brad Edmondson, who served as a magnificent editor of the final manuscript. How wonderful to have the founder of ePodunk and the former editor of *American Demographics* review the data and the trends and parse the prose.

Marty Silberstein, our project manager, who kept all the trains on track, helped manage the process from start to finish, and contributed greatly to the media and marketing chapter.

Maxine Paetro, friend and colleague, who confects words into icing and creates the scenes that all will understand; thanks for your guidance these past seven years and your help with our Introduction.

I could not have had the depth of content or breadth of subjects without the following writers: Paul Kleyman, editor of *Aging Today*, Marion Howard, Beth Witrogen McLeod, and Caroline Goldman.

Linda Dewey, our invaluable executive assistant, who rounded up all of the interviews and tracked entrepreneurs, investors, and corporate leaders around the world. Caitlin Carey, a Jill-of-all trades who transcribed; oversaw legal issues; and did the fact checking, copyediting, and permissions. Our key researchers, especially Michael Herskovic, Sam Shueh, and Chuck Nyren, who always found the elusive answers.

For their interviews, writing, and research for early versions of *Turning Silver into Gold*, I thank Brian O'Connell, Kathleen Cottrell, Lori Covington, Helen Gray, and Julie Penfold.

It is a privilege to have wonderful mentors who have provided invaluable guidance, insight, direction, and leadership. They include: Lloyd Morrisett, Myrna Blyth, Steve Newhouse, Mort Meyerson, Melinda French Gates, Fred Reynolds, Launny Steffens, Sen. Bill Bradley, and Jeff Zimman. I especially thank William Novelli for his inspirational leadership of AARP and for writing the Foreword to this book.

I humbly thank my friends and family who kept me going, among them Rad Dewey and Todd Healy, who were invaluable in support and entrepreneurial wisdom, and Bob McLeod, who fixed the fax and provided the humor. And everyone who so graciously gave of their time and inspiration through interviews, breakfasts, lunches, focus groups, dinners, facials, manicures, and emails: too numerous to mention here, but please accept my appreciation for contributing your expertise and leadership even if your name did not make it into the book.

Turning Silver into Gold is like a relay race that's just starting. The silver is the money we can make; the gold is the world we can create. I want to thank everyone who has worked to translate the silver into the good works that we can all accomplish, to help unleash the spirit, power, and voice of the boomers as we grow older. The gold is in how we treat one another and change the fabric of the world through products, services, and social contributions. I am grateful for the opportunity to help build community and to connect thought leaders, analysts, and entrepreneurs. The race isn't over; it's just beginning. Join in.

Twenty-five percent of the royalties from this book (silver) will be donated to the causes that matter to boomers (gold). Check out the website at MaryFurlong.com to cast your vote on a topic or issue or to suggest an issue or cause that matters to you.

INTRODUCTION

I remember a brilliant August day in 1995.

Microsoft was launching Windows 95 at a wildly exuberant expo held at their Redmond, Washington campus. I was there for SeniorNet, a non-profit organization I had founded in 1986 to help adults in their 50s and older get online. We had a 10-square-foot booth and a table of leaflets in the middle of the biggest product launch in modern history.

All around us were red and white market umbrellas, Cub Scouts carrying Microsoft briefcases, and tents filled with gourmet food. Bill Gates was running around in a golf cart with Jay Leno. There were hundreds of journalists snapping pictures, rolling film, and getting it all down. There was a Ferris wheel in the center of the expo and I took a ride. The wheel stopped at the top of the arc and I looked down on the carnival below. You could actually *see* a transition, a major shift in the way our world was going to be. It would be connected in ways we could not imagine. I knew then that it was time to build a new company, one that could leverage the power of this dramatic information revolution. I also knew that at age 47, it made sense for me to focus the brand and name of the company on my generation—the baby boomers—for I could sense at the top of that arc that boomers would seize the power of the Internet and technology in unprecedented new ways. It was my hope that this new company would grow large enough to endow the nonprofit SeniorNet. I am delighted to share that this dream was realized.

Demographers often describe the baby boom generation as a pig inside a python: a demographic bulge of 77 million people moving as a single unit down the length of time. The bump in fertility that started in 1946 and ended in 1964 is why the boomers' classrooms were always crowded, why it was so hard for me to get into college, and why we have rubbed shoulders with so many boomers at every stage of our careers. Now, with my bird's eye view from the Ferris wheel in 1995, I saw that boomers were moving *en masse* into the information age. And I saw what it would mean to the way we lived in this world.

I wasn't the only one to see it. Investors saw it too, and they began asking questions about this new market and what it could mean to them. They saw that one of the big applications of the Internet was going to involve baby boomers. They saw hordes of people who were moving into largely uncharted territory.

I was one of them.

With a stellar group of cofounders, I formed a new business, an Internet company called ThirdAge Media that was for and about the boomer generation. We listened to the stories of thousands of my peers from all walks of life and in all circumstances. We traded information with marketing giants like Procter and Gamble, IBM, Johnson & Johnson, Kraft, Ford, American Express, and many others. We discussed the changes that were taking place as the boomer generation moved toward what had once been thought of as retirement years. And we saw how these years would be different for boomers than they had been for their parents.

The oldest boomers faced a new reality in the mid-1990s, as the number 50 rolled up on the odometer of their lives. Now they have arrived at 60. It is a rude awakening for millions of people, a life-changing event that rattles the comfort zone. With a sharp intake of breath, boomers are gaining a new and clearer perspective on mortality. Searching for role models, boomers started with a look at how their parents dealt with the same time in their lives. They saw retirement parties followed by a life of leisure that looked like inactivity—and for the lucky ones, a handful of "golden years" in a two-bedroom condo in Delray Beach. The children of the '60s looked at that version of retirement and said, "Hell no, we won't go." They began to imagine a different kind of middle age, an extended and much more active time in which they could take the passion that ignited their youth and use it to ignite their 50s, 60s, and beyond.

The good news is, because of the advances of modern medicine, better nutrition, and decades of peace, the average life expectancy for a U.S. resident at age 65 has increased four years since the mid-1960s, and Americans reaching age 65 today can expect to live an additional 17.9 years (19.2 for females and 16.3 for males).[1] Even better, the share of people who reach age 65 with a chronic disability has dropped rapidly, from 26.2% in 1982 to 19.7% in 1999.[2] Affluence, medical technology, and better self-care have created an entirely new stage of life for millions of people. If you're 50 and have taken good care of yourself, you might get to enjoy an active lifetime a decade longer than the one you would have gotten in the 1960s. I call this new lifestage "the bonus round."

In the 1970s, 1980s, and 1990s, millions of boomers put their dreams on hold to do a full-court press for work and family. Now they are taking the reins of their own future and redefining their lives. People in their 50s are going back to school to obtain graduate and professional degrees. They are trekking in Nepal with their five best friends from the class of 1968. They are building their own sailboats, retiring the word "retired," and kicking down the fences previous generations put up around aging. Boomers are once again daring themselves to take risks, to touch and taste and listen in new, more informed ways. They want to learn to play again.

Boomers are also entering their regenerative, non-retirement years with plenty of spending power. Boomers earn more than $2 trillion in annual income and own more than 77% of all financial assets in the United States.[3] And they are going through more transitions now than at any other time in their lives. Each of those transitions is a tipping point for product and service decisions.

As boomers reach age 60 and prepare to leave the organized work force, they ask, "What should I do with my time?" Some still need income or crave the adrenaline kick of commerce. So they turn their spare bedroom into a home office, start a new business, open a frame shop or a Curves franchise, or sell real estate.

Children graduate from college or get jobs, and this transition frees up discretionary income that can be devoted to home improvement and self-improvement. Could this be why online sales of books and home accessories are going through the roof? Kitchen stores are springing up in multiples on Main Street. Empty-nest boomers are driving the market for plasma screen televisions, wireless Internet routers, and hybrid cars. One in four boomers is also buying a second home, partly so they can have an adventure when they have family reunions.

Some midlife transitions aren't as much fun. Older bodies must cope with menopause, arthritis, and the "trombone arm" response to vision loss. Boomers are keenly interested in medical breakthroughs that can lower blood pressure and cholesterol and are willing to spend vast amounts of money to stay healthy. Spending on prescription drugs rose from $40 billion in 1990 to almost $250 billion in 2005, and continues to increase faster than inflation.[4] Boomers know that the "bonus round" will come only to those who nurture their bodies now. So they buy Bowflex machines, free weights, and vitamin supplements. The weight-loss business represents a huge and growing market opportunity. Its annual revenues jumped from $100 million in the 1950s to $50 billion in the 1990s.[5] And since the launch of Viagra in 1998, sales of erectile dysfunction drugs have grown to more than $2 billion per year in the United States.

Boomers spent an estimated $42.7 billion on apparel in 2004, $14 billion of which they spent on clothing for others.[6] But they don't wear the same sizes they wore at age 18. In fact, the average adult American woman is 5 feet 4 inches tall, weighs 155 pounds, and wears a size 14.[7] Boomers will not ever have a teenager's body again, but they're dealing with it. Clothing stores are opening all across the country that specialize in great-looking apparel for women over 35, clothing that has verve as well as elastic waistbands.

The quest to maintain beauty and a youthful appearance occupies an increasing amount of time for many boomers. Millions of boomers, whether divorced or widowed, are dating again and will spend good cash to look and feel good. They want facials and spa days and an infinity pool in the sunroom. Not every boomer can afford these luxury items, but many boomers want them or a close approximation that they *can* afford.

I often ask conference audiences, "How many people have made time in their lives for play?" And in a hall filled with 1,000 people, maybe three will raise their hands. The rest of them say, "We got caught up in work. We forgot to play."

Well, the recess bell has rung again. Boomers' passionate interests are leading to a redefinition of identity. No longer just a suit or a soccer mom, they are now gardeners, writers, and digital photographers who, by the way, used to have an advertising career.

Travel is becoming one of our favorite ways to play. Millions of boomers who play tennis also have the time and the money to watch Wimbledon from courtside. Boomer golfers can realize their dream of playing a round at St. Andrews. The luckiest baby boomers can take the summer off to sail around the islands off the coast of Maine with their life partner of 30 years, or they can take the grandchildren skiing in Chamonix. Those who don't have quite as much money might go to a bed and breakfast for the weekend or take their grandkids to Six Flags. But they all want the same things: adventure, connection, and caring.

Boomers are the first generation in U.S. history of which more than 50% have obtained some form of higher education. Today, that education is translating into a hunger for travel that teaches. The readers of *Smithsonian* dream of traveling to India and China. They take Earthwatch vacations in order to do archeology in the Cotswolds or to protect the eggs of leatherback turtles in the Galapagos. Further down the income ladder, men who once spent their weekends at football games or stock-car races are now taking their grandchildren to Civil War battlefields.

Whether they are attached or single, rich or poor, boomers want to have "catered peak experiences"—that is, they want to create stellar, lifetime memories. They want to slowly troll across a lake in a pontoon boat or charter a yacht in Greece with the whole family. They want to enjoy champagne and chocolate fondue in a tree house or soak outside in a hot tub on a crisp December day. And they want to do this with like-minded souls.

Boomers spend approximately $157 billion on leisure travel each year, which is 80% of all U.S. expenditures on leisure travel.[8] And there's no end in sight. When they imagine another good, healthy 20 years, they vow not to squander this time. They look deeply into how they want to spend those years, asking, "What's worthy of me now?" In the third act of their lives, many boomers say, "I might have had a successful life, but what did I do that was significant?"

When they were young, millions of boomers embraced the Whole Earth philosophy. They believed in peace, civil rights, and protecting the quality of the environment. Their standard of life experience has deep emotional attachments. And that hasn't changed.

When it comes to giving, boomers are not just going to write a check to the United Way. They're going to contribute to causes that reflect their interests and matter to them—like my friend Larry, an ex-GI who returned to Vietnam to remove land mines. Call up the local chapter of Habitat for Humanity and you'll see that they have a long list of volunteers, many of whom are between the ages of 45 and 60. Boomers are looking for ways to give back. They want to leave a legacy they can be proud of. *The Economist* calls this "Billanthropy."

The enormous size of the boomer market—those between the ages of 42 and 60 in 2006 make up 25% of the U.S. population—translates into enormous business opportunities. But this market is misunderstood by many businesses that assume all boomers share the same tastes and passions, and that 60 "then" is the same as 60 "now." In fact, the boomer generation represents hundreds of market segments. The key to reaching this market lies in developing relevant services and products through understanding the demographic data, the trends, boomer psychology, and how to effectively communicate with the target audience. This book reveals where those opportunities are and how you can capitalize on them.

Turning Silver into Gold maps out the areas in which consumer demand is going to explode in the coming years. But it especially links these areas to critical social themes that are accompanying the boomer midlife transitions—issues that will guide you to create the best products and services for this market. Some of these areas include health and vitality; money and investing; play, passion, and travel; family, including grandparenting and elder care; entrepreneurship and technology; fashion and beauty; sexuality, romance, and intimacy; religion and spirituality; and philanthropy, along with other forms of community building. Each chapter reports the experiences and forecasts of venture capitalists and corporate executives in these key industries and provides case studies, statistical data, and insights on trends and market potential. We preview product innovations that will soon enrich boomers' lives and we examine ways in which smart companies are using the Internet and other new media to reach their markets.

Writer and film maker Norman Lear once told me you can make more of a difference in the for-profit world, and once you do, you can contribute to the not-for-profit one. This is one of the core principles that has guided me over the last 14 years. In this book, I hope to show you how to do good for society while doing well for yourself.

Experts estimate that more than 90% of net assets in the U.S. are in the hands of people age 40 and older.[9] This book aims to become the definitive guide for companies and entrepreneurs of any age who want to serve the boomer market. The opportunities are huge for those who both understand the boomer market and have the tools, resources, and data to build a business around it. If we can help develop the talent bank of entrepreneurs, brand managers, venture capitalists, and corporate leaders, we can envision a whole new world for boomers as they enter their third act. I believe that the entrepreneurs who find silver and spin it into gold through their companies will succeed mainly by doing good works.

Endnotes

1. U.S. Department of Health and Human Services, *Health, United States, 2005 with Chartbook on Trends in the Health of Americans* (Hyattsville, Maryland: 2005), 167, http://www.cdc.gov/nchs/data/hus/hus05.pdf.

2. National Institute on Aging, "Dramatic Decline in Disability Continues for Older Americans," May 7, 2001, http://www.nia.nih.gov/NewsAndEvents/PressReleases/PR20010507Dramatic.htm.

3. Carolyn Said, "Entrepreneurs Getting Hip to the Graying of America/Marketing Machine Out to Mine Gold in Boomers' Wallets," *San Francisco Chronicle*, May 11, 2005.

4. Alex Berenson, "Lipitor or Generic? Billion-Dollar Battle Looms," *New York Times*, October 15, 2005, A1.

5. Kai Ryssdal, *Marketplace Morning Report*, September 16, 2002 (Minnesota Public Radio).

6. Teri Agins, "Reshaping Boomer Fashion," *Wall Street Journal*, April 15, 2005, B1.

7. *Ibid.*

8. Bob Moos, "Boomer Market is Young at Heart," *The Dallas Morning News*, March 20, 2006, 1D.

9. Carolyn Said, "Entrepreneurs Getting Hip to the Graying of America/Marketing Machine Out to Mine Gold in Boomers' Wallets," *San Francisco Chronicle*, May 11, 2005.

1

A GLOBAL
OVERVIEW OF THE
BOOMER MARKET

We are on the cusp of a revolution. Since January 1, 2006, a baby boomer has turned 60 every seven seconds. This transition will continue for the next 19 years.[1] It will bring a revolution in longevity, and its impact will be felt for decades to come.

Millions of people who are now celebrating their 60th birthdays can expect to live longer and more active lives than 60-year-olds could expect a generation ago. What makes this "bonus round" especially compelling is the size of the potential customer base around the globe. There are 77 million baby boomers in the U.S., but the United States was not the only country that saw a sustained increase in fertility during the post-war years. In developed countries, one fifth of the population is currently 60 years old or older. By 2050, that proportion is projected to increase to almost a third.[2] In China, by 2025 the 50+ marketplace will be 525.8 million.[3]

Today, boomers around the world are reinventing their lives. They are finding new places to work, new places to travel to, new ways to spend their days, new fashions, new savings programs, new ways to spend time with their children and grandchildren, and new ways to stay vital and connected as they age. Each new choice represents a signal of enormous business opportunity.

Entrepreneurs, corporate brand managers and strategists, investors, and nonprofit executives want to know how to develop products and services that meet the boomers' changing needs. This book shares insights about boomers that I have gained from spending more than 20 years in the field of aging. I hope that reading it will inspire you to grab a notebook and sketch a business idea to serve this market. If you are an entrepreneur, you may be inspired to think up five or six ideas. If you are a corporate strategist, you will want to consider your company's core competencies and consider how they can be leveraged to create a new suite of products and services to support this marketplace. If you are an investor, you will want to identify ideas, such as healthy living, that can lead to market dominance across a range of categories. If you are a nonprofit executive, you will want to learn how to form programs that inspire boomers to get involved and support your cause.

Boomers' new values and attitudes have transformed consumer behavior at every stage of life so far, and the next stage will be no exception. Currently, 45% of the U.S. population is age 40 or older.[4] This group is the best educated, healthiest, and wealthiest generation ever to reach midlife and beyond. It is a force to be recognized and courted over the next decades as boomers move from midlife into old age.

Brad Edmondson was editor-in-chief of *American Demographics* magazine and is now the co-founder and vice president of ePodunk.com, a website that provides information profiles on more than 50,000 cities and towns in the United States, Canada, and the United Kingdom. He uses Figure 1.1 to help people visualize the business opportunities that will arise as the boomer "pig" continues to move through the life-stage "python."

"Older boomers are the focus of market opportunity in the next decade," says Brad. "The smart business is going to define a specific consumer target and aim for it with the best marketing information

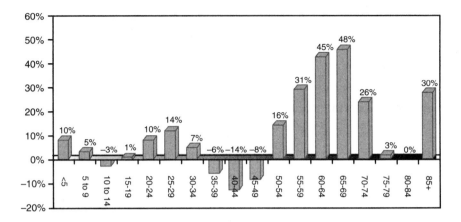

FIGURE 1.1 THE HOTTEST MARKETS (Percent change in U.S. 5-year age groups, 2005-2015)

Source: U.S. Bureau of the Census

available. The key concepts for reaching boomers around the globe are preservation and quality of life. The most important market segments among boomers are empty-nest couples and older singles."[5]

The key to success in this marketplace is life-stage marketing because the boomers will go through more transitions in their 50s and 60s than any other phase of life.[6] Each life-stage transition triggers business opportunities that revolve around family (empty nests, loss of parents, arrival of grandchildren); health issues (menopause, heart disease, vision and hearing loss, arthritis); housing (downsizing, rightsizing, remodeling, second homes); finances, work, retirement, and daily activities (time for passions and play); and perspective (the search for meaning).

The boomers are not a homogenous group. Many people who are in their 50s today face retirement, empty nests, grandparenting, and aging parents, but some of them have young children, and some are newlyweds. Today, millions of younger boomers (born from 1956 to 1964) are still pursuing careers and helping their kids through school. The boomers are also ethnically and economically diverse. For example, in the

United States, 12% of older boomers (those born between 1946 and 1955) and 15% of younger boomers are foreign-born.[7]

The emergence of a large, healthy, well-educated cohort of consumers in their 60s is a social and a business revolution the world has never seen before. Adults age 45 and older account for 77% of financial assets in the United States, control 70% of total wealth, and account for more than half of the nation's discretionary spending.[8]

The need for relevant products geared toward this aging population is growing daily because the demographic pressures are global. According to the Australian Bureau of Statistics, "The 'coming of age' of our baby boomers will challenge and perhaps totally revolutionize the stereotyped views people have about the habits, behavior, and tastes of people in their middle to senior years."[9]

The key to success in reaching baby boomers is tying your business idea to the social issues that surround aging, such as loneliness, empty nests, dating after 50, the death of a loved one, and retirement. *Turning Silver into Gold* explores these issues in terms of the emerging needs and desires of the boomer psyche. The most powerful insight we present is that for boomers today, amassing material possessions is not as important as having experiences that satisfy the mind, body, and spirit.

As you consider launching a new business for boomers, it is important to know that there are few barriers to entry for a new brand aimed at this generation. Surveys report that boomers are not brand loyal. They are educated consumers, and if they can find a smarter solution, they will switch brands. When you identify products that will serve their needs, there is a great potential for gaining market share. Some of the boomers' needs will be related to the challenges of aging. That is why we are seeing more performance-enhancing drugs related to sexuality and more spas and respite services to help people cope with the stresses around loss. Yet many of the opportunities will be centered on the joys of this lifestage transition. Boomers will have more time for travel and education and experiences shared with friends and family.

This book focuses on five key concepts and trends that will help increase your understanding of boomers and help you build a winning business strategy to reach this growing market. These areas—global markets, longevity, technology life-stage transitions, and spirituality/giving back—are woven throughout each chapter to bring perspective and to spark creative imagination.

Global Markets

According to CEO Linda Jenkinson of LesConcierges, Inc., it takes 10 languages to do business in the world today. Corporations, entrepreneurs, and non-profits routinely procure their boxes in Ghana, fabric in New Zealand, call centers in India, and programmers in Eastern Europe. Markets and teams are global. IBM has a global eldercare strategy. Intel holds its health care portfolio meeting in China. Fashion entrepreneurs launch their lines in Dubai and Macau. Microsoft's second largest company headquarters is in India. Roger Barnett, the CEO of Shaklee Corporation, travels to Asia and Europe and throughout North America serving a global market need for vitamins and natural products. The Internet makes it possible for companies to sell their products and services globally. The Internet also makes it possible to find a global team, and to respond to issues globally.

Longevity

Americans turning 65 today can expect to live to age 78, on average, but the ones who don't smoke, exercise, and eat right are likely to live well into their 80s. In 2000, people over 80 represented 1.5% of the U.S. population; by 2050, they are projected to occupy 5% of the total U.S. population, according to the Census Bureau.[10] There will be more than one million centenarians in 2050, up from 71,000 today. In fact, some gerontologists believe many baby boomers will have life spans of more than 120 years.[11]

And the longevity revolution is not just happening in the United States. The number of South Koreans age 65 and older is expected to surge from 9.1% to 24.1% in 2030 and to 37.3% in 2050—the highest in the world.[12] The number of people in Japan age 90 or older topped one million for the first time in 2005.[13]

Longevity has already had a huge impact on the marketplace, especially in health. Already, traditional companies are repositioning themselves. Intel is no longer just a chip company; it is a technology and health care company. Philips hit a home run with its home heart defibrillator and has now moved into the home alert space with its acquisition of Lifeline. Many consumer products companies are now looking into the lucrative home spa product and service business. The anti-aging space is taking off, as are businesses catering to the activities and passions that active adults enjoy. Each of the challenges of aging—from vision and hearing loss to heart disease, diabetes, and cancer—is also a market opportunity. The fact that many boomers have high cholesterol has led to giant sales of pharmaceuticals such as Lipitor and Crestor.

Longevity also means that with average life expectancy at an all-time high, more people over 50 are remaking themselves at midlife. They are leaving worn-out jobs to start their own businesses. They are traveling the world for catered peak experiences with like-minded souls. They are rekindling marriages or starting new romances after divorce, widowhood, and empty nests. They are buying second homes and nostalgic collectibles. And they are volunteering in greater numbers: Nearly half of all Americans age 55 and older volunteered at least once in 2005.[14]

Technology

The modern world has evolved from an industrial society into an information society. Technology is transforming how people date, manage money, shop, find support in their grief, educate themselves, connect with friends and family, and pursue their passions. And boomers and seniors are the fastest growing Internet user segments.

Technology enhances business practices in all kinds of ways. Managers who can think digital and cultivate a deep understanding of infrastructure and knowledge management will be able to ride the most important trend of a new aging marketplace. Technological innovations such as database marketing give businesses of all sizes powerful new ways to learn about their customers and target them with winning products and services. Technology also enables the growth of online communities, and it helps companies stay in touch with their customers.

Technology has to figure into your game plan as you create and manage your business, even if it's a small business. Are you getting as many sales as you can because you are listed in the right search engines, email newsletters, and portals? Do you use the capabilities of software tools and services to organize your team, conduct meetings, and manage your sales pipelines and customer database? Smart businesses will have a smart technology strategy.

Life-Stage Transitions

Exogenous shock, or *eshock*, is a term plucked from economics. It means a disturbance that comes from the outside and throws the status quo into chaos. We experience eshocks throughout our lives, whenever we are forced to evaluate who we are and where we're going. When someone gets an eshock around their 50th birthday, it is usually called a "midlife crisis." These eshocks are related to lifestage transitions such as remarriage and divorce, a death in the family, parents moving into a care facility, adult children moving back home, surviving a major illness, or caring for someone who is ill or dying.

When you understand what people are coping with in their 40s, 50s, and 60s (and beyond), you can plan a wealth of new products and services targeted for this demographic. The big winners in this marketplace will be entrepreneurs who care about the fears around aging—of loneliness, of being marginalized, of not giving enough back, of not having enough money or health, of no longer being attractive or youthful. And best of all, the big winners in the aging boom will also be able to smile when they look in the mirror. Their fortunes will be based on products and services that help improve quality of life for many people .

Spirituality

My first enterprise, SeniorNet, was a success partly because its members had a sense of spiritual efficacy. By engaging with computers while participating as volunteer learners and leaders, SeniorNet's members felt they were making a contribution. In this book, we define *spirituality* as building community and a culture of caring. At midlife, spirituality often arises when people take on the hard questions surrounding longevity and life-changing events, questions such as, "What is worthy of me now?" and "Did I give enough?"

How is a person's spirit unleashed? What satisfies his or her soul? More than likely, the answer will involve an experience—a vacation, a worship service, a pleasant time with grandchildren, a moment of joy and relaxation exploring a passion, or a morning walk with friends. One reason is that marketers have been selling "peak experiences" to boomers throughout their lives, and the boomers have listened. As a result, they demand authentic brands that free their spirits and respect their intelligence and creativity. If you can leave your customers with their spirits soaring when they talk about your product or use your service, you will win.

Spirituality also appears in the workplace in the forms of value creation and leadership. I often hear stories of midlife professionals who left their jobs because their boss made them feel as if they were not worth much. We have an opportunity to create a new generation of business leaders who will build teams that respect the spirit and dynamic contribution of all members of their companies. We have a chance to create business environments in which all members are respected for their ideas and contributions and challenges are dealt with openly and fairly. What the boomers won't stand for are environments that kill their spirit. So the best business lesson is to create companies that unleash the talent and inspire the spirit to let it shine each day.

This book explores eight key areas in which active older boomers will spend their money during their bonus round. The areas are health; travel; passion and play; sexuality and romance; fashion and beauty; housing; family; and eldercare. The good news is that the smallest entrepreneur and the largest corporation can both go after this market. This book outlines ways in which businesses large and small have leveraged these trends and made a footprint.

This book distills the business acumen and strategies of entrepreneurs, venture capitalists, corporate leaders, and nonprofits. Its goal is to inspire by telling stories of brand managers, entrepreneurs, corporate executives, and non-profit executives who combined in-house and outside experts to invent new products and services for the boomer market. It reveals how the largest companies on the planet bring in teams of experts to help plot an innovation strategy around this segment. It shows how companies reposition themselves in an entirely new space. It teaches how new brands are launched to help solve social issues such as the need boomers' parents have for accessible housing with a neighborhood feel. It also tells about energetic entrepreneurs who have created winning business plans, raised funding, and dealt with the ups and downs of launching a product or service.

This book's purpose is to give you the tools and resources necessary to help shape a business idea. I hope you will be inspired to take out a piece of paper and begin to plot your own business strategy as you go along. It's best to try this with four or five ideas and then toss them around with friends until you find the one that seems most promising.

There is also a "how-to" section that provides news you can use about reaching reporters who cover the "age beat," sales and marketing tips for creating a digital strategy, and advice from venture capitalists, business leaders, and nonprofits on ways to finance your dream.

Still, my intention for *Turning Silver into Gold* is greater than just assisting a business revolution. I also believe in the social mandate that boomers have carried since the Kennedy administration. Especially at midlife, when we are returning to these ideals of creating a better world, boomers want to embrace businesses that make a difference. They like the fact that IBM and Home Depot value older workers. They appreciate that JetBlue saves them money by having customers and employees clean the airplanes. They like brands that have a sense of social purpose as well as business purpose. They like companies that value them and don't marginalize them for turning gray. They buy products and services that help them age well. Companies that understand these sensibilities can do good while winning big.

This book is therefore partly a business guide and partly a social manifesto. It proclaims that a wealth of new businesses, new brands, and new funds can change what it means to grow older, and that this can be the catalyst for what author and boomer advocate Theodore Roszak calls "the longevity revolution." This third act of life is a time of opportunity. It is another chance for the exploration of both inner and outer lives. Ultimately, it is a time of generativity and making a contribution to others. It's about intimacy, creativity, and spirituality. This is where the real social and business revolution lies.

Businesses that combine doing good with doing well will capture market share in the aging boomer marketplace. They will understand the boomers' need for creativity and lifelong learning; their need for authentic and intimate relationships; their need for spiritual growth and personal expression; their need for adventure as well as cocooning; their need for connectivity, family, comfort, beauty, and security. They will understand that boomers want to make a life of their own choosing now, and that they are willing to pay for good value in the products and services that help them achieve these dreams.

For the past 25 years, the underlying theme of my work has been the restoration of the role of older adults as leaders in society. The industrial society marginalized elders because they had few ways to contribute to it. Today, our information society gives the opportunity to keep them connected, contributing, vital, and productive throughout their longer lives. As we speak of "turning silver into gold," then, the "silver" can be seen as a way to think about the money the boomers have or will inherit, as well as the color of their hair. The "gold" is a way to describe not just the wealth this generation will have to spend, but also the wisdom they have accumulated and how they will translate their financial worth into good works.

Once again, members of the baby boomer generation are acting as trailblazers, and the new ways they find to age will be the road map for generations to come. Now that boomers are in leadership roles, they have the opportunity to grow older in a different way. They can summon the same passion they had in youth, but now they have the time, money, experience, and desire to make a big difference.

Let's begin.

Endnotes

1. Lori Sturdevant, "The Baby Boom Turns 60," *Star Tribune*, January 10, 2006.
2. United Nations Population Fund. "Fast Facts," United Nations Population Fund, http://www.unfpa.org/pds/facts.htm (accessed April 9, 2006).
3. United Nations Population Division World Population Prospects. 1998 ed. New York.
4. "2005/2010 Demographic Trends," *ArcNews Online*, Summer 2005, http://www.esri.com/news/arcnews/summer05articles/2005-2010-demo-data.html.
5. Brad Edmondson (lecture, Silicon Valley Boomer Venture Summit, Santa Clara, CA, June 21, 2005).
6. Emilio Pardo (panel discussion, Silicon Valley Boomer Venture Summit, Santa Clara, CA, June 21, 2005).

7. Kim Campbell, "The Many Faces of the Baby Boomers," *The Christian Science Monitor*, January 26, 2005. Further, "Twelve percent of baby boomers are black, 9 percent are Hispanic, 4 percent are Asian or Pacific Islander, and less than 1 percent are American Indian or native Alaskan." *Ibid.*

8. Laura Pedersen, "There's Gold in Senior Years," *Orange County Register*, August 11, 1996.

9. Australia Bureau of Statistics. "Western Australia's Baby Boomers a High Priority for Planners," June 27, 2003 (quoting Seniors Minister Sheila McHale).

10. U.S. Census Bureau. "Table 2a. Projected Population of the United States, by Age and Sex: 2000 to 2050," http://www.census.gov/ipc/www/usinterimproj/natprojtab02a.pdf (accessed April 9, 2006).

11. Bruce J. Klein, "This Wonderful Lengthening of Lifespan," January 17, 2003, http://www.longevitymeme.org/articles/printarticle.cfm?article_id=11 (accessed April 9, 2006).

12. Bae Keun-min, "S. Korea Will Become Most Aged Society in 2050," *The Korea Times*, May 22, 2005, http://times.hankooki.com/lpage/nation/200505/kt2005052221402311990.htm.

13. "People Aged 90 or Older Top 1 million in 2004," *Japan Economic Newswire*, June 3, 2005.

14. Civic Ventures. "Fact Sheet on Older Americans," http://www.civicventures.org/publications/articles/fact_sheet_on_older_americans.cfm.

2

THE BUSINESS OF HEALTH

Introduction

Life can turn on a dime. As boomers turn 60, this is often the health care dime.

The number boomers used to worry about most was the one that sent them to Vietnam. Today it's prostate and cholesterol and blood pressure counts. Boomers see their friends become isolated after a cancer shock, and they wonder who will be next. One by one, they are being tested to find the compassion they will need to deal with the health challenges of aging.

Yet boomers are also on the cusp of a revolution in health care. They are the first generation to hold their health destinies in their own hands. Gone are the days of my grandmother's generation, when Dr. Bryce made house calls and delivered babies. The health care world did not figure much in her day-to-day experience; when a person got sick, he either got better on his own or he died. But as baby boomers have grown older, they find that health care questions are always on their radar screens.

Businesses are well aware of the connection. They see dollar signs in the rising rates of obesity, high blood pressure, and diabetes—because, after all, a person is going to spend down to his last dollar if that's what it takes to make his or her loved one well. Intel and Philips have changed their brands and core product lines from technology to technology *and* health care. New phrases like *consumer-directed health care* are springing up to capture the movement.

Most businesses are not looking at this subject broadly enough. The revolution in the health care marketplace is a shift from health care as a medical topic to health care as a blend of entertainment, fitness, beauty, and spiritual well-being. Industries are merging as doctors' offices come to look more like spas, and spas take on medical-type services. Resorts are offering fitness, weight loss, and stress reduction programs.

Boomers are just beginning to shift their agendas from full-time work and raising a family to spending more time doing what they love. Longevity is the goal and fitness is the key. The deep questions for business leaders are how boomers can best organize their lives around self-care and caring for others. To inspire boomers toward health, businesses must combine motivation and aspiration with socialization and fun. Healthy living and aging is not only one of the most attractive spaces for business to invest in, it is also the bottom line for everything else they do.

This chapter profiles market opportunities and shares strategies of some of the leading venture capitalists, entrepreneurs, and corporations leveraging this trend, from market segmentation to medical devices. Its goal is to explain why Richard Rosenberg, former chairman and CEO of Bank of America, describes his investment focus as "health care, health care, health care."[1]

Market Analysis

As age-beat journalist Paul Kleyman says, "It's time to wake up and smell the demographics."[2] To understand healthy living and aging, we have to look at the lifestage transitions that happen at midlife and beyond. The most visible transition is what happens to the body as it ages. Boomers face the loss of libido, vision, hearing, muscle tone, and hair. Health conditions such as hypertension, heart disease, and arthritis can become chronic.

About half of Americans who were age 65 and older in 2001 had hypertension, and close to 40% had symptoms of arthritis. About one in three in this age group has heart disease, and one in five has had a brush with cancer (see Figure 2.1). Even if these percentages decrease somewhat by the time boomers reach age 65, the absolute numbers of older Americans with chronic conditions is almost certain to rise due to the massive size of this generation.

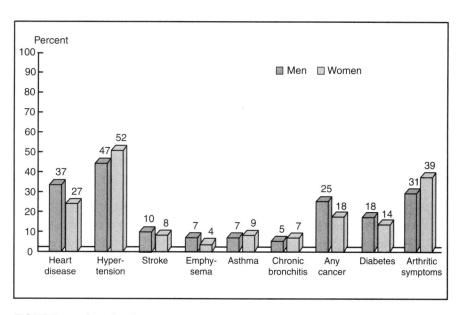

FIGURE 2.1 CHRONIC HEALTH CONDITIONS (PERCENTAGE OF PEOPLE AGE 65 AND OVER WHO REPORTED HAVING SELECTED CHRONIC CONDITIONS, BY SEX, 2001–2002)

Source: Centers for Disease Control and Prevention, National Center for Health and Statistics, National Health Interview Survey

The leading causes of death among people age 65 and older are heart disease, cerebrovascular diseases, chronic lower respiratory diseases, cancer, influenza, pneumonia, and diabetes.[3] Depression is alarmingly prevalent among older Americans, with the percentage rising as age rises.[4]

Gender does seem to matter in health as we age. More women than men rate their health as good or excellent. Alzheimer's is the fifth leading cause of death for women, but it doesn't rank in the top five for all Americans because men suffer from Alzheimer's less frequently than women.[5] Twenty-four percent of men are smokers, whereas only 19% of women smoke.[6] Women are almost twice as likely as men to suffer from depression,[7] but men are more likely to suffer hearing loss (55% of boomer men, but only 44% of boomer women, already report some form of hearing loss).[8] And at every age, more women than men have arthritis.[9]

In a 2001 poll, 57% of boomers said they were concerned about getting cancer and 54% were concerned about having a heart attack. But the good news is that most Americans ages 45 to 65 were positive about their overall health, physical appearance, sex life, and even the way they manage stress.[10] When baby boomers enter the next stage of life, they will fuel greater enthusiasm and spending around learning how to age well.

This is where opportunity is born. There is growing recognition that many health problems can be reduced, delayed, or avoided by lifestyle changes, and marketers are increasingly looking to people with chronic ailments as a new must-reach demographic. It is part of a cultural shift that increasingly views health problems not as diseases, but as lifestyle issues. For example, supermarkets are devoting sections of cereal displays to heart health, sugar-free sections for diabetics, and gluten-free foods for people with wheat sensitivities.

Natural Marketing Institute

Steve French, managing partner at the Natural Marketing Institute (NMI), has looked at boomers' changing definitions of health and wellness, and the attitudes driving those changes. Twenty years ago, NMI's survey showed that the boomers' top priorities were maintaining an active, healthy sex life, having a successful job, and balancing work and family. Steve reports these top boomer concerns today:

1. Enough money to retire.
2. Overall financial health.
3. Enough energy to do what they want.
4. Enough money for health care expenses.
5. Taking action to prevent disease.
6. Good advice from their doctors.

According to NMI, boomers said they feel that having a healthy lifestyle is important, but they find it difficult to establish that lifestyle. For example, most boomers would like to eat more healthfully, but many don't know how. Most believe that exercising is important, but not everyone is motivated to be disciplined. Most think supplements are worthwhile, but they are also confused by conflicting information about what supplements to take.

Steve says that the market opportunity here is to create integrated lifestyle approaches. "Those companies or individuals who develop and market a cohesive package of products and services under one umbrella will have a competitive edge," he says. For example, a health care practice might be comprised of medical doctors; alternative practitioners such as chiropractors, nutritionists, and dieticians; and a retail store with health-care products and organic foods and beverages, all in one location.[11] One example of this concept is Solana MedSpas, a medical spa group that opened more than 50 locations in one year.

Elephant Entrepreneur: North Castle Partners

At the 2005 Silicon Valley Boomer Venture Summit in Santa Clara, California, Chip Baird shared why he has invested heavily in the healthy living and aging space. Chip is the founder and CEO of North Castle

Partners, a mid-market private equity fund that has invested more than $1.5 billion in more than 40 consumer-oriented companies, all in the fast-growing area of health and wellness.

"I began to think about what happened when I hit 50," he said. "I was losing my hair—by 50, about half of men begin to go bald. I was beginning to need glasses—90% of people over 50 need some type of vision correction. Hearing loss begins to affect people by 50, and it impacts 83% of men over 70. My teeth were yellowing, my joints ached—40% of people over 50 suffer from arthritis and 60% of people 65 and over do. It's the number-one cause of disability in the United States. I gained a little weight—from age 30 on, a pound of muscle turns into a pound of fat each year. It had been rumored that I needed a little help from a blue pill—44% of men over 50 have experienced some degree of erectile dysfunction."

"What you want at 50 is a vacation, a second home, and a fast car. What you get at 50 is the wheels start to come off. I may be fat, bald, deaf, blind, and have yellow teeth, but I am not senile—and therein lies the opportunity."

Segmentation within one market space is a powerful way to understand market opportunity, and this is how Chip and North Castle understand where to invest. Their investment principle is to focus on healthy living and aging, which means deal identification, effective due diligence, value creation, and company synergies in this sector of the market. Focusing on one market space also means developing an enormous inventory of knowledge and network, which leads to proprietary deal flow and greater efficiency when it's time for due diligence. North Castle's chart (see Figure 2.2) segmenting the healthy living marketplace clarifies this approach. "The economic space of healthy living and aging is an enormous engine of investment opportunity," Chip says. "This is a $500 billion space comprised of between 15,000 and 20,000 companies. By 2020, healthy living and aging will be well over a trillion dollars."

Chip says that the convergence of four major forces drives this consumer marketplace. First, there is an emerging science and consumer awareness of the importance of exercise, nutrition, and stress management for long-term wellness. Second is the aging population, with a boomer turning age 60 every seven seconds. Third is increasing longevity. The fourth market driver is a shifting concentration of wealth and spending.

"If you look at the things that happen to an aging population, whether it's the $40-billion weight management business or the single product Rogaine that's $117 million, the almost billion-dollar hearing aid business, the $23-billion vision correction business and so on, what you see is that this aging baby boom creates enormous opportunities for products and for businesses. It is everywhere. We don't invest just behind the aging theme, we also invest behind the healthy living theme."

Chip says, "You want a space where one person can't come in and trump all of your hard work. You want a sector with an attractive

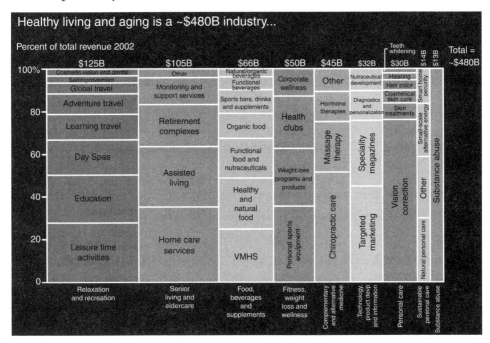

FIGURE 2.2 NORTH CASTLE PARTNERS $480-BILLION MARKET DIAGRAM

Source: North Castle Partners

growth rate. For us, the issue of industry structure and fragmentation in life-stage was very important. If you look for businesses with a high level of fragmentation and where a lot of the companies are early on in their life-stage, you have the opportunity to come in and to consolidate and build a market leader without staring into the face of someone with a 60% market share."

"Finally, as an investor, you always have to think about exit. We looked for businesses that had a very high degree of interest from strategic buyers. Just about every consumer products company, every technology company, loves this space because of its growth, but they can't invest in it because the companies are too small. But if you can build a company of $100 million or $150 million, they're willing to pay outrageous multiples of your money."

Chip Baird and the North Castle team have been way in front of the curve. "By 1999, we had invested in the travel business, the day spa business, a bunch of leisure-time activities, organic food, vitamins, and health food," he says. "Since then we have continued to invest and have 10 major platforms."[12]

Elephant Entrepreneur: WebMD

Sometimes the fastest way to change consumer behavior is to create a new online community. I saw this work directly when ThirdAge Media challenged its members to eat Quaker Oats every day as a way to lower their cholesterol. Within 24 hours of the online announcement, members joined the campaign with amazing rates of compliance. There is great potential to inspire and motivate health care behavior changes through an online community.

The Internet has revolutionized information and entertainment, and it is also revolutionizing health care. One of the reasons the online world is so compelling for consumers is its anonymity. It is difficult to talk about incontinence, impotence, infertility, or irritable bowel syndrome over lunch, but it is easy to learn about them online. It is amazing to see the click-through rates for some of these more widespread but sensitive disease states.

And if a second opinion is what people want, they will go online to get it—even though the quality of the advice might be questionable. In a recent Merck Institute of Aging & Health study, 69% of people age 50 and older with Internet access at least occasionally used it to look for health information. However, 38% found it hard to assess the credibility of health information on the Web, and almost 25% of respondents didn't know how to use that information to make decisions about their health care.[13]

Boomers are three times more likely than those over age 65 to go online, with more than 33.2 million people ages 50 to 64 surfing the Web. Fifty-three percent of adults ages 50 to 64 get health information online, according to a 2005 survey by eMarketer.[14] "Nearly half of seniors say they don't trust health information they find online," says eMarketer Senior Analyst Debra Williamson. "Boomers are less worried; about a quarter express mistrust. That still leaves lots of room for improvement."[15]

As consumers are asked to pay a greater share of the cost of their health care services, they look for more information. They want "news you can use," support groups, and interactive tools that guide them through the different phases of diseases. They also want blogs, email newsletters, and online support communities.

WebMD is often the first place consumers turn for health information. In 2004, the site had more than 100 million users and revenue of $1.16 billion, up from $964 million a year earlier.[16]

The site is growing steadily because it understands what consumers want from their health care relationships. Many older people want information and support, but they feel invisible and hurried along. WebMD reassures them with its interactivity and its wealth of informative resources and tools.

Consumer desire to take personal responsibility for health care will only grow as boomers age. Nan Forte, WebMD's executive vice president of consumer services, describes how the company identified the market opportunity and moved to capture that market space. "One of the most significant changes we saw in the health-care market was the individual's need to know and understand more about their own personal health, so we looked at health in the broadest spectrum possible."

WebMD's materials are measured against clinical guidelines for doctors, so that when a patient comes to an appointment with questions relating to a medical condition, the doctor has confidence in the patient's findings. WebMD has also launched a magazine distributed in medical offices, another sign of its acceptance in medical circles.

Nan says that WebMD knew there wasn't a brand established in this category. With no competition but tremendous need, the company had an enormous opportunity to build a brand based on three tenets: credibility and trust, community and caring, and optimism and action. By building community around health subjects that matter to the individual, it laid claim to a gold mine while building a community that will last.[17]

Intel Inside Health

Sometimes a change in consumer sensibilities is big enough to cause a large company to change its core identity. Intel has long been known as a maker of computer chips, but the company's interest in health care also came early, when founder Andy Grove went public with a personal story about his search for answers after a diagnosis of prostate cancer. Now Intel has redefined itself as a participant in the health care revolution.

In recent years, the company has sprouted five business units that focus on markets other than silicon chips.[18] One of these units aims to make health care as digital as possible, partly by designing medical devices and nanotechnologies to keep older people in their homes longer. It plans to invest $1 billion in this field globally in the near term, starting with sensors and diagnostics.

Intel's Digital Health Group comprises three units: personal health care, the digital hospital, and biotech (like biodiagnostics).

"We do a lot of start-up deals," says Sean Cunningham, director of strategic investments at Intel Capital. "Being a corporate investor, we invest from a financial, strategic, and from a viability standpoint. We've been very successful."

"The nearer-term opportunities will be sensors and diagnostics," Sean says. "The longer term will be therapies and blood stream robots that you hear about in science futurism. We're pretty far from that today, so the things we're investing in are stepping stones to that vision. It tends to motivate the best and brightest scientists of the field who really want to explore these frontiers of the unknown. There's lots of excitement."[19]

Emerging Entrepreneur: Fitness Together

You don't have to be a giant like Intel to build a franchise that successfully addresses the health and fitness trend. Thomas Peeks made his move after spending more than 30 years in corporate America. His work was uninspiring, he says; he felt that his efforts "did nothing for the greater good of mankind."

Thomas says he has long lived "with the goal of continuously improving [him]self physically, mentally, and spiritually. Spiritual improvement is most important and rewarding, and it is also the most difficult. It requires you to constantly work outside of the comfort level and to constantly adapt."

Thomas was struck by reports that 90 million Americans are overweight or obese, and that the problem is worst among boomers. Using some of the equity in his home, Thomas bought a Fitness Together franchise in 2003. He applied his business acumen accrued in sales and operations to helping people improve their lives through health and fitness. He estimates that 80% of his clientele are boomers. And although his revenues at the start-up stage were less than $250,000 per year, business and profits have steadily increased each year.

"I wanted to do something that not only would bring in income, but also something I would enjoy doing," Thomas said. "I thought I could fill a huge need, which is helping people be healthy." Thomas offers complete fitness assessments every six weeks because accountability is a key to success. His tools include comprehensive weight, cardio, and flexibility training; continuous one-on-one coaching; a private workout suite; calorie-controlled meal plans; and regular progress training.

Thomas has brought a class of grandmothers, soccer moms, and out-of-shape boomers back into strength training and exercise and diet. Bonnie, 68, is a role model. "For our 47th anniversary, my husband said the best present would be for me to take care of myself. I'd never worked out. I couldn't walk to the mailbox without stopping three times. Now I'm stronger in every way. My family is so proud." Thomas put Bonnie on the home page of his website and features her testimonial in one of the four direct mail pieces that he sends out to potential customers. His marketing messages are simple but powerful: "Only your trainer sees you sweat. All the world sees you fit."

Thomas says the secret to his success "is that my clients know that I really care about them getting into shape. And that is more than just a business—it's kind of like a calling. I feel good about seeing people come through the door. More importantly, I feel good seeing them when they leave. People are usually smiling and radiating good feelings because that's what you get when you're in good shape."[20]

Posit Science Corporation

Jeff Zimman watched the ebb and flow of deals through the 1990s as a top corporate lawyer and investment banker in San Francisco. Then he saw a deal he could not pass up.

Since 2002, he has been the CEO and president of Posit Science Corporation, a San Francisco-based company that develops and markets software programs to improve memory and cognitive performance. A global consortium of university-based scientists design, test, and evaluate exercises that rejuvenate the brain through intensive and progressively challenging exercises that engage the brain in new ways. By signing on with Posit Science, Jeff became a leader of a revolution in health. Posit Science blends a sharp understanding of demographics with groundbreaking research in neuroplasticity—the brain's ability to change physically at any age in response to new learning—to discover how to improve brain health as we age.

More than 25% of people over age 65 are at risk for mild cognitive impairment and Alzheimer's disease. Add to this the hundreds of millions of people worldwide who suffer from brain disorders, such as Alzheimer's disease, mild cognitive impairment, schizophrenia, depression, bi-polar, traumatic brain injury, repetitive strain injury, stroke, and Parkinson's disease—plus the fact that even healthy people lose cognitive abilities as they age—and you see the potential for Posit Science to make a difference.

"As we age, things get 'noisier,'" Jeff says. "Information from our senses becomes less reliable, because our processing speed and accuracy are diminishing and because we are producing fewer neuromodulating chemicals that help encode information.... Our programs are designed to improve the speed and accuracy with which we process signals (such as incoming verbal information), while stimulating the machinery that produces key brain chemicals that strengthen learning and memory."[21]

Research has shown that actively engaging in new learning throughout life can mean less cognitive decline with age. Yet most people don't know what it is they should do as they age. Does this mean we should keep working? Take up new hobbies? Do crosswords? Learn a foreign language? The latest research from Posit Science shows that brain exercises can actually improve cognitive performance.[22]

"Through brain exercise we can improve cognitive function in older adults by decades," Jeff says. "It is also highly likely that we can delay, arrest, and even reverse the effects of many brain disorders. Our ability to enhance brain function as we age changes everything. It dramatically reduces costs for care; it moves our focus on technology from addressing failure to promoting success; and it recognizes that hope and self-actualization should stretch across the entire lifespan."[23]

Posit Science has raised more than $31 million in venture capital and holds more than 50 issued U.S. patents, most for inventions by its co-founder and Chief Scientific Officer Michael Merzenich, Ph.D., Merzenich, Ph.D., a professor of neuroscience at the University of California, San Francisco a professor of neuroscience at the University of California, San Francisco.

One investor, Steve Jurvetson of Draper Fisher Jurvetson in Menlo Park, California, says his firm likes companies that have a vision to change the world—even if the company doesn't have a product. Steve felt that Posit Science was targeting an untapped market need. But it ultimately was the energy and quality of Jeff's team that convinced these venture capitalists to invest. Steve says, "Lifelong learning is not just about enlightenment, it's an economic imperative."[24]

Posit Science is in the early stages of marketing its programs, including software for computers and interactive game and television platforms. Its goal is distribution through retirement communities, learning centers, associations, insurers, and medical providers. Jeff envisions a world in which individuals can access brain exercises any where, at any time, to stay mentally fit.[25]

Body Monitoring

Entrepreneur Astro Teller chose the health and wellness trend when he created his first company. BodyMedia, Inc. focuses on mobile monitoring of vital signs, such as energy expenditure, sleep, and automatic journaling of daily activities such as time in a moving vehicle. It has created reliable and comfortable body monitors that use state-of-the-art, easy-to-use software and display technologies. The tools can help manage weight and cardiac disease, monitor elders, and help with stress and sleep issues. For example, the bodybugg is an intelligent calorie monitoring system for weight loss.

Astro says that consumers will demand personal health tools that decipher the choices that either create wellness or cause disease. The technology to do this will require monitoring physiological information through wearable body monitoring devices.

Patterns of use among wearers of BodyMedia's products show the exciting news that boomers and seniors who wear fitness monitoring devices do a better job of exercising and eating right than do younger wearers of the same products. This is especially true among people ages 55 to 59 who are trying to kick their health up a notch. BodyMedia is a company that has a bright future. It combines attractive technology with an important consumer health outcome.

Medical Spas

Medical spas are comfortable facilities that provide consumers with convenient access to non-surgical aesthetic procedures, such as chemical peels, that are now usually performed in a dermatologist's or plastic surgeon's office. These new facilities can be found in malls and shopping centers. Revenues are expected to exceed $1 billion by the end of 2006, according to the International Medical Spa Association.[26]

"Eastern Europe and Scandinavia have had medical spas for several years," says John Garcia, an investor in Solana MedSpas. "The demand for these services in the U.S. has increased by 450% over the past four years, with estimated annual revenues of $450 million for doctor-run medspas and an annual growth rate of 11 to 14%."[27]

A typical retail medspa offers five services: laser hair removal; skin rejuvenation through intense pulsed light lasers; injectibles such as Botox, Restylane, and collagen fillers; prescription-strength facials and peels; and cosmeceuticals, pre- and post-treatment. All MedSpas require a physician medical director, although the laser and injectible procedures are performed by a nurse under the supervision of the medical director. Facials and peels are performed by a medical aesthetician.[28]

Clients spend 380% more in medspas than in traditional day spas. They are also an all-cash business, with repeat visits as high as 90%.

Clients spend an average of $700 on each trip to a medical spa, compared with $150 at a traditional day spa, says Dana Caruso, founder of the Long Island Nail and Skin Care Institute in Levittown, New York. Men make up about 10% of the industry's clientele.[29]

John Buckingham, CEO of Solana MedSpas, has developed a turnkey development blueprint for this industry. The five "success triggers," he says, are committed and entrepreneurial owners; ideal location; experienced, well-trained staff; safe, effective, and high-return aesthetic treatments; and aggressive marketing/sales programs.

"As a baby boomer, a career health care CEO, and a serial entrepreneur, I could not resist a company that capitalizes on the boomers' infatuation with anti-aging, especially if we offer ways for people to hold onto the appearance of youth with new, noninvasive technology approved by the FDA," John says. "Boomers are willing to spend whatever it costs to remove unwanted hair, reduce wrinkles, and eliminate sun damage."[30]

Boomers also want to own their own businesses, make money, and have fun. John's turnkey MedSpa Development Program allows professionals a chance to build their own cash health care business. The number of MedSpas is projected to increase from 700 in 2005 to 5,000 by 2012, says John.[31]

Hannelore Leavy is the founder and executive director of the Day Spa Association and the International Medical Spa Association, both of which are trade organizations comprised of spa owners, managers, industry professionals, and equipment, skincare, and other suppliers. The organizations track the trends, products, and services that are winning in this space. Basing her insights on 20 years of promoting the spa lifestyle of health, well-being, and beauty and selling cosmetics and beauty, health, and spa products, Hannelore says that what people are buying is "hope—the promise of health, beauty and youth."[32] Those who are selling spa products need to appeal to women's underlying values and speak to their needs for belonging, esteem, and self-actualization.

Tibion

Boomers are going to embrace medical devices the way they have embraced designer reading glasses. Cell phone earpieces are the new hearing aids, so expect these to become hip, cool accessories. "We're entering a period of exponential growth in technological learning where the power of biotech, infotech, and nanotech compounds the advances of each domain," says investor Steve Jurvetson.[33]

Each year, Santa Clara University, in conjunction with the American Society on Aging, hosts the Boomer Business Plan Competition, which brings together investors, analysts, corporate leaders, and entrepreneurs to explore opportunities in the boomer marketplace. Tibion, Inc., winner of the 2005 Boomer Business Plan Competition, produces "active orthotics" for people with impaired mobility. To serve the many Americans who get knee operations each year,[34] this bionic technology firm created a motorized leg brace called the PowerKnee. Its patented technology augments the quadriceps muscles by employing compact, lightweight sensors along the leg to help movement.

Tibion recognizes that boomers are physically active and will want to stay that way. Founder and CEO Kern Bhugra is looking to angel investors for $3 million to produce a prototype, and another $7.5 million to launch a commercial platform.

Alternative Health Care

More than 33% of Americans choose to treat their illnesses with alternative therapies such as spiritual healing, acupuncture, guided imagery, massage, and chiropractic, according to a study in the *New England Journal of Medicine*.[35] Boomers and older adults are more willing to seek out holistic health care. A study at Ohio State University concluded that 71% of adults age 50 and older used some form of alternative medicine in 2000. Chiropractors were the most commonly used alternative therapy, followed by acupuncture, massage therapy, breathing exercises, herbal medicine, and meditation.[36]

In the United States, 158 million adults use these "complementary" therapies. According to the USA Commission for Alternative and Complementary Medicines, consumers spent $17 billion on these remedies in 2000. In the United Kingdom, the annual expenditure on alternative medicine is $230 million. The global market for herbal medicines currently stands at over $60 billion annually and is growing steadily.[37]

The alternative medicine boom further evidences the revolution in health care. Technology is the engine and the boomers' thirst for solutions and vitality is the fuel.

Endnotes

1. Richard Rosenberg (lecture, What's Next I, San Francisco, CA, April 13, 2004).

2. Paul Kleyman, interview by author, June 5, 2005.

3. Federal Interagency Forum on Aging Related Statistics, "Older Americans 2004: Key Indicators of Well Being," www.agingstats.gov.

4. *Ibid.* Eighteen percent of women age 65 and older and 22% of women age 85 and older have symptoms of depression. For men of the same ages, there is a jump from 11 to 15%. *Ibid.*

5. Department of Health and Human Services, *Health*, United States, 2005. *U.S. With Chartbook on Trends in the Health of Americans* (Hyattsville, Maryland: 2005), 178, http://www.cdc.gov/nchs/data/hus/hus05.pdf#031.

6. *Ibid.*, 32.

7. Mary Duenwald, "More Americans Seeking Help for Depression," *The New York Times*, June 18, 2003, A1.

8. "Baby boomer men more prone to hearing loss." *Life Science Weekly*. June 7, 2005. Page 930.

9. Marilyn Linton, "Women and Arthritis Comprehensive New Report a 'Wake-up' Call for Government." *Toronto Sun*. Page 5. Feb. 27, 2000.

10. "*Newsweek* Focuses on Living Longer: 72% Say They'll Live to Be 80 Years Old," *SeniorJournal.com*, September 10, 2001, http://www.seniorjournal.com/NEWS/Aging/Arch-Aging01/09-10-1Newsweek.htm. Eighty percent described their health as good to excellent. *Ibid.*

11. Steve French, National Marketing Institute's "Healthy Aging/Boomer Database" (panel discussion, 2005 Silicon Valley Boomer Venture Summit, Santa Clara, CA, June 21, 2005).

12. Chip Baird (panel discussion, 2005 Silicon Valley Boomer Venture Summit, Santa Clara, CA, June 21, 2005).

13. Almost 40% of Older Americans Find it Difficult to Determine Credibility of Web-Based Health Information: Healthcompass.org Provides 'How To' Program to Better Evaluate Health Information on the Internet, The Merck Institute of Aging and Health, June 21, 2005, http://www.miahonline.org/press/content/6_21_05_surveyforhealthcompass.html.

14. eMarketer, *Seniors Online: How Aging Boomers Will Shake up the Market*, June 21, 2005.

15. Debra Aho Williamson, "Boomers and Seniors: Big Differences in Online Usage" (lecture, 2005 Silicon Valley Boomer Venture Summit, Santa Clara, CA, June 21, 2005).

16. WebMD Corporation, "WebMD Reports Fourth Quarter and Full Year 2004 Results Company Increases First Quarter 2005 Guidance," March 8, 2005, http://phx.corporate-ir.net/phoenix.zhtml?c=116708&p=irolnewsArticle&t=Regular&id=683104&.

17. Nan Forte, interview by author, April 10, 2005.

18. Jeffrey Burt, "Intel Reorganizes Around Platforms," *eWEEK.com*, January 18, 2005, http://www.eweek.com/article2/0,1895,1752191,00.asp.

19. Sean Cunningham (panel discussion, 2005 Silicon Valley Boomer Venture Summit, Santa Clara, CA, June 21, 2005).

20. Thomas Peeks, interview by author, July 15, 2005.

21. Jeff Zimman, email message to author, September 18, 2006.

22. Henry Mahncke, et al. "Memory enhancement in healthy older adults using a brain plasticity-based training program: A randomized, controlled study," Proceedings of the National Academy of Sciences, 103, no. 33 (August 15, 2006): 12523-28.)

23. Jeff Zimman (panel discussion, 2005 Silicon Valley Boomer Venture Summit, Santa Clara, CA, June 21, 2005).

24. Steve Jurvetson (panel discussion, 2005 Silicon Valley Boomer Venture Summit, Santa Clara, CA, June 21, 2005).

25. Jeff Zimman (panel discussion, 2005 Silicon Valley Boomer Venture Summit, Santa Clara, CA, June 21, 2005).

26. Elaine Walker, "Medical spas a growing trend in S. Fla.," *Miami Herald*, October 11, 2005, http://www.miami.com/mld/miamiherald/business/12868704.htm?source=rss&channel=miamiherald_business.

27. John Garcia (panel discussion, 2005 Silicon Valley Boomer Venture Summit, Santa Clara, CA, June 21, 2005).

28. John Buckingham, conversation with author, Wisconsin, October 11, 2005.

29. Dana Caruso, conversation with author, Wisconsin, October 11, 2005.

30. John Buckingham, conversation with author, Wisconsin, October 11, 2005.

31. *Ibid.*

32. Hannelore R. Leavy, conversation with author, Wisconsin, October 12, 2005.

33. Steve Jurvetson (panel discussion, 2005 Silicon Valley Boomer Venture Summit, Santa Clara, CA, June 21, 2005).

34. There are 850,000 knee operations each year just for meniscus tears. "Extra Pounds Equate to Knee Damage," HealthCentral.com, April 29, 2005, http:/ /www.healthcentral.com/newsdetail/408/525281.html.

35. James L. Eng, "Large Number of Patients Seek 'Unconventional' Therapy; Medicine: Naturopathy, which Emphasizes the Healing Power of Nature, Is Among the Popular Alternatives for Treating and Preventing Ailments," *Los Angeles Times*, May 2, 1993, B3.

36. "Almost 70 Percent of Older Adults Use Alternative Medicine," *SeniorJournal. com*, April 9, 2005, http://www.seniorjournal.com/NEWS/Health/ 5-04-09AlternativeMedicine.htm.

37. World Health Organization, "Fact Sheets: Traditional Medicine," 2003, http:// www.who.int/mediacentre/factsheets/fs134/en/.

3

Travel: An Adventure for the Heart, Mind, and Soul

Introduction

Homer lost his wife of 60 years and was not sure how to cope. So shortly after his 77th birthday, he took a trip to Africa and met a new partner while riding an elephant. Sarah, at age 49, thought her partner was going to ask her to marry him. Instead, he told her she was letting herself go. So she hopped a plane to Costa Rica, had cosmetic surgery, went on a nude cruise, and danced with the captain—all in celebration of her 50th birthday. Barbara, a young widow at 61, didn't want to just sit on a beach anymore—she wanted her travel to *mean* something. So she jumped at the chance to set up at a sewing school for young girls in Kenya.

These people are not alone; they are part of a new trend in meaningful travel.

When people ask the question, "What business should I create for the boomers?" my answer is always the same. It's travel.

Travelers age 50 and older are yearning for romance, leisure, life-long learning, and giving back. They represent the hottest market for

tours and independent vacations, according to the United States Tour
Operators Association (USTOA).[1]

Midlife travelers are adjusting to the fact that the kids have left
home, and they may also be healing after a divorce or a death. Their
work life may be winding down, so now it is time to create a new life
of their own choosing. After age 55, the number of childless married
couples increases dramatically, and so does the number of women who
live alone. Demographers call this pattern *life cycle messiness* because
the living options for this stage of life are so diverse (see Figure 3.1).
But no matter what their household arrangements may be, most people want the same thing when they hit age 55. They want to renew
themselves. They want to see, taste, tour, learn, chill, film, connect,
play, and serve. In other words, they want to travel.

Recently, Eurail offered a special package aimed at boomers who
remember wandering around Europe on $5 a day. Europe wants
the boomers back—but this time they have better backpacks and
silver in their hair. As this generation moves into its new lifestage, the
passive, leisure-oriented view of retirement is fading. Boomers are

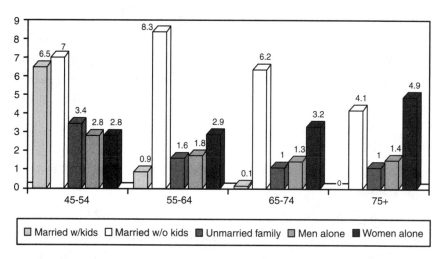

**FIGURE 3.1 LIFE CYCLE MESSINESS (Households by type aged 45 and
older, in millions, 2002)**
Source: CPS

less interested in acquiring material assets and more interested in acquiring life-changing experiences. "Catered peak experiences with like-minded souls" is their new mantra.

Niche businesses that are cultural, educational, and service-oriented are redefining travel to fit boomers' needs. As the most educated generation ever, boomers want to enjoy local cuisine the way the locals do. They want learning for its own sake, like cooking classes with an Italian chef or a walk through an English garden with a top designer. They want to rekindle marriages, take the grandchildren to the Galapagos, and build a beach house in Newfoundland. They want to go behind the scenes of history, teach their peers, or hop in the RV and boldly go where no one has gone before, just like Captain Kirk did on *Star Trek*.

After retiring from Microsoft, Larry spent half a year in Vietnam cleaning up the land mines left from decades earlier. When the tsunami hit Asia in December 2004, Tom immediately put his Texas State Department job on hiatus and went to Thailand. Within three weeks he had helped locals set up a boat-building business in a fishing village. The experience fueled both his spirit and the local economy.

Travel is the one business category that covers all the themes outlined in this book. It is a global business; it benefits from increases in longevity, health, and wellness; it caters to the boomers' hunger for family and community; it is being transformed by online services and other technology; it is a purchase that often accompanies life transitions; it offers learning and enhances creativity; and it feeds a hunger for spirituality and service.

In this chapter, we look at what motivates boomers to travel at midlife, where they go, and who is capitalizing on this market. We will see who has captured the sensibilities and trends of educational travel, intergenerational travel, luxury travel, disability travel, adventure travel, and health and wellness travel. We will also look at entrepreneurs who are developing niche markets, and we will offer other "market slices" and tips.

Scoping Out the Travel Markets

Most categories of consumer spending peak between the ages of 45 and 54, but travel is an exception. Spending on hotel and air travel is highest among households headed by persons age 45 to 54, according to the Consumer Expenditure Survey, but spending on cruises doesn't peak until ages 65 to 74. And spending on hotels and airlines remains above average in the 55 to 64 and 65 to 74-year-old household groups, so there's plenty of money in this market now—and when the boomers move into it, there will be a lot more (see Figure 3.2).

Analyst Heather Hardwick, vice president of Menlo Consulting Group in Palo Alto, California, says boomers are fueling key growth segments in travel: family/intergenerational, adventure, meaningful travel, luxury, cruising, and health and wellness. "Boomers' age and lifestage impact their travel behavior," Heather says. "Younger boomers tend to stay closer to home, favor sun and sand destinations, travel less frequently, prefer short breaks, and have longer planning lead time. Older boomers tend to travel farther afield, travel more often, take longer trips, are concerned with the pitfalls of travel, and reflect the values of 'mature travelers.'"[2]

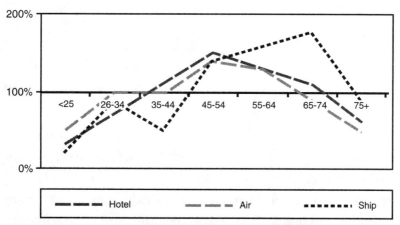

FIGURE 3.2 VACATION SPENDING BY AGE (INDEX OF AVERAGE ANNUAL HOUSEHOLD SPENDING ON AIR TICKETS, HOTELS, AND SHIP TICKETS BY AGE OF HOUSEHOLDER)
Source: Consumer Expenditure Survey

Baby boomers are certain to boost spending on travel because they are the most educated generation in U.S. history, and education goes with travel the way baseball goes with Crackerjacks. Household spending on hotels and airlines increases steadily with the educational attainment of the householder, and spending on cruises is much higher among college graduates than it is for any other group.[3] In part, this is because college educated people tend to earn more money. But it's also because educated people are more curious about life (see Figure 3.3).

Americans over age 50 account for 45% of trips in the United States,[4] and they are spending more than $30 billion a year on travel.[5] They consume 80% of all luxury travel.[6] They take 72% of all RV trips and account for 70% of cruise passengers.[7] They spend 75% more money per vacation than do travelers under 50.[8] Persons age 65 and older account for 31% of all trips taken in the United States, spending on average $507 on overnight trips.[9] Even when they are single, boomers spend more on their trips than do single people in other age groups.[10]

Where do boomers go to have fun? Ann Thomas, former chairman and CEO of the National Tour Association (NTA) and owner/manager of Western Discovery LLC, in Reno, Nevada, says

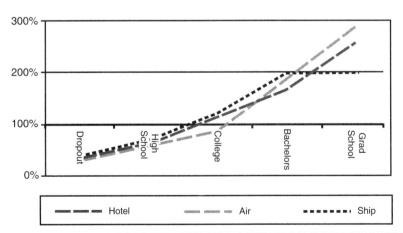

FIGURE 3.3 VACATIONS BY EDUCATION (INDEX OF AVERAGE ANNUAL HOUSEHOLD SPENDING ON AIR, HOTELS, AND SHIPS BY EDUCATIONAL ATTAINMENT OF HOUSEHOLDER)
Source: Consumer Expenditure Survey

the hot growth areas are cruises, national parks, and experiential tours to almost anywhere. "Experiential travel is huge right now. It's no longer enough to simply visit a place," Ann says.[11] Instead, boomers want to get involved with their destination by learning about it or giving something back. The NTA reports steady growth in tours and packages offered for families (up 31% from 2003), wine tasting (up 23% from 2003), and learning tours (up 35% over 2003).[12] *Voluntourism*, which describes a visit on some type of service mission, is also joining the travel mainstream.

Ann says that the boomers want three things when they travel: good value, engaging all their senses, and lots of options. "They seem to be traveling in smaller groups or special interest groups or with their families. They consider travel a priority and see educational experiences as key. But really, the boomers are unlike any other generation in terms of travel. By the time they reach midlife, they consider travel a necessity, not a luxury. Boomers have also traveled more extensively as young adults than any other generation has, so they arrive more savvy and wanting more exotic and deeper experiences to fulfill the dreams they have put on hold. And they want these deferred dreams even if their bodies are reluctant to go along."[13]

Boomers are also growing accustomed to handling their own travel arrangements using the Internet. There is a wealth of choices now that they can research and book trips online. About 68% of boomers now use the Internet.[14] As websites are redesigned by companies to become more readable and usable by older adults, we can expect the 50+ demographic to travel even more.

The trend is one-stop shopping for air, hotel, and car reservations for an overall travel package. According to Nielsen/NetRatings, which analyzes Internet audiences, leisure travel shoppers tend to begin their research with agencies and online meta-search providers such as Kayak.com or Sidestep.com before visiting individual suppliers. Southwest Airlines, American Airlines, and Delta are the three most visited airline websites. Expedia leads the three top online travel agency sites, followed by Orbitz and Travelocity.[15] In addition, the one airline that seems to be doing everything right is JetBlue.

Elephant Entrepreneur: JetBlue Airways

David Neeleman has asked the right questions and created the right boomer travel experience for the next two decades. Where do boomers in New York want to go for the winter? Try Florida. Try California. Offer a great experience with low prices and clean air in the cabin. Do this with a cheerful crew and you will soon have profits and customers who cheerfully help you clean up. While JetBlue may not be targeted at boomers per se, it has become one of their favorite brands. And it will stay that way because JetBlue makes it easy to travel with the grandchildren.

David hatched the idea for JetBlue back in 1993 when he sold his first airline, Salt Lake City-based Morris Air, to Southwest Airlines. Two personal experiences were crucial to forming his vision for JetBlue. After getting assigned to a urine-soaked seat (solution: leather seats for JetBlue) and a nightmarish layover in the wee hours (solution: discount coupons for future flights for inconvenienced JetBlue passengers), David knew he could do better by bringing "humanity back to air travel." His industry experiences taught him that innovative, high-quality service combined with low fares could attract a loyal market.

JetBlue secured $130 million in capital funding from five investors, including George Soros, Chase Capital, and Weston Presidio Capital. David kicked in several million of his own funds. He handpicked his management team and created a unique culture in the travel market, building community around principles and values.

JetBlue, which began service in 2000 between New York City's JFK International and Fort Lauderdale, is the first and only U.S. startup airline to launch with more than $100 million in capital, the first to be 100% e-ticketed, the first and only airline to offer live satellite programming free at every seat, and the first and only low-fare U.S. airline to operate a fleet of brand-new aircraft. Customers get roomy, all-leather seats, LiveTV, and biscotti snacks.

JetBlue has been profitable since its first year.[16] It doubled in size and then doubled again during its first nine quarters. Its operating margin is the highest of any major airline. Given the recent woes of the domestic airline industry, this is an impressive accomplishment.

Several lessons can be drawn from this startup. First, JetBlue started with a lot of money to invest in the best product possible. It hired top people by screening and training them rigorously. Most importantly, it focused on service for the best experience possible.[17]

David says the essence of JetBlue is "something you can trust; it is comfortable and consistent. You are treated well. We will do the right thing for you. We stay in the gate a bit longer to make sure the planes are clean."

Boomers have a deep desire for travel and play. Their desire to connect with children and grandchildren is even stronger. Reasonable airfare puts this all in reach. A friend flew all six of her grandchildren to New York—which was not a problem because JetBlue offered her low fares, individual TV sets, and comfortable seats.

"I felt strongly about equal treatment. Do things right," David says. "Treat our own crewmembers well and they will treat the customers well. It is a better place to work when people value you." All of JetBlue's more than 5,000 employees participate in profit sharing, and employees can buy company stock at a 15% discount.

David instills loyalty and trust by being a highly visible CEO. He visits every incoming flight attendant training class and teaches the values of crew relationship management, where people learn how to cooperate. When he flies, he chats with passengers, asks for feedback, and doles out cookies and chips. He handles complaints, takes time to find a pet carrier for a passenger with a cat, and even helps clean up after the plane lands.

David's business acumen is more than just about profitability. Giving back is also a key theme for him, as it is with other boomers. "Some people say that happiness is acquiring more and more [things]. I think that it matters if you are helping others. I learned this when I was a missionary in Brazil." David donates his entire salary to JetBlue's employee catastrophe fund. He has even helped a widowed employee make a down payment on a house.

JetBlue's business strategy focuses on building a system that is consistent and clear in delivering top service all around. That way everyone believes in the culture and practices it. Whether it's encouraging a pilot who buys McDonald's Happy Meals for kids when his plane is grounded or a manager who helps a family whose employee father had a heart attack, David flies his talk.[18]

Emerging Entrepreneur: Travel Learning Connections

If you want to have an experience to treasure, put Travel Learning Connections' (TLC) annual Education Travel Conference on your calendar. There is so much enthusiasm, as the conference provides a place to broker programs for tour planners and operators; travel suppliers; international and domestic destinations; and museum, education, and cultural groups.

TLC started in 1986 to link nonprofits with for-profits. It also provides a forum to facilitate professional development and community for people developing lifelong learning programs with an educational bent for travel. Mara DelliPriscoli founded the conference for travel planners for nonprofit organizations like museums, and she expanded into alumni associations and conservation groups. Then tour operators came on board; then destinations and suppliers. More than 500 people now go to the annual conference and there is a larger community active online.

Mara became a key player in the affinity travel market by continually asking how to serve it. Recently she launched an online community because she saw that her people wanted to continue talking with each other.

TLC is a great example of a company with a smart leader who knows that global reach, lifelong learning, family connections, giving back, and building community are key themes in the boomer midlife lexicon. TLC is also tapping into the lifestage themes of wanting to follow one's passions, create a family of one's own choosing, and find meaningful experiences.

That sensibility is driving explosive growth in exotic, niche destinations like Libya, Madagascar, Mongolia, Tibet, and India. This growth is enhanced by changes in marketing and vision among alumni associations, where the median age of customers was in the 60s, but is now younger. Tour operators are capturing more boomers by offering more flexibility on trips, more freedom, more interaction with the leader, more behind-the-scenes visits, and more options for self-directed pre- or post-conference programs.

Mara points to new trends that include service learning, such as volunteer vocations in which participants can take a day to work with locals on a project. This is the experience economy at its best because it gives customers the chance to experience a culture by participating in it, provides the opportunity for transformational experiences, and is the vehicle that allows travelers to give back in a direct, personal way.

This boomer desire to make connections is also feeding an explosion in intergenerational travel. Even universities are offering family adventures. Mara says, "I have colleagues who have retired from their positions as travel planners and the one thing they ask me is, 'What are the operators that do intergenerational?' I want to take my grandchildren who don't live close by. I have the money and the time, but I don't want to do the work that is involved in creating an educational program. I don't want just the standard fare travel. They want an educationally focused safari or a trip to the Galapagos, where they can share an incredible experience together."[19]

Now let's take a closer look at the travel industry segments where the opportunities shine brightest.

Intergenerational/Family Travel

Boomers are hitting the road with their grandchildren in record numbers, says the American Automobile Association (AAA). In fact, the number of websites catering to family travel is exploding, with Grandtravel and the Family Travel Network among the top sites.

According to several surveys, the changing composition of the U.S. family has led to a greater demand from both older and younger travelers for multiple-generation trips. One study found that 20% of grandparents took a trip with their grandchildren in 2000. And 56% of children age 6 to 17 said they "would really like to" take a trip with their grandparents. Travel with grandparents and grandchildren represented one-fifth (21%) of all trips taken with children in 2000, up from just 13% in 1999.[20] In addition, grandparents and older Americans, in general, are using the Internet more frequently for their travel plans. According to a Pew Internet survey, 41% of older Americans had made travel reservations online by the end of 2003. That was a 64% increase from 2000.[21]

The range of family-oriented trips includes cruising, sun and sand, educational, and outdoor activity. REI offers trips to the Canadian Rockies with ghost stories around the campfire, or you can go elsewhere for cruises to Alaska, Antarctica, or the Galapagos.

Generations Touring Company offers family tours of historic ballparks, so visitors can watch the Yankees and Red Sox pursuing their rivalry in both Boston and New York. Grandparents can take their grandchildren to dine with a sportswriter and then head to Cooperstown to visit the National Baseball Hall of Fame.

When boomers travel with their families, they don't always need a luxury environment. More often, they prefer a friendly, quality atmosphere at an affordable price. This is why more bed and breakfast inns and motels feature accommodations tailored toward both old and young. Someone interested in this new niche might consider whether their venue has enough activities to keep children interested—or if there is wheelchair accessibility onsite and bathtubs equipped with safety handles.

Adventure Travel

Adventure travel used to mean roughing it in some faraway place, but today it can mean almost anything. Heather Hardwick of Menlo Consulting Group says the category is cross-pollinating with other segments such as health and wellness, family travel, women-only travel, luxury travel, ecotourism, and cultural immersion. Adventure operators are refining their products to appeal to a broader audience. They are integrating more cultural pursuits; even cruising is getting more adventurous, with new options and destinations. Heather says "white linens and wilderness" is an example of how adventure travel is blending with luxury travel. Honeymoons are blending with adventure travel as well: now a honeymoon may be a hike on the Inca trail or a visit to Cuba.[22]

Travelers visiting historic or cultural destinations grew from 192.4 million in 1996 to 216.8 million in 2002, according to the Travel Industry Association. Households headed by boomers are most likely to take historic or cultural trips, accounting for 41%.[23] And the typical adventure traveler is not who you might expect: she is a 47-year-old female boomer who wears a size 12 dress.[24]

Boomers are looking for once-in-a-lifetime experiences. They want champagne flights to the North Pole, travel to Timbuktu, sea kayaking through the Panama Canal, a stay with a Mongolian family in the Gobi Desert, cage diving with great white sharks in South Africa, and caravanning by camel across the Sahara Desert. The South Pacific, Eastern Europe, China, Australia, and New Zealand are also popular destinations for boomers.

Cruise Travel

Cruising used to be something baby boomers did down Main Street on Saturday nights. Menlo Consulting Group finds that today, ocean cruising is the star performer of the travel industry. New destinations, luxurious new ships, specialty and theme packages, and even smaller vessels (yachts and canal barges) mean that cruises now provide a variety of activities, events, classes, meals, and entertainment. Top destinations are the Caribbean, Mexico, and Alaska. Destinations with the highest ratio of interest to past experience are Australia, New Zealand, Fiji or Tahiti, Hawaii, Scandinavia, and the Mediterranean.[25]

Heather Hardwick notes, "Boomers are not currently cruising at the levels of other travelers. But boomers' demand for cruising is equal to that of other travelers'. Boomers are a great potential market for future growth in cruising."[26] Cruise lines are banking on wealthy boomer travelers in the coming years. The industry is building new ships with more diverse amenities, services, and ports. Post-cruise tours and excursions to experience destinations in more depth are a growing market. Another is the smaller cruise line selling to group companies to leverage the brands of those operators. The website CruiseCritic.com offers good insights into the cruise marketplace.

Education and Culture Travel

Since the earliest days of SeniorNet, I have heard one travel brand consistently mentioned in meetings with corporations: Elderhostel. This is America's first and the world's largest education travel organization for adults age 55 and over. It serves nearly 200,000 adults each year with over 10,000 programs in 90 countries. The business model is based on strong database marketing. Most of their community members self-identify as Elderhostelers and are repeat customers. Elderhostel is one of the most trusted brands for the 50+ market.

Among the things that Elderhostel gets right is the sensibility of the consumers age 55 and older. Its language involves the traveler actively: "Learn to paint on Nantucket" or "Investigate hot air ballooning with your grandchildren" or "Join a student orchestra." It has learned that adults want to share their experiences and contribute to conversation. Thus, many of the instructors are peers and the method of learning is collaborative.

Elderhostel has adapted over the years. To capture the emerging boomer market, it opened a second brand called Road Scholar. This program offers "Snapshots and Weekenders," two- to four-night programs that delve into topics such as the ecology of Puget Sound. It also emphasizes hands-on service to community and conducting wildlife and marine research to protect endangered species.

Elderhostel discovered that as the boomers age they still want adventure, but with more comfort. So they have changed the accommodations over the last 20 years. Now tours offer comfortable rooms with private baths in hotels, inns, retreat centers, and campuses. Elderhostelers often say that this kind of travel provides more than an adventure. It also provides a family of your own choosing.

A few other travel companies catering to the over-50 set are Saga, Silver Sneakers, Backroads Active Travel, Odyssey Travel, and 50Plus Expeditions.

Another key player in the education and culture travel market is High Country Passage, a company that provides educational travel programs with a focus on smaller groups and exclusive access to people and events. Don Kendall and his father, who was the marketing chief at Pepsi Cola when the company created the "Pepsi Generation" ad campaign back when the boomers were young, purchased the company in 2003, having previously founded a marketing services company called Affinity Expeditions. They knew that the boomer market was going to drive huge growth in travel, and they got out in front of the trend.

The family's connections allow them to invite world leaders such as Mikhail Gorbachev along on trips to European capitals. The chance to discuss world affairs with Gorbachev is a catered peak experience, which is the very thing boomers are looking for.

High Country Passage understands the boomer sensibility and creates unique, quality experiences. In addition to expert-led education, its trips have a bit of soft adventure, such as hiking, biking, and snorkeling, followed by a gourmet lunch and dinner and a bed with 500-thread-count sheets.

Health and Wellness Travel

Health and wellness travel is one branch of the anti-aging industry. Bicycling vacations have attracted more than 27 million travelers in the past five years. Bicycling is the third most popular outdoor vacation activity in America, after camping and hiking.[27] Boomers are flocking to fitness and spa facilities such as The Chopra Center for Wellbeing in La Jolla, California; the Green Valley Spa and Tennis Resort in St. George, Utah; and The Aspen Club in Aspen, Colorado.

The industry is also beginning to accommodate special health needs with services such as specialized diets and accommodations for people with sensory and mobility impairments. One example of this is Level Travel.

Emerging Entrepreneur: Level Travel

One of the finalists in the first Boomer Business Plan Competition was a Wharton graduate named Jamie Sharples, who is a great example of someone who saw a huge social issue and is doing something that not only creates a viable business, but also helps solve a problem.

Jamie uses a wheelchair, and his business idea came from personal experience. He recalls, "I was trying to make dinner reservations for my grandfather's birthday. I called seven restaurants. Finally, the seventh one said that they were wheelchair accessible. So we were all surprised when we got there and there were eight steps to get into the front door. The maitre d', who was standing at the top, said, 'Ah, it's not a problem. We pick you up. We carry you. It's accessible. It's not a problem.'"

Jamie's definition of "accessibility" was rather different. The seed of his business, Level Travel, was planted. He began building a database of rating criteria for disabled travelers and their companions and families—a kind of *Consumer Reports* for hotels and restaurants. In his due diligence, Jamie discovered there is no comprehensive resource for special-needs travelers, no independent group that verified compliance with the Americans with Disabilities Act (ADA). Even the barrier free travel guides from AAA and Fodor's use varying criteria to rate facilities. Travelers still have to contact each destination directly to find out about accessibility, and the answers are subjective.

Jamie says that 94 million Americans comprise the mature and disabled markets. Within this large group are 62 million people over the age of 50; 29 million who have some type of sensory impairment, like vision or hearing loss; and another 9 million with some type of significant mobility impairment that keeps them from mounting steps or walking long distances. As boomers turn 50, this market size may grow to approximately 40% of the U.S. population by 2020, or about 135 million people.

Jamie also found that mature and disabled travelers spent $35 billion on travel and tourism in 2003. This is a fraction of what is possible. A Harris Interactive study in 2002 estimated that disabled Americans would spend another $13 billion on travel if there were better and more accessible conditions available. "Accessibility is not something businesses should do out of the benevolence of their heart. This is a very large market," says Jamie.

Level Travel segments the disability travel market into four categories: people with mobility impairments; people with vision loss; those with hearing loss; and mature travelers. Level Travel has developed a set of comprehensive rating criteria, called the Level Ratings, which assess the level of disability access provided by hotels and restaurants in major locations. "We have an objective and transparent set of rating criteria so that anybody that comes and looks at our data can see exactly what we're looking at," he says. For example, a hotel rating would look at the elevators, pool, business center, parking, interior quarters, desk, entrances, and bathrooms.

Jamie has staffed Level Travel with experts in hotel management, venture capital funding, and mature and disabled travel. He plans a subscription-based Internet site that will allow users to access the database of rated facilities similar to the models employed by Consumer Reports and Zagat Survey. He plans to have polls on his website to ask visitors where they would like to travel and what places they would like to see rated.

"There's a terrific amount of upside to it, not just from the social benefit side," he says. "There's also a strong business case because it is such a large marketplace and it is so untapped. I think some businesses can be singularly focused on creating a financial juggernaut, but it's really not going to improve society in general. Others might improve society, but they will just be lifestyle business for one or two people. I think Level Travel bridges both of those worlds. I think it can have a huge societal impact, and I think there's also a tremendous amount of potential to turn this into a for-profit company."[28]

Other Market Slices

Women-only travel: This market has grown into one of the most innovative and creative opportunities in group travel. Gutsy Women Travel's Gail Golden likens her trips to pajama parties. She says, "By the end of the first night, women are hugging each other and telling their life stories."[29] Single women like to travel together because they feel safer in groups than they do alone. So there are adventures to a

Montana dude ranch to be a cowgirl for a week, to Sedona for a retreat, and cuisine and culture tours to Tuscany. Travel geared specifically toward women in mid-life is also on the rise. Teresa DeLillo, founder of web-based Menopausal Tours, notes that women over the age of 40 are more likely to travel during mid-life than their mothers, confirming the company philosophy that travel is "for women of a certain attitude." Trips are both domestic and international, and clientele include a lot of mother/daughter duos, sisters, and best friends who want to re-energize while enjoying the experience of adventure. Tours are designed for the "midlife lust for life and curiosity about new locales."[30]

Special interest travel: Experts see a lot of opportunity for continued development in special interest travel. Architecture, wine, and food top the list. Travel is even crossing categories as retailers get in the act. Sales at the travel division of Orvis, a retailer of fly-fishing gear and apparel, have increased from less than $200,000 in 1999 to about $2 million per year. The company served fewer than 1,000 travelers in 2002, but expects 10,000 per year within five years.

The revenue stream linked directly to travel amounts to less than 1% of Orvis's overall revenue, but it plays a significant role from a marketing perspective by helping build brand loyalty. The philosophy is simple, says Dave Parker, managing director of travel at Orvis: "If you're selling a guy fish hooks and tell him a good place to go fishing, chances are he's going to buy more fish hooks."[31] Outfitters like REI, Orvis, L.L. Bean, and Cabela's—each of which has a travel division—expect these trends to increase demand for fishing, hiking, and hunting in the coming decade. As a further incentive, many outfitters offer catalog-wide discounts to customers who book trips with them.

Gay and lesbian travel: According to the Altus Group's David Jefferys—who did Philadelphia's successful gay travel market campaign with the slogan "Keep Your History Straight and Your Nightlife Gay"—gays and lesbians between the ages of 35 and 60 average three to four trips per year, spend $54 billion a year, and tend not to buy group tours. Compared to heterosexuals, more gay travelers hold a valid passport, travel by plane and train, are college educated, and have household incomes above the national average. Gay men prefer event-driven travel, and more than half spend between $2,500 and $10,000 per person on each vacation. Lesbians prefer privacy and family-friendly planned itineraries, with 60% spending $1,500 per person.[32] This is a space to watch.

RVs: Forty-four percent of RV buyers are age 55 or older. In 1991, industry retail sales hit $6.7 billion;[33] by 2005, that number had shot up to $14 billion, and it's still climbing. Eight and a half million U.S. households are expected to own RVs by 2010.[34] And it's not only RV makers and retailers who are benefiting. Manufacturers and retailers of aftermarket gear, campground operators, and others are getting in on the trend.

Singles travel: Almost 96 million American adults are single or unmarried.[35] Singles account for 27% of all domestic trips taken over 50 miles from home. Working singles age 55 and older are more likely than younger singles to visit historical places or museums or to attend cultural events or festivals.[36] An increasing percentage of solo female travelers are boomers and single mothers.[37] They usually travel with their girlfriends or join a singles mixer group.

Summary

Boomers will travel throughout their bonus years, but they won't go in station wagons. They will explore new destinations. They will reconnect with their families, bring their grandkids, and reignite their marriages. They will want to savor those fleeting moments that create lifetime memories. Travel means lots of connections, but at midlife, boomers also need time for personal retreat.

How will you build a business that taps into the deep desire boomers have for adventures that are meaningful? Here's what the experts say.

"It's all about packaged travel with a personal touch," says Ann Thomas. "Successful agencies walk their guests through the selection process and offer lots of options. They also take the time to find out what their guests really want. Consumers are demanding more flexibility and unique destinations, so customizing tours and tailoring activities to the tastes of the traveler are imperative."[38]

Single boomers present an opportunity for travel companies because the loss of a partner or a divorce can serve as a catalyst for travel. Newfound singlehood often inspires older adults to travel, but many are reluctant to travel alone and thus seek additional amenities when they do travel. Travel companies will do well to tune in to the needs of single travelers and offer a human touch. Companies should note that many singles are newly widowed and may need extra help or attention during the trip. Also, travel companies should keep singles in mind while planning activities. Singles won't want to go on a cruise where the only social activity is a couples' dance. It would be better to plan activities where singles can meet the locals, play golf, or learn a craft—anything that doesn't require having a partner, but rather facilitates finding a new one or making a new friend.

Tie passions and pursuits to your offerings. Boomers are going to become avid bird watchers, surfers, chefs, and gardeners. They will want to use travel to see the world to explore these passions. Remember that boomers influence the travel plans of their children and grandchildren. And remember to market to them online. Provide discount emails with bargains. Build a travel community around your product or service.

Endnotes

1.   United States Tour Operators Association, "USTOA Names Italy, Alaska Top Vacation Destinations For 2004, Baby Boomers Hottest Growing Demographic Group for Packaged Travel," http://ustoa.com/consumernews/04survey_c.cfm.

2.   Heather Hardwick, Menlo Consulting Group, Inc., "The Analyst Perspective: Trends in Boomer Travel" (lecture, 2005 Silicon Valley Boomer Venture Summit, Santa Clara, CA, June 21, 2005).

3. U.S. Department of Labor, Bureau of Labor Statistics, *Consumer Expenditure Survey*.

4. Travel Industry Association of America, "Executive Summaries—The Mature Traveler, 2000 Edition," http://www.tia.org/researchpubs/executive_summaries_mature_traveler.html.

5. Joanne Fritz, "The Yen to Travel," December 23, 2005, http://second50years.blogspot.com/2005_12_01_second50years_archive.html.

6. Suddenly Senior, "2002 Senior Market Facts," http://www.suddenlysenior.com/seniorfacts.html.

7. Joanne Fritz, "The Yen to Travel," December 23, 2005, http://second50years.blogspot.com/2005_12_01_second50years_archive.html.

8. Leslie M. Harris, "Baby Boom Travel Emphasizes Adventure and Relaxation," in *After Fifty: How the Baby Boom Will Redefine the Mature Market* (Paramount Market Publishing, Inc., 2003).

9. Travel Industry Association of America, "Mature Traveler," 2000.

10. Travel Industry Association of America, *Domestic Travel Market Report*, 2003. Baby boomer households (ages 35–54) are more likely to stay in a hotel or motel on overnight trips (59%), travel for business (32%), and fly (22%) than other lifestage segments. Baby boomer travelers are the most affluent among lifestage segments: 44% having an annual income of $75,000 or more. Boomers spend more on their trips than other age groups, averaging $491 per trip, excluding transportation to their destination. Fourteen percent spend $1,000 or more on a trip, excluding cost of transportation. With an average age of 45, this group represents baby boomer singles. This group generated 47 million trips in 2001. They spend the most of all singles age groups, with an average of $462 per trip, not including cost of transportation. They have the highest household incomes of the singles groups. Trips made by middle singles are more likely than those by other singles to be taken for business travel (32%). Trips are more likely to be by air (28%) and, or include a hotel, motel, or B&B stay (55%). *Ibid*.

11. Ann Thomas, email message to Lori Covington, May 20, 2005.

12. Sara Morton, "Special Interest Travel Increases for National Tour Association Tour Operators," July 6, 2005, http://www.ntaonline.com/index.php?s=&url_channel_id=24&url_subchannel_id=&url_article_id=2337&change_well_id=2.

13. Ann Thomas, email message to Lori Covington, May 20, 2005.

14. Anick Jesdanum, "Boomers Closing Digital Divide," *CBS News*, April 8, 2004, http://www.cbsnews.com/stories/2004/04/08/tech/main610937.shtml.

15. Tracy Yen, "Online Travel Purchases Split Evenly Between Travel Agencies and Suppliers' Web Sites; Airline Supplier Sites Nearly Doubles Conversion Rates of Online Travel Agencies, According to Nielsen//NetRatings," NetRatings, June 21, 2005.

16. Perry Flint, "It's a Blue World After All: JetBlue Rewrites the Rules of the Game and Has the Majors on the Run to Keep Up," *Air Transport World*, June 2003.

17. Arlyn Tobias Gajilan, "The Amazing JetBlue," *Fortune Small Business*, May 2003; JetBlue Airways Corporation, Form 10-K/A, Annual Report Pursuant to Section 13 or 15(d) of the Securities Exchange Act of 1934, 9, http://64.106.229.11/jetblue2004/10k.pdf. JetBlue had sales of $635 million and grew to an operating revenue of $430 million for the second quarter 2005—34.5% higher than the same period of 2004. *Ibid.*

18. David Neeleman, interview by author, July 11, 2005.

19. Mara DelliPriscoli, interview by author, August 6, 2005.

20. "The New Family Vacation—Demographics, United States—Statistical Data Included," *American Demographics*, August 1, 2001.

21. Susannah Fox, *Older Americans and the Internet* (Pew Internet & American Life Project, March 25, 2004), ii, http://www.pewinternet.org/pdfs/PIP_Seniors_Online_2004.pdf.

22. Heather Hardwick, Menlo Consulting Group, Inc., "The Analyst Perspective: Trends in Boomer Travel" (lecture, 2005 Silicon Valley Boomer Venture Summit, Santa Clara, CA, June 21, 2005).

23. National Assembly of State Arts Agencies, "Cultural Visitor Profile," http://www.nasaa-arts.org/artworks/culture_profile.shtml.

24. "Women Travel Statistics," *The Gutsy Traveler*, http://www.gutsytraveler.com/mbbStatistics.html.

25. Menlo Consulting Group, Inc., *TravelStyles USA: Americans as International Travelers*, 2004, http://www.menloconsulting.com.

26. Heather Hardwick, Menlo Consulting Group, Inc., "The Analyst Perspective: Trends in Boomer Travel" (lecture, 2005 Silicon Valley Boomer Venture Summit, Santa Clara, CA, June 21, 2005).

27. Travel Industry Association of America, "Domestic Travel Fast Facts—Travel Trends from 'A to Z,'" http://www.tia.org/pressmedia/domestic_a_to_z.html.

28. Jamie Sharples (lecture, 2005 Silicon Valley Boomer Venture Summit, Santa Clara, CA, June 21, 2005).

29. Nancy Gibbs, "Midlife Crisis? Bring It On! How women of this generation are seizing that stressful, pivotal moment in their lives to reinvent themselves," *Time*, May 16, 2005, 52.

30. Teresa DeLillo, interview by author, 2005.

31. Brad Foss, "Outfitters cater to aging baby boomers with travel," *Northwest Indiana Times*, May 12, 2003.

32. David Jefferys, "Gay and Lesbian Travel Market" (lecture, What's Next II, Philadelphia, PA, March 9, 2005).

33. Robert McGarvey, "Gray matters: seniors to sway future trends—baby boom generation," *Entrepreneur*, January 1999.

34. Recreational Vehicle Industry Association, "RV Business Indicators," February 3, 2006, http://www.rvia.org/Media/RVBusinessIndicators.pdf.

35. U.S. Census Bureau, "Special Edition: Unmarried and Single Americans Week," *Facts for Features*, July 19, 2004, http://www.census.gov/Press-Release/www/releases/archives/facts_for_features_special_editions/002265.html.

36. Jim Thompson, "No Babysitters Needed; Singles Take One-Fourth of U.S. Trips," *Travel Journo*. February 12, 2003, http://www.traveljourno.com/TravelBriefs.cfm?varR=132.

37. "Women Travel Statistics," *The Gutsy Traveler*, http://www.gutsytraveler.com/mbbStatistics.html.

38. Ann Thomas, email message to Lori Covington, May 20, 2005.

4

IT'S YOUR PASSION: MAKE IT HAPPEN

Introduction

Do you make enough time for play?

Most boomers don't. For several decades they have been so directed toward career and family that they have missed recess. They have often lost the lilt in their smiles and the sparkle in their eyes that come from a day of play. By this stage of life, some boomers have graduated to size 14 and have lost their hair, libido, and health. The big house doesn't lift the heart anymore. Money doesn't rekindle the soul.

But as boomers age, the times they are a-changin'. Ralph and his brother Frank stopped by my house recently, on their way home after placing decoys for the start of duck-hunting season. My friend Beth spends more time these days taking pictures of her two passionate interests: water polo and water birds at dawn. Carlos skis down "corduroy" slopes specially groomed to reduce stress on aging boomer bodies. Karen takes time out to paint a few watercolors on the weekends. Play may mean a walk along the beach or tea at a favorite spot. It is simply time to stop and reconnect with one's soul.

Mythologist Joseph Campbell urged people to follow their bliss, but that quest usually doesn't begin until the children leave home, careers change, or a person has endured great personal loss. These changes tend to clean out the cobwebs that veil one's true self. At midlife, people want to reconnect with the things that anchor them and give them zest. They still have to earn an income, but they don't want it to interfere with play anymore.

Play has become a necessity for baby boomers because it is how they explore and share the deep joys of their lives. Look at Max, who checked out of the corporate world early to pursue a writing career and to have the time to explore her passion: gardening. She bought a Cape Cod home in the Hudson Valley surrounded with dirt. Two decades later she has created a "garden of note" that is a highlight of the Garden Conservancy's tour each year. Like many who start to explore a hobby, Max learned from the masters. She read books about gardening, traveled to English gardens, and hired a top-notch expert to guide her.

In midlife, boomers will make a difference in their lives by making a difference in someone else's life. When you do what you love, it becomes a gift to the world. Nurturing, growing things, and tending one's garden—both in a real and in a metaphorical sense—are how boomers will bring forth their spirit.

In his acclaimed 1999 documentary *Surfing for Life*, filmmaker David Brown showed us people who knew how to grow old while staying young in spirit. David describes the attitude of two teachers by day, pioneer big-wave surfers by late afternoon who he featured in his film: "Fred Van Dyke and Peter Cole were reluctant to attend mandatory post-school meetings at the prestigious Punahou School when the surf was breaking 25 feet at Waimea Bay. They would never miss class, but these mandatory meetings when the surf was up were difficult to attend." Brown said about the central theme of Surfing for Life: "The overriding key we found to healthy aging was passionate involvement and following one's bliss as you age. Surfing is a resonant metaphor for that."[1]

This pursuit of passion and play is fueling new market opportunities as boomers revamp traditional industries such as travel and create new ones like scrapbooking. This chapter profiles businesses that are leveraging boomer passions. They have reaped huge rewards by helping boomers pursue their deepest loves.

Market Analysis

The business opportunity around passion and play is to help boomers return to the things they loved when they were younger and to build support around those pleasures. When you build community, business will follow.

Gardening is the number-one hobby for adults age 50 and older, followed by eating out, crosswords, music, books, shopping, sports competitions, and pets.[2] AARP understands that boomers are returning to nostalgic interests, so it has launched motorcycle insurance. Boomers have driven major expansions in motorcycle sales during the last 40 years.[3]

Boomers are buying cool toys and collectibles they couldn't afford while they were raising families. They're buying electric guitars, model trains, and other trinkets that rekindle good memories. They are pursuing hobbies with zeal, especially on online auction sites such as eBay, where they build communities—and sometimes businesses—around these passions. In fact, crafts and hobbies are a thriving $25.7 billion industry, in large part because of boomers. The most popular crafts are cross-stitch, home décor, painting, scrapbooking and memory crafts, floral arranging, and crocheting, according to the Hobby Industry Association.[4]

The Elephant Entrepreneur: Sega Group

You can expect older boomers to climb on their Harleys; take out their golf clubs; and get into biking, hiking, sculpture, and glass blowing. But, you may not know about the gaming market and younger

boomers—people who are now in their 40s. Younger boomers are going to take video gaming into the next phase of their lives, and that will
create a mega-market opportunity—an entertainment industry like
we've never seen before.

Online gaming is no longer the denizen of teenage boys, as
more women and older people are participating in sites such as
GameSpot.com and Pogo.com. In fact, women over the age of 40
spend nearly 50% more time each week playing online games than
men or teenagers.[5] Men tend to play for the challenge, but women
play for escape and relaxation. Investment firm Bear Stearns reports
that the online gaming industry is rapidly growing and presents a major investment opportunity.[6]

In 2005, half of all U.S. households played video games, and half of
those households had high-speed Internet access. Some 19% of gamers
are over 50, up 9% in five years, according to Peter D. Hart Research
Associates. And 53% of game players expect to be playing as much, or
more, 10 years from now. To the aging gamer, this isn't a fad—it's a permanent part of his or her lifestyle. And with total U.S. hardware and software sales nearing $10 billion, it's eating up a growing portion of his or
her entertainment dollar. PricewaterhouseCoopers projects spending on
the global video-game market will reach nearly $55 billion by 2009.[7]
"When we look at today's market, we do not have a lot of people aged 55
and older playing games," says Shinobu Toyoda, chief strategist at Japan's
Sega Group, the leader in a $12 billion U.S. gaming market. "But there's
a potential demand for the 50-year-old. The youngest boomers continue
to play videogames because they are not intimidated by holding a control pad and playing interactively with a game," he says. The most popular interactive title today is John Madden's football game, especially
among men. Women are playing Tetris and other puzzle games.[8]

More women than men will live alone in their old age. Thirty-two
percent of women between ages 65 and 74 live alone, and 57% of those
over age 85 live alone. This compares to just 13% of men between ages
65 and 74 and 29% over age 85.[9] As educated boomer women enter this

stage of life, more will go online at night to play interactive games. Multi-player role-playing games in which both women and men can engage will become a hot trend. Another place to start is with trivia because that has long been an interest of the boomer generation. Expect boomers to purchase record numbers of interactive toys, such as the learning game Leapfrog, for their grandchildren.

Emerging Entrepreneur: LesConcierges

One of the most innovative companies catering to affluent boomers' leisure interests is LesConcierges, Inc., whose CEO and founder Linda Jenkinson knows how to translate boomer passions into ultimate experiences.

All businesses today need to have a strong customer database. LesConcierges has information on three million affluent consumers between the ages of 35 and 55. Linda knows what luxury consumers are buying on a global basis—and she is able to interpret those data to provide targeted and original services.

Linda had been the CEO of Dispatch Management Systems, the world's largest on-demand delivery service. She rang the bell on Wall Street the day she took that company public. She was also co-founder and CEO of a web-enabled personal services company. Ramesh Patel, Linda's business partner for many years, says she has always created memorable experiences for herself that other people aspire to. The two of them created LesConcierges, a global company that serves large companies and the luxury marketplace.

Linda and Ramesh know that boomers will pay for peak experiences and exceptional service, whether they can afford extravagance or just want a singular memory. So LesConcierges can arrange for a private jet or meet you at the airport with a clean set of clothes. It can arrange breakfast with Cinderella at Disneyland for a client's daughter or make sure that your grandson's name appears on the big screen when you take him to the ballpark for his fifth birthday.

LesConcierges' list of key accounts includes RCI Cendant (the world's largest timeshare operation), and Jaguar.

"The whole concept is knowing your customer and using that information to bring more value into the relationship," says Linda. "They want community, they want intimacy, and they want quality services based around their needs."[10]

Let's take a look at other top segments of the passion and play market to learn who is doing a good job of building a business and how they are doing it.

Other Market Slices

Gardening is already a $36.8 billion industry[11] and it will grow even larger as boomers find themselves with more time to dig in the dirt. Gardening is part of the boomer passion for creating sacred spaces at home and for reconnecting with nature.

The average U.S. homeowner today is age 52.[12] During this decade, as leading-edge boomers move into their 50s and 60s, spending on plants and flowers will surge. Homeowners age 55 to 64 already spend more on horticulture than any other age group. But the changing demographics of this cohort—the combination of rising incomes and the increase in the number of boomer households—should more than double spending in this category. Peter Francese, the founder of *American Demographics* magazine, has predicted that the 48% increase in the number of 55- to 64-year-olds projected by the Census Bureau for the next decade should add about $2 billion a year to spending on plants.[13]

One of the leaders in serving gardening interests is Steve Lacy, CEO of Meredith Corporation, whose properties include *Better Homes & Gardens* (with 40 million readers, 20% of whom are men) and *MORE* magazine (1.2 million subscribers, all between the ages of 40 and 60). *Better Homes* also has about 10 million website visitors, most of whom are boomers.[14]

Meredith is one of the most successful companies in leveraging boomer interests. Its strategy is to build a large customer database and then analyze it to find new customers. Customer profiles include purchase activity from Meredith overlaid with data from surveys and customer feedback. For example, when someone subscribes to *Better Homes*, Meredith searches its database of about 85 million names and finds people who are likely to have similar interests. "It's not one-to-one marketing. I would call it one-to-many," Steve explains.

Steve says that Meredith focuses aggressively on building magazine circulation via the Web because consumers usually come to Meredith through a search engine or partnership link. "People type in their passion and then find Meredith. They don't type in 'Meredith,' they type in 'gardening.' They are not coming just to look, they are coming to *do* something like plant a perennial garden or redo their kitchen. So Internet visitors come to our website already inspired. They want help in taking action. This is an important thing about the baby boom generation."[15]

Music

"Baby boomers were probably conceived with music playing in the room. They will probably die with music playing in the room, too," *ABC News* columnist Michael S. Malone told the 2005 Silicon Valley Boomer Venture Summit.[16]

Since 1990, older adults have steadily increased their share of the music market. In 2004, Americans age 35 and older bought 44% of all music sold, compared with 28% in 1991.[17] A similar trend is occurring in the U.K., where consumers age 40 and older represent the largest percentage of music buyers. In 2003, this group accounted for 43.4% of album purchases, an increase of 10 percentage points since 2000.[18] Music customers in their 40s and older are more musically active than they were 10 years ago, says David Weyner, general manager of Bertelsmann's adult-oriented RCA Victor Group. He cites boomers' early music education as a key to this market trend.

And boomers are buying more than just The Rolling Stones' greatest hits. They are also key to the success of genres such as soundtracks—a collection of traditional folk songs from the movie *O Brother, Where Art Thou?* sold more than five million copies. Boomers are also driving the demand for roots music, jazz, and new age.[19]

Boomers' love of music is also influencing the housing and home renovation industries. Some families are adding recording studios to their homes, as digital technology makes the process easier and more affordable. Prices range from a few thousand dollars for a basic package to $10,000 for state-of-the-art studios, which cost nearly $50,000 15 years ago. One in every five U.S. households has at least one musician, which means the potential market for home recording studios is significant.[20]

Sales of musical instruments hit an all-time high in 2004, at almost $7.4 billion. That was an increase of 5.2% from 2003, according to the International Music Products Association. Fretted instruments, drum kits, portable keyboards, and digital pianos lead this "unprecedented" consumer interest in making music. The reason for the surge, according to the survey, is growing enthusiasm among baby boomers and adults in their 30s.[21] AARP recently launched a music initiative and features top performers such as Elton John at its Life@50+ events.

Books

One never-ending boomer passion is the pleasure of books. People usually find more time to read after they become empty nesters. As the boomers move into this lifestage, there will be "a huge opportunity for marketers," says Harry Balzer, vice president of the NPD Group.[22] In fact, Americans over 50 clock nearly twice as much time per day reading as younger people do.

Harry says the market opportunity lies in creative development of material that people want to read in the format they want.[23] For example, the Time Warner Book Group[24] has a new imprint targeting boomers, called Springboard Press, that specializes in "self-help at midlife" books that focus on emotional well-being, nutrition and diet, fitness, age-related beauty, relationships and sex, caring for aging parents, reinventing living space, personal fulfillment, and financial planning.[25]

Doubleday has a large-print book club, with plenty of Danielle Steele, Sandra Brown, and John Grisham. Its Editor's Picks currently include *Living in God's Love* by Billy Graham, and *90 Minutes in Heaven* by Don Piper and Cecil Murphey. Random House's large-print division features such books as *The South Beach Diet* and *Ted Williams: The Biography of an American Hero*, though they don't have a large-print club.

The nonprofit SeniorNet Book Club was inspired by older readers' desire to have literate, cordial conversations about books with people all over the world whom you never would have met otherwise, says coordinator Ginny Anderson. Thanks to its volunteers, the club has grown from book discussions to contests, travel, online talks with authors, a Great Books series, National Book Festival presentations, and book exchanges. It sponsors the PBS Program Club discussions as well as Bookfests, where members meet with authors. An online discussion with Wally Lamb inspired a nationwide SeniorNet.org drive to supply books to prison populations, including South Carolina libraries where nearly 2,100 books have been donated.

Reflecting the older adult's passion for lifelong learning, the club sponsors classes in literature, often taught by retired college professors. A book discussion of Julius Caesar's *Gallic Wars* led to several online courses in Latin and Greek, which enrolled more than 650 students from 12 countries.[26] Having celebrated its 20th anniversary in 2006, SeniorNet has become a global organization.

Pets

Pets are another boomer passion. As children leave home for college, boomers fill their empty nests with new family members—dogs, cats, and birds—which is one reason 39% of Americans age 55 to 64 and 25% of those 65 and older own a pet.[27] According to the American Pet Product Manufacturers Association, Americans spend $35.9 billion per year on their pets, which is more than they spend on toys or candy.[28] Spending on pets by Americans age 55 to 64 is expected to grow faster than all other age groups over the next few years.[29]

As important as pets are to children, they are even more important as an antidote to the loneliness that often comes with age. After the shock of an empty nest or loss of a partner, the pet's wardrobe, grooming schedule, and diet usually get upgrades. Two Boomer Business Plan Competition finalists who understand this market are Chris and Natasha Ashton. In their homeland of England, most adults purchase pet health insurance—but there are just four insurance providers for 140 million dogs and cats in the United States.

One in three pets unexpectedly requires veterinary care each year, and every six seconds, someone spends $1,000 or more on a veterinary bill. Yet spending on pet health insurance in the United States accounts for less than $130 million.[30] The Ashtons, through their company Fetch, Inc., obtained exclusive licensing rights for the use of the U.K. Petplan brand and logo in the U.S. The Ashtons created unique policies to meet the needs of American pet owners and have received awards and recommendations from vets in the U.S.[31] The Ashtons recognized how important a pet is in the life of an older adult. They created a solution for the problem of expensive veterinary bills that won the hearts of customers as well as the enthusiasm of veterinarians.

Lifelong Learning

Lifelong learning is another key to the fountain of youth. Psychologists Carl Jung and Erik Erikson knew that a passion for self-discovery is part of how successful older adults fill out their years. As waves of boomers ease into retirement, their higher incomes, better health, and higher education will translate into greater interest in continuing education.

Elderhostel is the world's largest learning adventure organization serving older adults. Providing 8,000 programs in more than 90 countries to 170,000 older adults each year,[32] it sets the agenda for the lifelong learning industry. Elderhostel focuses on providing stimulating academic content, a warm social environment, and simplicity.

Jim Moses, who heads Elderhostel today, says that the people who choose Elderhostel decide that "learning is a more exciting way to spend their time than shopping or lying on a beach. They are people who care more about what is on the inside than what is on the outside. Learning is fun, especially when it is shared with good people." To that end they've developed Road Scholar in anticipation of the baby boom's arrival. The average age of a Road Scholar participant is 64, almost 10 years younger than the average Elderhosteler.[33]

Older adult learning is also a growing presence in traditional classrooms. In the past 30 years, the number of part-time college students has more than doubled, and about 20% of them are age 50 and older.[34] In response, many institutions of higher learning are creating nontraditional models for lifelong learning, and other organizations are targeting older adult education. Among the most popular are the Osher Lifelong Learning Institutes (there are now more than 70 across the country), the OASIS programs (now available in 26 U.S. cities), the Shepherd's Centers, the SeniorNet Learning centers, emeritus programs at junior colleges, and programs run by local Jewish community centers. U.S. county Area Agencies on Aging keep lists of local resources.

College towns are becoming popular places to retire, and more than 300 universities have responded by creating academic courses specifically for older adults. States like Ohio offer free classes without credit at state schools for residents over 55. Look for the cutting edge of this trend in small college towns like Ashland, Oregon; Las Cruces, New Mexico; Iowa City, Iowa; Athens, Georgia; and Brunswick, Maine.

Harvard and Duke universities both founded institutes for learning in retirement in the mid-1970s. Today, there are almost 500 similar programs nationwide, and that number is growing. At Harvard's Institute for Learning in Retirement, students age 55 and older pay $325 per semester for courses such as "Love and War in Classical Japanese Literature" and "Boston Architecture Since 1930."

"When they started careers and families, they had to set things aside, and now in their 60s or 70s or 80s they're saying, 'I never did read Plato,' or 'I always wanted to learn Italian,'" says Michael Shinagel, Harvard's dean of continuing education.[35] Expect this trend toward learning in retirement to increase as well-educated boomers age.

Sports

Boomers are also swelling the ranks of weekend athletes. The player base for tennis is aging, with 23% of frequent players (at least 21 times a year) and 16% of regular players (4 to 20 times) age 50 or older.[36] Biking is also growing in popularity among aging Americans, in part because boomers have more disposable income. The percentage of American cyclists who are 45 and older increased from 17.6% to 21.4% of all cyclists between 2001 and 2004, according to surveys by the National Sporting Goods Association. "The baby boomers want to exercise so they don't become obese. They can work out on a bicycle without the impact that hard pavement has on knees and joints," says Frank Dryer, operator of Hank and Frank Bicycles shop in Lafayette, California.[37]

Sports doctors and physical therapists are reporting a surge in office visits as boomers develop knee problems and other conditions that limit their activities. They have even given the phenomenon a term—*boomeritis*. The American Academy of Orthopaedic Surgeons (AAOS) estimates that more than $18 billion per year is spent on medical costs stemming from sports-related injuries to baby boomers, and the number of boomers who went to hospital emergency rooms for sports-related injuries jumped 33% from 1991 to 1998.[38]

And here is the opportunity: Because they cause so many aches and pains, boomers will be forced to turn away from high-impact sports like tennis, running, basketball, and racquetball that twist and turn the joints. They will turn increasingly toward smooth, low-impact activities that are easier on the joints, such as yoga, swimming, cycling, Pilates, walking, golf, and mountain biking.[39]

Motorcycles

Motorcycles are a passion for many boomers, who came of age watching *Easy Rider* and listening to Steppenwolf. "Because boomers have the most money to spend on discretionary purchases such as motorcycles, that's the right bracket to be in," says Tom Watson, marketing director for Harley-Davidson. "Our demographics mirror America. Baby boomers are buying most of the big ticket items."[40]

In fact, the median customer for a new Harley is a 46-year-old man. This means that the guy saddling up for a weekend ride is likely to be a dentist, doctor, or mortgage banker.[41]

The popularity of Harley motorcycles is fueling sales of peripheral Harley-branded products such as clothes, boots, and cat toys. It's as much a lifestyle as a product. Harley has also tapped boomer sensibilities at midlife by supporting their desire for community and connection. "Harley groups are very, very involved in civic engagement and fundraising," says Brent Green, a marketing consultant and author of *Marketing to Leading-Edge Baby Boomers*. "[I]t's tapping into people's later-life needs to make a difference, to have relevance, to leave a legacy. Those are the themes that (companies) need to be marketing to."[42]

Boomers are also boosting sales of Vespa motor scooters—especially the top-of-the-line models with all the trimmings. Much to the company's surprise, consumers age 50 and older buy one-quarter of the scooters Vespa sells in the United States.[43]

Wine

In the United States, adults age 50 to 59 are the biggest wine consumers, followed by those age 40 to 49. Consumption has grown at a rate of 8 to 10% per year in recent years, but the strong influence of demographics on wine consumption potentially could increase consumption 80% by 2015, according to *Wine Business Monthly.*[44]

AARP has set up a wine club, through which participants attend wine events and subscribe to wine newsletters. Peter Granoff, the founder and former "chief cork dork" at wine.com, has positioned himself for America's growing love of wine by opening a new kind of wine store in San Francisco's landmark Ferry Building, a former transportation hub that now houses a farmer's market and dozens of owner-operated retail shops and restaurants.

Peter studied European wine stores and bars to build his store, Ferry Plaza Wine Merchant, and the cornerstone of his effort is a way to simplify wine selection. Peter was frustrated by the pretentious terms often used in the industry, as well as Robert Parker's numerical scoring system. He developed a seven-point qualitative taste charting system, making it easy for beginners and collectors alike to judge their choices. Now he is creating a friendly website and online store for the new business. The result will be a hybrid, with a stellar store in a prime location linked to a friendly place online. Passion for wine combined with a great location and a cyberspace storefront is a winning combination.

Summary

At a 15th high school reunion, everyone passes out business cards. At that stage of life, it's all about networking. Boomers are at a different stage now. People at their 40th high school reunions are more likely to talk about their passions, and savvy entrepreneurs are building business models that leverage those passions.

The real juicy part of life is in learning how it feels to be alive, according to human potential movement founder and aikido master

George Leonard. That is the message and the opportunity of this lifestage. As the wave of baby boom retirements peaks around 2019, there will be time to fulfill this deep hunger for something more.

In his book *The Third Age: Six Principles of Growth and Renewal After Forty*, William Sadler discusses the need to "step into more purposeful living." He suggests that the long third age ahead of us is an opportunity to design our own mosaic.[45] The potential for a much longer period of healthy old age challenges baby boomers to think creatively about how we want to spend our time.

When we step out of our work shoes and into our passions, what will we create? Whether your business model is doing better than the competition like PetPlan, database marketing like Meredith, or a developing nonprofit that serves its members well like Elderhostel, you will find market opportunities.

Think about how people will use technology to manage their passions. More and more consumers are using wireless broadband devices to connect their friends and family and support their passions. In a book I coauthored in 1999 titled the *Grown-Up's Guide to Computing*,[46] I discovered that pioneering older adults were going online to research their genealogy, plan their trips, shop, use business accounting software, do financial planning, garden, and look at the news. Now these activities are mainstream.

Expect boomers to get involved in online tools that promote social networking. It was no surprise that social networking was a key part of Eons.com, a website geared toward boomers, when it was launched in July 2006. Its founder, Jeff Taylor, who also founded Monster.com, knew the power of peer-to-peer connection and support.

Expect to see many websites and companies create online and real-life solutions to help boomers work around their passions. As boomers begin to volunteer in greater numbers, expect them to go online to participate in organizations like NetAide and the SeniorNet Technology Volunteer Corps. New social groups and advocacy connections will take place across a wide variety of platforms.

Endnotes

1. David Brown, interview by author, 2005.

2. Millennium Research Bureau, *Mature Thinking*, 2003.

3. Rick Barrett, "How Long Will the Boomers Cycle Last? Solid Sales Expected Until," *Milwaukee Journal Sentinel*, March 28, 2005.

4. Melody Vargas, "U.S. Craft and Hobby Industry Valued at $25.7 Billion," Retail Industry, About.com, http://retailindustry.about.com/od/statistics/l/aa020522a.htm.

5. Ben Berkowitz, "Women Over 40 Biggest Online Gamers," *Reuters*, February 10, 2004, http://www.msnbc.msn.com/id/4235270/. More than a quarter of women surveyed play their favorite games between midnight and 5 a.m. and tended to favor word and puzzle games. *Ibid.*

6. Grant Eastbourne, "Bear Stearns Report: Online Gaming Continues to Grow," *WINNERonline.com*, March 16, 2001, http://www.winneronline.com/articles/march2001/bearstearns.htm.

7. Cliff Hahn, "Attack of the Gaming Grannies," *Business Week*, October 19, 2005, http://www.businessweek.com/print/innovate/content/oct2005/id20051018_173699.htm.

8. Shinobu Toyoda, interview by author, September 8, 2005.

9. U.S. Census Bureau, "Sixty-Five Plus in the United States," May 1995, U.S. Census Bureau, http://www.census.gov/population/socdemo/statbriefs/agebrief.html.

10. Linda Jenkinson, interview by author, July 26, 2005.

11. National Gardening Association, "Garden Market Research: Could the Lawn and Garden Business Be Doing Better?" National Gardening Association, http://www.gardenresearch.com/index.php?q=show&id=2542.

12. Peter Francese, "The Second Home Boom," *American Demographics*, June 2003.

13. Peter Francese, "Horticulture Is Hot," *American Demographics*, May 2002.

14. Steve Lacy, interview by author, August 29, 2005. Forty percent of the visitors are in the 40 to 50 age group, and about 60% are in the 50 to 64 age group. *Ibid.*

15. *Ibid.*

16. Michael S. Malone (panel discussion, 2005 Silicon Valley Boomer Venture Summit, Santa Clara, CA, June 21, 2005).

17. David Lieberman, "Baby Boomers Give Second Life to Older Rockers," *USA Today*, February 18, 2002.

18. The Canadian Independent Record Production Association, "International Markets—United Kingdom," http://www.cirpa.ca/Page.asp?PageID=376&ContentID=683.

19. David Lieberman, "Baby Boomers Give Second Life to Older Rockers," *USA Today*, February 18, 2002.

20. Beth W. Orenstein, "Homeowners Convert Rooms to Sound Studios," *Allentown Morning Call*, March 6, 2005.

21. NAMM, the International Music Products Association, "Music Products Sales in U.S. Hit Record $7.3 Billion in 2004," April 19, 2005, http://www.amc-music.com/news/pressreleases/record-sales.htm.

22. NDP Group, "Aging Boomers Could Drive Reading Boom, Says NPD Study," July 14, 1999, http://www.npd.com/press/releases/press_990714.htm. There are four key changes in the way older Americans spend time once their children leave the nest: 1) less time working, 2) less time on child care, 3) more time watching television and 4) more time reading. No other daily activities change more than these four. *Ibid.*

23. *Ibid.*

24. Time Warner Book Group was purchased by Hachette in 2006.

25. Steven Zeitchik, "Warner Goes Boomer," *PW Daily*, August 1, 2005, http://www.publishersweekly.com/article/CA631237.html.

26. Ginny Anderson, interview by author, September 20, 2005.

27. Rebecca Gardyn, "Animal Magnetism—Survey Results on Pet Ownership—Statistical Data Included," *American Demographics*, May 1, 2002.

28. American Pet Products Manufacturers Association, "American Pets Making Dollars and Sense," March 14, 2005, http://www.appma.org/press_releasedetail.asp?id=51

29. Rebecca Gardyn, "Animal Magnetism—Survey Results on Pet Ownership—Statistical Data Included," *American Demographics*, May 1, 2002.

30. Chris Ashton and Natasha Ashton, interview by author, April 13, 2004.

31. Fetch, Inc., "Fetch, Inc. Launches Petplan, the World's Leading Pet Health Insurance Brand, Into the US Market," Yahoo!Finance, August 28, 2006, http://biz.yahoo.com/prnews/060828/sfm094.html.

32. Elderhostel, "About Us: What Is Elderhostel?" http://www.elderhostel.org/about/what_is.asp.

33. Jim Moses, e-mail message to author, September 30, 2005.

34. University Continuing Education Association, *Lifelong Learning Trends: A Profile of Continuing Higher Edducation*, 5th edition (University Continuing Education Association: 1998), 11.

35. Jenna Russell, "Thirsty for Learning, Seniors Fill College Programs," *The Boston Globe*, November 17, 2004.

36. James Martin, "Research: Reaching Out—The Industry's Groundbreaking Participation Study Can Help You Expand Your Customer Base," *Tennis Industry*, August 1, 2003, www.tennisindustry.com.

37. Denis Cuff, "Cycling's Growing Popularity, Changing Perceptions," *Contra Costa Times*, February 18, 2006, www.mercurynews.com/mld/mercurynews/sports/outdoors/13904775.htm.

38. Stephanie Smith, "'Boomeritis': A Generation of Sports Injuries," CNN.com, May 15, 2003, http://www.cnn.com/2003/HEALTH/05/15/boomeritis/.

39. American Academy of Orthopaedic Surgeons, "Care of the Aging Knee: Baby Boomers May Need Lifestyle Changes," October 2002, http://orthoinfo.aaos.org/fact/thr_report.cfm?Thread_ID=389&topcategory=Knee.

40. Rick Popely, "Growing Older with Harley," Knight Ridder Tribune News Service, June 26, 2005, http://homepage.mac.com/gegomez/blogwavestudio/LH20050304120358/LHA20050629101038/index.html.

41. "Disposable Incomes Create New Markets in Search for Toys from Youth," *Charleston Post and Courier*, May 1, 2003.

42. Andrea Coombs, "Off the Radar: Aging Boomers Derided, or Ignored, by Ad Campaigns," CBS Market Watch, December 14, 2003, http://www.boomerproject.com/news1.html.

43. Louise Lee and David Kiley, "Love Those Boomers; Their New Attitudes and Lifestyles Are a Marketer's Dream," *Business Week*, October 24, 2005.

44. David A. Goldman, "Significant Conclusions from the STES Wine Industry Conference," *Wine Business Monthly*, November 1, 2000, http://www.winebusiness.com/html/MonthlyArticle.cfm?dataId=3583.

45. William Sadler, *The Third Age: Six Principles of Growth and Renewal After Forty*, (Cambridge, MA: Perseus, 2000), 171.

46. Mary Furlong and Stefan B. Lipson, *Grown-Up's Guide to Computing*, (Microsoft Press, 1999).

5

SEX AND ROMANCE: I'LL HAVE WHAT SHE'S HAVING

Introduction

A new sexual revolution is taking place. Love, for the baby boom generation, isn't about the first time anymore—it's about making love *feel* like it did the first time, despite their aging bodies. What kinds of romantic, sexual, intimate experiences do people want at midlife and beyond? As boomers answer that question, they are going to change society's sexual standards once again. Hundreds of business opportunities will emerge as a result.

Sex and romance at 50 are not the same as sex and romance at 20. As boomers were raising their families and building careers, they didn't anticipate how different it would be when the kids left home and they downsized their work lives. Their primary relationships may have taken a beating just getting to midlife, but boomers still want the rush of the touch and that dopamine high that only sex can bring. As the dining patron said after watching Meg Ryan fake an orgasm in *When Harry Met Sally*, "I'll have what she's having."

Whenever boomers negotiate a new stage of life, they change things—and as they change things, they create global business and marketing opportunities. The key trend pushing change in the field of sex and romance is better health and increased longevity. During the next few decades, the romantic lives of millions of boomers will be impacted by such transitions as divorce, remarriage, empty nests, widowhood, and loneliness.

Boomers liked sex, drugs, and rock 'n' roll when they were young, and they may still. But now they are less interested in the Erica Jong days of quick hook-ups; they want more time for connection and sharing with a partner or lover. Their drugs of choice will no longer offer escape, but enhanced intimacy.

The aspirational key is that there are more opportunities than ever to rekindle marriage, romance, and sensual vitality at midlife. Boomer bodies may show the effects of gravity and childbearing, but what boomers have lost in springy muscle tone has been gained back in the courage to express their desires. They now have a heightened capacity for intimacy.

Baby boomers are using their new powers to enrich their sexual experiences with their lifelong partners. They are becoming more inquisitive and experimental: they are joining the mile high club for the first time, having sex play in exotic locations, making love nests before the fireplace or in the treehouse, and discovering sex toys. They are clicking onto online stores like Good Vibrations and cruising the bestseller lists for copies of the *Kama Sutra* and *Sex Over 40*. They are exploring weekend getaways. They are taking salsa and ballroom dancing lessons, and they are going to cooking school. They are using books, music, yoga, erotica, massage, and videos to help them reach a heightened sensuality.

The best intimacy at midlife comes from the knowledge that caring and being cared for is one of the most important things in life. No matter how wildly boomers lived during the sexual revolution of the 1960s, or whatever the state of their relationships today, sex will always be the most powerful method of human connection. Every human being needs touch and deep emotional connection to feel fully alive, and the need for this experience only deepens with age.

These insights are important in understanding the boomer customer. Successful businesses in this space are organized around four main themes:

- **Drugs.** Pharmaceuticals, "cosmeceuticals," and "neutraceuticals" are a growing category because many drugs can ease the challenges of aging. The question is how to frame the marketing so that it speaks to the customer.

- **Dating.** Many boomers are finding themselves single and looking for a new connection. They are going online in growing numbers to find dates and mates.

- **Education.** Boomers' relationships and marriages will move through multiple phases, from child care to elder care to caring for each other. As people live longer in their marriages, how will they reinvigorate them?

- **Gifts, travel, and experiences.** There are business opportunities in travel, jewelry, flowers, restaurants, retreats, greeting cards, and spas. Any grace note that reveals appreciation, respect, and care will find appreciative customers.

Market Analysis

When I was the CEO of ThirdAge Media from 1996 to 2002, one of the most heavily visited channel on its website was "Romance, Intimacy, and Sexuality." There were many forums on this topic and the community was very involved in the discussion. One of the most "clicked on" headlines was "Rekindle Your Marriage at Midlife."

Sexuality remains an essential element of the lives of adults age 45 and older, according to a 2004 AARP study. More than half of the respondents said sexual activity is critical to a good relationship and that a satisfying sexual relationship is important to quality of life. Among those age 45 to 59 who have sexual partners, 63% said they have sexual intercourse at least once per week. Among those age 60 to

74 with sexual partners, 30% of men and 24% of women have sex at least once per week, as do more than one-quarter of those age 75 or older.[1] Other studies have found that nearly half of all Americans age 60 or older have sex at least once per month but want it more often. Older women are less sexually active than are older men, but this is often because they lack a partner or have a medical condition.[2]

Health and Vitality

"If you stay interested, stay healthy ... and have a good mate, then you can have good sex all the way to the end of your life," says Dr. Walter Bortz, a professor at Stanford Medical School and co-chair of the American Medical Association's Task Force on Aging. "People that have sex live longer. People need people. The more intimate the connection, the more powerful the effects."[3]

The healthier a boomer is, the more likely he or she has a healthy sex life, according to the AARP survey. And as the years go by, older people are likely to say they still view their partner as romantic, physically attractive, or both. Two out of three respondents who had sexual partners told AARP they were either "extremely" or "somewhat" satisfied with their sex lives. And while a majority (56%) of people age 45 and older agreed that a satisfying sexual relationship is important to one's quality of life, most of them also said it wasn't the number-one priority. Good spirits, good health, close ties with friends and family, financial security, spiritual well-being, and a good relationship with a partner were all rated as more important than a fulfilling sexual connection.

Not surprisingly, men place a higher value on sex than women do: 66% of men in the AARP survey, compared with 48% of women, said that satisfying sex is important to their quality of life. This gender split changes with age, however. In the 45 to 49 age group, men and women place almost equal (and high) importance on sex. By age 60, the gender gap is noticeable.[4]

Contrary to common assumption, menopause does not mean the end of female sexuality. In fact, many women find that intimacy is enhanced in midlife because the capacity for satisfying sexual relationships does not disappear with age. Although menopause does bring physiologic changes that may slow down response time and affect sexual activity in a variety of ways, 70 to 80% of women in one survey said they did not experience a reduction in sexual activity or satisfaction after menopause.[5]

Loneliness, Empty Nest Marriages, Divorce, Widows

Almost a third of women age 65 to 74 and 57% of those over age 85 live alone.[6] Some are happy and independent. For others, there are nights of abiding loneliness. Sharing a pillow for 40 years and then losing a partner is one of life's most devastating experiences, especially when support systems are lacking and one must start over to build a new life.

For others, marriages die from within. You can be lonelier inside a marriage than without one. Empty marriages defined more by habit than by deep affection burden millions of couples as they reach midlife. There is a prevailing need for intimacy and meaning, especially among women. Jane Glenn Haas, founder of the nonprofit WomanSage, has found that more women than men leave their marriages at midlife.[7]

Many empty-nest boomers are searching for adventure and a new future. One of the prime targets for the Jaguar X series, which is the most popular car in the line, is women age 50 and older with household incomes of $50,000 to $100,000. Jaguar got me with its pitch and my car gets 99.9% of its compliments from women over 50. We no longer need to carry around our son's rugby team in an SUV. Our goal now is luxury, excitement, and a sense of freedom. But the empty nest also can mean too much freedom, as some couples break apart when the children leave. The children may have been the glue.

Marriage and family therapist Alexandra Kennedy says that when children leave home, especially the last or only child, "It's the end of a whole phase of your life. You have raised a family. It's been tremendously consuming, and suddenly they're out of the nest. Part of this process is that it calls on parents to look at their own lives and what they set aside in order to raise their kids—their dreams, or intimacy, or what they want to nurture in their own lives. So it is common for long-term problems in the marriage to surface at this point."[8]

For companies, a market that is significantly less dominated by married couple households with children brings new and different opportunities than it had in the past. When marriage is no longer at the center of one's life, housing, travel, and recreation choices all change.

Boomers are more likely than previous generations to live on their own in midlife. Of the 97 million Americans age 45 and older, almost 40%—36.2 million—were single in 2003.[9] The majority of singles between the ages of 40 and 69 are separated or divorced, but 31% have never been married. Fifteen percent of Americans in their 50s are divorced, and 70% of divorced people have been single for five or more years.[10]

According to the Current Population Survey (CPS), older adults who live alone are more likely to be widowed than divorced. About one-third of women over the age of 55 are widowed, while just 15% are divorced, separated, or never married. In addition, 14.5 million Americans age 65 or older are unmarried. In another decade, baby boomers will push these numbers much higher.

Nearly 16% of people age 35 to 44 have never been married, compared with just 6% of this group in 1970. Even boomers who have married are more likely to be divorced by the time they reach retirement. Boomers make up nearly 60% of all divorced people over the age of 15 in the United States, which means that they are more likely to be living alone than previous generations of elders, according to AARP.[11]

Entrepreneurs want customers with money and a need to spend it. Boomer singles are going to be one of those markets. There will be many businesses formed to serve their needs. A good example is online dating.

Online Dating

Consistently, the number-one goal for boomers when they go online is a search for intimacy and connection, friendship and support, and "wall-socket sex" with a spiritually connected soul mate.

Sites like Match.com, eHarmony.com, Yahoo! personals, and Matchmaker.com are the first places people now look for romance online. A 2005 Yahoo! singles survey found that older daters are using email, instant messaging, and online dating. More than 75% are looking for long-term relationships, with those age 45 to 49 leading the way.[12] When people 55 and older date, what they want most is companionship, especially after the death of a partner. "Women grieve, and men replace," says Zella Case, owner of a matchmaking service for people ages 18 to 80. Women wait longer to begin dating because they have women friends with whom they share intimacy, she says. Men are lonelier.[13]

And in Europe, a recent report by Intel on digital lifestyles found that in some countries, as many as 13% of those with computers have tried Internet dating. A report from Nielsen/NetRatings found that one in every three Internet users in the United Kingdom would use the Web to meet a potential partner.

Nielsen/NetRatings found that English men and women differ on what they look for in an online date. Women want friendship or shared interests, while men want a long-term relationship, an intimate relationship, a short-term relationship, or marriage. Men are also four times more likely to be looking for a no-strings fling than were women.[14]

Elephant Entrepreneur: eHarmony.com, Inc.

Because boomers are now older, they require more information about a potential love interest before a first meeting or date. Online services provide the perfect opportunity.

With more than 8 million registered users, eHarmony bills itself as the Internet's top relationship service. Its user base is doubling every quarter, adding 10,000 to 15,000 new users each day. It now attracts 2.7 million visitors per month, according to ComScore Media Metrix, while Yahoo! Personals draws 5.9 million visitors and IAC/InterActiveCorp's Match.com draws 4 million. But 10% of eHarmony's current membership is over age 55.[15]

"Single seniors, over a third of whom are widowed and nearly 8% divorced, are turning to the Web for a chance at love," says eHarmony founder Neil Clark Warren. "We are seeing an explosion in the numbers, and we expect that to continue as baby boomers enter their golden years with greater life expectancy and disposable income. We are extremely honored to serve our mature customers in their search for a soul mate."[16]

In a 2005 interview by Salon.com, Neil said, "My agenda is to try to do two things: to change the world and build a business." eHarmony tallies a 28 to 30% conversion rate between those who visit the site and fill out the free profile, to those who spend $50 to $250 to become active members. Accordingly, eHarmony was looking to spend $80 million in 2005 on national advertising, up from $50 million in 2004.[17]

"eHarmony walked into a vacuum and created a brand that catered to serious daters," says Nate Elliot of Jupiter Research. "They did a great job of differentiating themselves."[18]

eHarmony's patented Compatibility Matching System technology is based on 35 years of empirical and clinical research on what makes a relationship successful. It is focused on helping users build long-term, solid relationships. The site establishes a personality profile with 436 questions developed by psychologists. It identifies a person's key characteristics, beliefs, values, emotional health, and skills. Then eHarmony runs the technology to find a pool of compatible candidates and guides users through a four-stage process for meeting their matches.

As the lucrative boomer dating segment grows, you can expect all the portal players to enter this market. Yahoo! and Match.com have already gone after an online dating niche that eHarmony passed up.

Both companies accept gay and lesbian subscribers, a group that eHarmony excludes.[19]

Personals

There is big business in online personals and dating. People will pay subscription fees to meet others. In fact, personals and dating are the largest paid content category on the Web, bringing in $469.5 million in 2004.[20] The most likely visitor is male, about age 45, with an income between $50,000 and $75,000.[21] Today, boomers list their personals with descriptions such as, "sexy and bold, solid pension, and health-care benefits with a low co-pay."

Investors delight at businesses that have steady subscription revenue. The one that's most likely to grow as boomers get older is online personals. This is because of the high chance of losing your partner as you age. Technology gives boomers a new way to hook up.

Elephant Entrepreneur: Lilly

Another way to serve the boomers' needs for sex and intimacy is through performance-enhancing drugs. Just as we jumped onto the birth control bandwagon in record numbers when we were 18, we are again jumping onto drugs that enhance performance.

Sexual performance and interest can decline as we age. Erectile dysfunction (ED) affects an estimated 189 million men and their partners worldwide. Experts believe that 80 to 90% of ED cases are related to a physical or medical condition such as diabetes, cardiovascular diseases, and prostate cancer treatment, while 10 to 20% are due to psychological causes.[22] The probability of impotence increases as men age. According to a study conducted from 1987 to 2004, the prevalence of complete impotence triples, from 5 to 15%, between the ages of 40 and 70.[23]

Since Viagra's debut in 1998, Pfizer has spent over $100 million to gain its 75% share of America's $2 billion erectile dysfunction market.[24] According to a Reuters survey of Americans age 45 and older taken for Viagra, one in every four men reported being either completely or moderately impotent, and 15% of those said they had tried Viagra to improve sexual performance. Most who took the drugs said that sex became more satisfying, if not necessarily more frequent, and the drugs improved the relationship.[25]

Viagra was a blockbuster for Pfizer, but Eli Lilly soon matched it with Cialis, a drug made in partnership with ICOS. My colleagues and I had a chance to talk to the leaders of the Cialis brand team shortly after the drug's launch. We told them that intimacy and connection were a better approach than stressing the performance-enhancing aspects of the drug. A third competitor, Levitra, was running ads that showed a middle-aged man throwing a football through a tire. We told Cialis that this was the wrong approach.

Cialis launched in the United States with a bang, with several spots during the broadcast of the 2004 Super Bowl. The spots showed couples in a bathtub sharing a conversation. The mood was right. "When the time is right," the ad said, "will you be ready?" A voiceover disclaimer at the end— "If an erection lasts for more than four hours, see your doctor"—caught the audience by surprise. The commercial was the subject of conversations and jokes for weeks.

Within six months of launch, Cialis (tadalafil) was already challenging Viagra (sildenafil citrate) for market share of the ED market. According to ImpactRx, United States urologists initiated treatment with Cialis at a rate of more than two-to-one over each of the other oral ED treatments. In fact, Cialis represented 56% of new treatment initiations by urologists in April 2004, compared to 21% for Levitra (vardenafil HCl) and 23% for Viagra.[26] Cialis started generating a profit less than two years after its U.S. launch.[27]

Expect sex-enhancing businesses to continue growing as the population ages. Also expect new solutions for women. Over-the-counter female sexual enhancement products are showing explosive growth as a mass market category. Trojan, the nation's largest condom manufacturer, has launched a new line of condoms marketed to women. Johnson & Johnson is transforming its traditional K-Y brand into a line of warming gels and massage oils. The K-Y name is on 7 of the 10 top-selling lubricants on the market, and it accounted for more than two-thirds of the category's $92 million in sales in 2005, according to Information Resources, Inc., a Chicago market research firm.[28]

Stephen Mare, brand manager for Durex Consumer Products, Inc., the maker of the 4Play line of lubricants and vibrators, says many of today's sex enhancement products are similar to ones that have been around for years, but today they're being marketed differently. "The old products were really sold as a solution to a medical problem," he says. "What we've been selling is sexual intimacy."[29] Pioneering this trend is Suzie Heumann, a small entrepreneur who is using education about sexuality as a way to build her boomer business.

Emerging Entrepreneur: tantra.com

Suzie is the founder of tantra.com, a web portal about sacred sexuality that celebrated 10 years online in 2005. Her online visits have grown exponentially, thanks to her useful blend of ancient wisdom and modern technology. A search for "'tantra'" in most search engines usually brings up her site as number one.

"I decided to have a membership premium content area and offer better and deeper information online," she says. "Our stats and email told us that we had a lot of international visitors, and shipping costs are high. I wanted to build a business with low environmental impact. Having a premium content area with global access fit the bill."

Suzie says it's turned out to be a brilliant revenue model. Most of her marketing dollars are put toward getting a higher position on Google and other search engines. She kept the teachers' listings free, and the premium content area costs $14.99 a month. That buys hours of streaming educational video and audio. Visitors can also purchase and download hundreds of articles, book reviews and excerpts, and ideas for creating intimacy, ritual, and ceremony around lovemaking. DVDs, books, and videotapes are also selling well. The biggest sellers revolve around the tantric principles. "Anything to do with the G spot, even female ejaculation, massage techniques, and touch both for men and for women, does well," she says.

Suzie's customer base is not typical for a sex site. It is mostly boomers, with equal proportions of men and women age 40 to 60. About 10% of subscribers are over age 60. This is because she is selling more than sexual techniques or pornography. She's selling to the desire to connect with the spirit of your partner in a sexual way.

"We are looking for an authentic bond—the elixir that something deeply meaningful brings," Suzie said. "Sexuality has gotten bigger than sex. Men and women are looking to expand their techniques, but integration is a bigger part of it. And that's what boomers are striving for. You see people taking a look at their personal history and asking, where did I lose my creativity? Tantra is about expanding the you or the me into we."[30]

Other Market Slices

Safe sex: Many women in their 50s stop using protection during sex because pregnancy is no longer an issue, says Jan Fowler of HIV Wisdom for Older Women, a national program of prevention and support. But after menopause, a decrease in lubrication and a thinning of the vaginal walls puts them at higher risk for HIV transmission. When Jan speaks to groups of older men and women, she stresses safe sex with an emphasis on condom use. Sex education is a business opportunity with books, websites, and promotions.

Spas/retreats: Ultra-luxury spa Canyon Ranch, with locations in Arizona and Massachusetts, is one of a growing number of spas that have incorporated sex education into their programs. Canyon Ranch dubs their offering Sex: Body & Soul as "a unique program for couples who want to enhance their intimacy by learning medical facts, sexual techniques, and creative approaches to love-making." The resort also offers a weekly, complementary sex workshop called Awakening Sexual Passion.[31]

Older Women, Younger Men: Older women have more economic power than they've ever had in history. Female executives in Silicon Valley used to joke that if your valuation was high enough, you didn't need perfume. Younger men are discovering this, along with the fact that older women are secure, creative, and independent and enjoy intimacy and sexuality. Thus, older women are dating younger men in record numbers without eliciting too many sideways glances. As Gray Panther founder Maggie Kuhn said, "We may get older, but we still get hot."

Almost 33% of women between ages 40 and 69 are dating men 10 or more years younger than they are. According to a recent AARP poll, one-sixth of women in their 50s prefer men in their 40s.[32] These women want fun and companionship, but not necessarily marriage. Many have recently been divorced. Sex therapist Dr. Lonnie Barbach, author of the best-selling books *Going the Distance* and *For Yourself*, says that "in past decades a younger man might have been interested, but the older woman wouldn't have thought it was possible. So she wouldn't have acted on it. Today, however, women have a lot more options. The dictates of social norms don't run our lives like they used to."[33]

Summary

Loving, sexuality, and intimacy have the power to call forth our deepest and most powerful emotions. At its best, sex overwhelms a couple with a wave of positive sensations that makes them feel intensely bonded. No one wants to give this up. It's good for our spirits and our well-being, and it keeps us young. Here are the key ideas about how to create a business that serves this need.

First, realize that there will be a large market of singles as the boomers get older. Provide special programs that serve the needs without a penalty, such as single rooms on a cruise.

Use your advertising to show couples engaged and conversing in experiences that they dream about, such as cruises. Show them 15 years younger than the target market you're going after because they like to think of themselves as younger than they are.

This is the best-educated generation ever. They will buy books and tapes and take classes to learn about how to improve intimacy and performance and pleasure. Boomers have experimented with things their whole lives, so expect them to order drugs, toys, books, and more online. They will also be able to afford the finest silk lingerie, although they may need it in a larger size. In fact, I was just sent a product sample of Jockey's new "boomer thong" with "moisture management features and support for targeted shaping for everyday." Seriously.

Endnotes

1. NFO Research, Inc., *AARP/Modern Maturity Sexuality Survey* (AARP, August 3, 1999), http://assets.aarp.org/rgcenter/health/mmsexsurvey.pdf.

2. National Council on Aging, "Half of Older Americans Report they Are Sexually Active; 4 in 10 Want More Sex, Says New Survey," September 28, 1998, http://www.ncoa.org/content.cfm?sectionID=105&detail=128.

3. Loren Stein, "The 70-Year Itch: Seniors and Sexuality," Consumer Health Interactive, 2000, http://healthresources.caremark.com/topic/srsex.

4. NFO Research, Inc., *AARP/Modern Maturity Sexuality Survey* (AARP, August 3, 1999), http://assets.aarp.org/rgcenter/health/mmsexsurvey.pdf.

5. Laurie B. Rosenblum, "Sex after Menopause," EBSCO Publishing, 2006, http://www.beliefnet.com/healthandhealing/getcontent.aspx?cid=14512.

6. U.S. Census Bureau, "Sixty-five Plus in the United States," May 1995, http://www. census.gov/population/socdemo/statbriefs/agebrief.html.

7. Jane Glenn Haas, interview by Beth Witrogen McLeod, July 23, 2005.

8. Alexandra Kennedy, interview by Beth Witrogen McLeod, July 2005.

9. Sarah Maloney, "Seeking Love," *AARP Magazine*, December 2003, http://www. aarpmagazine.org/lifestyle/Articles/a2003-09-23-seekinglove.html.

10. AARP, "Results from our Singles Survey," 2003, http://www.aarpmagazine.org/lifestyle/Articles/a2003-09-23-survey_results.html.

11. Highbeam Research, "The Next Big Singles Market (Baby Boomers in the Future)," August 20, 2001.

12. "Yahoo! Personals Announces Results of its Third Annual Singles' Voice Survey in Celebration of National Singles Week; Survey Reveals More Mature and Older Daters Are Looking For a Special Someone While West Coast Singles Are Social Butterflies," *Business Wire*, September 19, 2005.

13. Mary Vinnedge, "Men and Women 55 and Older Have Different Needs and Expectations in Dating," *Dallas Morning News*, November 12, 1996.

14. eMarketer, "Falling in Love Online," September 15, 2005.

15. David Colker, "Sounding Out the Singles Set; Neil Clark Warren Has Made eHarmony.com a Success But Still May Face an Image Challenge," *Los Angeles Times*, May 1, 2005.

16. eHarmony.com, "Seniors Logging on to eHarmony to Find Love," October 13, 2004, http://www.eharmony.com/singles/servlet/press/releases;jsessionid=FE97 91C2396BB8BD5627DEDE550C47D7.14 -1?id=30.

17. Rebecca Traister, "My Date with Mr. eHarmony," Salon.com, June 10, 2005, http:// archive.salon.com/mwt/feature/2005/06/10/warren/index.html?pn=4.

18. David Colker, "Sounding Out the Singles Set; Neil Clark Warren Has Made eHarmony.com a Success But Still May Face an Image Challenge," *Los Angeles Times*, May 1, 2005.

19. *Ibid.*

20. Online Publishers Association, *Online Paid Content U.S. Market Spending Report*, March 2005, http://www.onlinepublishers.org/pdf/paid_content_ report_030905. pdf.

21. "Personal Ad Websites Not Drawing Seniors, but Boomers," *SeniorJournal.com*, October 15, 2005, http://www.seniorjournal.com/NEWS/Sex/5-10-15Personal-Ads.htm.

22. "Cialis (tadalafil) Reaches $1 Billion Global Sales Milestone," *Medical News Today*, July 26, 2005, http://www.medicalnewstoday.com/medicalnews.php? newsid=28003.

23. New England Research Institute, "Massachusetts Male Aging Study on Impo-tence," *Abstract of: Impotence and its Medical and Psychosocial Correlates: Re-sults of the Massachusetts Male Aging Study*, http://www.junkscience.com/jun99/ feldman.htm.

34. "The Power of ED Drug Advertising Challenges the Hippocratic Oath," *PRN ewswire*, June 13, 2005, www.prnewswire.com.

25. "Survey: Aging Boomers Pushing Sexual Revolution into Older Age," CNN.com, August 3, 1999, http://www.cnn.com/US/9908/03/sex.over.45/.

26. "Lilly ICOS' Cialis (tadalafil) Makes Impressive Strides in First Six Months on the U.S. ED Treatment Market," *PRNewswire*, June 2, 2004, www.prnewswire.com.

27. Eric Fetters, "Joint Cialis Venture Reports its First Profit," *HeraldNet*, January 21, 2006, http://www.heraldnet.com/stories/06/01/21/100bus_cialis001.cfm.

28. Bruce Mohl, "CVS, Others Fill Shelves to Meet Growing Demand," *Boston Globe*, November 6, 2005.

29. *Ibid.*

30. Suzie Heumann, interview by author, February 7, 2006.

31. Kathy McCabe, "Romantic Getaways," Travel Channel, http://travel.discovery.com/ideas/romance/articles/getaways.html.

32. Star Lawrence, "Older Woman, Younger Man Relationships," WebMD, December 29, 2003, http://www.msnbc.msn.com/id/3679116/.

33. Dr. Lonnie Barbach, interview by Beth Witrogen McLeod, 2003. This quote originally appeared in Beth Witrogen McLeod's "Older Women, Younger Men," *Consumer Health Interactive*, 2003, reprinted by permission of author.

6

Jeans, Jeans, You're Young and Alive

Introduction

"I bought Chico's," Sally smiled at the women in the focus group, and they wished they had had her foresight. The other women had all shopped at Chico's, but only Sally was smart enough to purchase the stock. Sally is an attractive, well-dressed woman in her 60s, and she knew that Chico's, a clothing store that appeals to women over 35, would be a grand success. She also knew that there are a lot of women like her. "We're not Barbie dolls," she said.[1]

The image of a reed-thin blonde as the poster child for fashion and beauty was never realistic, but now it's ridiculous. "There's a point where denial no longer can succeed," says David Wolfe of the Doneger Group, a market research company that focuses on apparel and accessories markets. "Once the boomers started passing 50, they couldn't kid themselves anymore. They don't want to look like Paris Hilton."[2]

The midlife shock around beauty and fashion hits men and women equally. Hair turns gray and begins to fall out. Wrinkles and age spots appear where tan lines used to be. Waistlines increase and other parts sag. For both men and women, the 50th birthday is a time for identities to shift.

As 60 becomes the new 40, the whole notion of style is changing. Baby boomers will become less dependent on what others think of them, and they will be more focused on how they feel about themselves as they step into midlife. After their 60th birthdays, boomers will adjust to a new face, a new rhythm, and a new sense of self. "We don't want to look younger; we want to look better," says Myrna Blyth, former editor-in-chief of both *Ladies Home Journal* and *MORE* magazine.[3]

Traditional marketing focused on attracting consumers when they are young and keeping them as they age. But that concept had a serious shortcoming because it never addressed the ways consumer behavior changes as lifestyles change. At midlife, fashion becomes a reflection of lifestyle. Instead of fitting in with cliques, people at midlife are more interested in being their own person.

Seventeen magazine got to the baby boomers when they were young. Tommy Bahama and Chico's get them today. These companies succeed through lifestage marketing, which transforms the shopping trip into an experience and a statement of self. In this chapter, we will look at several fashion and beauty brands that tap into the boomers' desire for inspiration and spirituality. We will also look at other ways the new boomer sensibility is transforming style, beauty, and personal identity.

Market Analysis

Conventional wisdom holds that people largely ignore fashion and beauty once they reach a certain age, but this isn't really true, and it certainly will not be true of baby boomers. Eighty-one percent of women age 45 to 54 feel their clothes express who they are, according to a Roper ASW Survey, as do 76% of women age 55 to 64 and 70% of those age 65 and older. Since 1999, the proportion of women age 65 and older who follow changes in clothing styles has increased 24%.

About two-thirds of women age 45 to 64 and about half of those over 65 say they have a superior sense of fashion, and the proportion of women age 55 and older who hold this opinion increased rapidly between 2000 and 2002.[4]

Baby boomers know that their youth is fading. Two-thirds of those age 45 to 54 say that on any given day, they look "middle-aged." But they aren't all giving up on their looks. One in four midlife women is on a weight-loss diet, and 17% of boomer men also say they're trying to drop a few pounds.[5] More than ever, health is the foundation of beauty for boomers. The urge to feel healthy and vital influences how and why they buy beauty products, and it also controls what they wear.

Baby boomers have always used particular products to define themselves. Blue jeans became a worldwide fashion phenomenon in the 1950s when they came to symbolize youth and rebellion—and for boomers, they still hold great symbolic power. Japan's baby boomers are creating a new culture around jeans, according to a survey of midlife Japanese called "Jean 50s." The survey found that Japanese boomers see themselves as having good fashion sense and being trend pioneers. They want to be known for their "sense of style, oneness with themselves, and youthfulness." They want a new lifestyle with more focus on greater connectedness with loved ones and greater sensitivity toward fashion and trends.[6]

Although they are nearly ignored by marketers, American boomers still spend heavily in the fashion and beauty markets. American women in their 40s and 50s spent an estimated $27 billion on clothes in 2004, according to The NPD Group/SDS Research. Sales of anti-aging products are estimated to hit $30.7 billion by 2009, up from $20.2 billion in 2004.[7]

Let's take a look at two fashion giants who saw the baby boomer "elephant" coming and built businesses that captured it. These entrepreneurs listened to their customers to improve on their original ideas. They also understood that the boomers' bodies were changing, so they found clothes that fit and make them feel good.

Elephant Entrepreneur: Tommy Bahama

Tommy Bahama is a boomer-targeted brand that made fashion an experience.

President and founder Tony Margolis, along with his partners Bob Emfield and Lucio Dalla Gasperina, created a fantasy character that appealed to the boomer desire to escape from stress. The brand became a major hit in fashion retail, restaurants, and home furnishings.

Tony and Bob worked together on the Generra and Brittania brands for more than 17 years. They also had beach homes near each other in Bonita Springs, Florida. When they were sitting on the beach watching the water, the seagulls, and the clouds going by, they kidded with each other, asking "Why do we have to go back north and do what we do for a living?" Tony recalls.[8] They began to fantasize about a guy who didn't have to go back. He spent his days on the beach, and all he needed was cold beer, wax for his surfboard, and gas for his old VW convertible. He would sell his old Hawaiian shirts when he needed some quick cash.

That character became Tommy Bahama. Tony and Bob brought in their friend Lucio for product design, and the brand took off. The three apparel industry veterans blended their visions into an overall spirit of the relaxing life. They understand that boomers want fun, comfort, and luxury, and they also want to feel good. The brand became an icon for casual, tropical elegance with its motto, "Life is one long weekend."

The team initially saw a line of products just for the beach. They started out in 1992 making shirts as an upscale brand of men's sportswear for boomers, using breezy fabrics like linen and silk. They played up the lifestyle element at an early trade show, and the results confirmed they were on the right track. They built their booth as a thatched roof bar, but with clothing samples on the shelves instead of liquor bottles. Buyers got it right away, and Tony understood that they had to build a prototype store rather than be part of someone else's retail chain.

They opened their first retail store in Naples, Florida. Then they opened a juice bar. Their new landlords liked their vision so much they offered them more space, which led to the Tommy Bahama Tropical Cafe in 1996. They served 250,000 meals in the first year. Their first licensing adventure, selling Tommy Bahama beer in local bars, was a flop because the big-name beers had more clout with the bartenders, so the Tommy Bahama taps kept mysteriously disappearing from the bars. But the successes kept coming. Now the brand has added accessories, women's sportswear, footwear, swimwear, and upholstered home furnishings.

Tony says that the target customer has always been a baby boomer who sees himself as a nonconformist. Tommy Bahama's fashion collections sell at more than 60 retail locations around the world, including Dubai and Canada. They are also available in specialty stores, golf shops, and resorts. There are seven cafe/emporiums in Florida, Texas, California, and Hawaii.

The brand's success goes beyond its great products. It is successful because Tony and his team base their strategy on changes in boomer lifestyles. For example, they know that boomers are buying second homes in warm climates. So they have a license with Lexington Homes to make furniture in rattan and other "island" components. The venture has been a huge success because of the leaders' willingness to risk evolving into new niches.

The nonconformist vision also extends to marketing. Tommy Bahama doesn't base its marketing just on ads and commercials. Instead it uses sports sponsorships—golf, auto racing, speedboat racing, sailing, and equestrian riding—to extend the brand[9] and give back to the communities in which it operates.

Tony says there are three keys to building a successful brand in fashion retail. First, he says, create shops that people enjoy going to and treat them well: "We teach employees to behave as if someone has come into their home to be entertained for the evening." Second, create a product that touches the senses, to make it exactly right: "Is this the best weight of silk, the best finish? Is the pattern playful and going to bring somebody to a good place? Is it relaxed, does it fit comfortably, feel good on the skin?"

Third and most important, he says, is to "stay true to the vision. Do not allow the pressures of survival to force you to walk away from your vision. When customers see that you are the real deal, they will come back. Repeat customers are the full circle.

"I believe that Tommy Bahama is a generic name for a vision of apparel, both men's and women's," says Tony. "We have people who are discussing building homes and resorts with Tommy Bahama. So the vision that we had for apparel has been applied to other industries. Not all of our efforts have been home runs, but more times than not, the ones that failed didn't fail because the vision was wrong. They failed either because of poor execution or not having the right guys doing it. If we had gone to Budweiser, we might be the biggest name in beer."[10]

Chico's

Chico's is a brand that got it right for boomer women. Chico's understands that the average American woman at midlife is size 14, has a tummy, and prefers a look that smoothes her curves rather than exhibits her pudge. So they removed the emotional obstacles around fit. Sizes come in 0, 1, 2, and 3 to reflect extra-small through large, but eliminate the fear of needing a "large." Chico's understood that its customer does not need a mirror in the dressing room but does like an honest sales clerk to say, "That color works for you." It created clothing that was comfortable for women who no longer fit into girls' clothing.

For customers who are tired of being anonymous, Chico's emphasizes personal attention through loyalty programs offering lifetime discounts, gifts, and private shopping events for "members" who have purchased over $500 of merchandise. It offers incredible personal service for regular customers: the salespeople know what your daughter's name is or that your sister is a size 1 and looks good in blue. Chico's also offers an extensive selection of accessories so customers can put together an outfit at a single store.

Chico's FAS, Inc., began in 1983 on Sanibel Island, Florida, with Marvin and Helene Gralnick selling Mexican folk art and cotton sweaters. Today the company carries a diverse range of styles, from comfortable everyday clothes to elegant eveningwear, all designed for the over-35 crowd. Its growth has been phenomenal. In 2005, the company reported sales of $327 million, a 27% increase from the previous year.[11]

Chico's success turned heads in the fashion industry, bringing other major players into the game. In the summer of 2005, Gap launched five Forth & Towne stores selling clothing for women who need a more forgiving fit.[12] The line offers traditional career clothes like structured suits along with dressier knit tweed pants and cropped jackets with fur trims. It hires sales associates who have experience serving customers from a variety of industries, including spas. Gap is playing catch-up, however. The company has a significant market share for female shoppers younger than 35, but less than 3% for women over 35.[13]

Now let's turn to two clothing entrepreneurs who are also grasping the boomer market. Snowy Peak's natural products and Butterfly Dreams' emphasis on inspiration show that these two small businesses are also on the right track.

Emerging Entrepreneur: Snowy Peak

Peri Drysdale grew up on the slopes of New Zealand's Snowy Peak, with breathtaking views of the Southern Alps right out her kitchen door. Her grandmother worked closely with the indigenous Maori and wrote books on native plants and trees. This deep-rooted passion for nature is behind every product in Peri's New Zealand-based company, Snowy Peak, and her brand, Untouched World.

Peri was a burned-out cardiology nurse when she got a vision for a business that could change the world through fashion and beauty. Today she creates products using only natural ingredients, including body products made from pure plant extracts and organic wool clothing.

The Untouched World brand began at her kitchen table in 1981. Now it employs more than 100 people and sells worldwide. Peri's daughter Emily, an award-winning designer, creates the designs that go into elegant merino leather, and also fur clothing from "nuisance" animals— invasive species, such as possum and wallaby—that are being eradicated by the New Zealand government.

The desire to give back also drives Peri's vision. She puts it this way: "Through fashion, to lead the way in what is possible for people and planet."[14] In 2002, Untouched World published a five-year plan to switch to renewable resources for its energy needs. The company also helps protect New Zealand's native species, educates children about conservation, and creates employment opportunities in rural areas that typically offer only limited job prospects.

Peri integrates the image of New Zealand purity into her brand to evoke feelings of safety and well-being in her customers. She is also a product placement genius. At her request, former President Bill Clinton entered an economic summit meeting in Auckland wearing an Untouched World polo shirt. Clinton said that Peri's silk shirt is the best clothing he's ever worn and you'll find his photograph in the Snowy Peak marketing materials.

According to Peri, "What's important about these brands is that they come from the heart and there is someone who will make sure that the brands stay true to where they want to go." She says, "You have to be able to feel it. If you can feel it, that gives you the energy to take hold of these opportunities when they come."[15]

Emerging Entrepreneur: Butterfly Dreams

"Feeling pretty is part of healing," says Lynn Madonna of Butterfly Dreams, a company that designs and manufactures specialty apparel and get-well gifts for women who are coping with chronic illness and surgical recovery. This means camisoles with pockets and buttonholes in the side seams to accommodate drains for post-breast surgery recovery, for example. It's clothing that can make you feel good when you're not feeling well.

Lynn is a former public relations executive who left a career in health care and venture capital to "repurpose" her life in Scottsdale, Arizona. Her partner Susan Feagler is a breast cancer survivor and an artist who moved to Scottsdale with her husband for semi-retirement. Butterfly Dreams, which launched in 2004, also includes Capri pants, wraparound nightgowns, and Get Well Gift Totes.

Its strategy has two marketing channels: business-to-business and business-to-consumer. "We made a strategic decision to go to our customer as directly as possible, so we started the business through an Internet store," says Lynn. "We also sell direct to healthcare organizations and those that have a special emphasis on addressing specific diseases."[16]

Large companies like Avon and Estée Lauder have also done a good job of combining beauty and cause-related marketing. Their support of breast cancer research has poured millions into the cause. This commitment helps these companies win the loyalty of their customer base because customers feel good when they support inspirational brands.

Beauty

Boomers no longer focus solely on their looks because they have learned that health is the true foundation of beauty. Healthful lifestyle behaviors such as proper rest, diet, exercise, and nutrition have increased in importance among women age 45 to 64, according to a 2002 survey by AARP. But this doesn't mean that boomers are ignoring their looks. Most of the employed women age 50 and older in the survey said they would use hair color and regular exercise to keep looking young; 24% would use anti-wrinkle creams, 11% would consider having cosmetic surgery, and 9% would wear a wig.[17]

These statistics show how far boomers will go to feel shine in their hair and glow in their cheeks. Boomers know that while true beauty comes from within, "face value" is what people see.

"Every woman knows that life is better for women in their 40s than it used to be," says Myrna Blyth. "Women remember how hard it was for their mothers, and they don't want to look like their daughters. Beauty products should sell the notion of agelessness. That can mean everything from creams to plastic surgery. This audience is also interested in experience, which means challenging themselves physically to be fit."[18]

Emerging Entrepreneur: Dayle Haddon

Dayle Haddon has come to represent the beauty of an older woman. Thirty years ago, she was a top model. Now she is back at the top of her game again—in both the United States and China. Her first modeling career ended when she was fired for being too old at age 38. Dayle dropped out of the industry until she realized that she was in a position to get beauty industry executives to pay attention to women over 40. Then she spent years educating beauty industry executives about how women feel invisible and marginalized as they age. Now Dayle's face advertises a line of anti-aging products for L'Oréal. She regularly contributes to CBS's *Early Show*, and her book *The 5 Principles of Ageless Living* was a best-seller in China.

"What I'm doing is shifting the balance," she says. "A lot of people reach out to me because they want to look younger. But they walk away with other things that are more important. What I bring is inspiration about the spiritual side of life. It's about deep value and how we find meaning."[19]

Emerging Entrepreneur: Entourage Day Night Spa Salon, Café Wine Bar

"We are a repair stop," says Gino Chiodo, owner of the Entourage Day Night Spa Salon, Café Wine Bar in Northern California.[20] Boomers are especially drawn to spas and salons once their schedules become flexible enough to allow it, their purses still support it, and their stressful lifestyles demand it. Spas and salons are a $14-billion market, according to North Castle Partners, and growth is accelerating at double-digit rates.[21]

Gino has been in the beauty industry for 25 years. Even though his initial hair salon was a success, he felt something was missing. He began to notice customers coming in with coffee in the morning, having lunch while they were having their hair done, or having a glass of wine in the evening. He thought, "Why not put all these things together by design and create a concept to allow customers to do what they need to do?"

The first Entourage opened in 2002, and it was an immediate hit. It offers a sense of community and entertainment along with high-end services. It features a living room with couches; a bar with cappuccino and fine wines; a manicure and pedicure area; and rooms for massages, Jacuzzi, facials, and waxing. Gino hosts after-hours spa parties for teens, working women, moms and daughters, and work groups. A holiday event with 17 corporate lawyers resulted in 16 new customers. The Valentine's Day Sweetheart package has couples lined up to drink wine, walk down a rose petal-lined hallway for their massage, and join the party in the living room afterward.

Between 2002 and 2005, Entourage's customer database grew from 1,700 customers to 7,000. The average customer spent about $120 in 2005, up from about $40 three years earlier. The gender gap has closed as well—Gino's customer base has changed from 20% men to a solid 50-50.[22]

Gino could have been a restaurateur or a tavern keeper, but he chose to become a community builder. He is using the platform of Entourage to bring people together and to relieve their stress. It is a trend to emulate.

Other Market Slices

The fashion and beauty market contains dozens of opportunities for entrepreneurs who understand the boomers' sensibility. Cynthia

Robins, for example, makes elegant jewelry under the name Cyn City Designs in Las Vegas. "Jewelry used to be something that men bought women," she says. "But the minute that women entered the workforce, it became a perk they bought to adorn themselves with." Now luxury marketers score by encouraging women with means to reward themselves. "A woman will go out and maybe buy herself a Porsche or a BMW, but more than likely she will buy something intimate," says Cynthia. "There are some classic things that most women want for themselves: shiny studs for the ears and a good set of pearls."

Cynthia understands that boomer women take care of themselves and build their own style through jewelry purchases: "It's not about the man. It's about being feminine, about having something that can take you anywhere."[23]

Another promising market targets the unique needs of menopausal women. A handful of companies, including CoolDryComfort, HotCool Wear, Wicking J Sleepwear, and DryDreams, are reaching the 75% of menopausal women who suffer sleepless nights due to hot flashes with materials that wick moisture away from the body. Several of these companies were started by boomer women who were tired of waking up drenched in sweat. Others have expanded their lines to include workout clothing as well as bath and body lines.[24]

Summary

Overall consumer spending on apparel in the United States has been stagnant or declining since the 1990s. Conventional wisdom says that the aging of the population is the reason because older adults don't spend as much on clothes as younger ones do. But boomers are changing things, and fashion entrepreneurs who understand how can find profitable niches.

Boomers will fuel rapid growth in apparel sales through the Internet, for example. Apparel has lagged behind other e-commerce categories because, so far, most consumers have preferred to touch and try on clothing before buying it. But as people become more familiar with online shopping, e-commerce will become a complementary distribution channel for store-based retailers. Increasingly, consumers are browsing online for clothing. Internet penetration is growing quickly in Europe and Asia, and reports indicate that affluent consumers are happy with their online clothing purchases. This bodes well for luxury fashion brands.

Look for more e-tailers to tweak their sites with virtual dressing rooms, 3D models, zoom capability, and other sophisticated selling tools. Savvy entrepreneurs will look at the Internet not as an independent channel or a standalone business, but rather as an integral component of a multichannel strategy for attracting customers, building brands, and cultivating consumer relationships.[25]

"Our customers seek the newest skin regimens on the market to help them look and feel younger," says Kent Anderson, President of macys.com. "The power of the Internet accelerates the process of getting these state-of-the-art advances in skin care into customers' hands."[26]

Cosmetic surgery will also take off as boomers age, but it has to be done right. Ages 55 to 64 are the "age of cosmetic surgery," according to an AARP survey that revealed that nearly 1 in 10 women in this age group, more than twice that of any other group, has had some cosmetic surgery. Even more significant, the survey discovered, is the fact that 16% of 55- to 64-year-old women expect to have cosmetic surgery eventually.[27] The true trendsetter might be the 95-year-old woman who attends a symphony opening dressed in red sequins, pearls, gold shoes, and a candy-apple red walker to match. The desire to dress up for special events does not decline with age. Neither does the desire to stay in the game.

Part of understanding fashion and beauty is simple: We feel good when we look good. As we age, it may take more effort to do so. But for an increasing number of baby boomers, beauty is tied to deep personal issues related to the themes of self-worth at midlife. As fashion forecoster David Wolfe says, "Fashion is starting to look grown up. It's not just about acceptance of aging—there is also a celebration. People don't want to look young; they want to look as healthy as possible. It's such a positive time, such an exuberant time, and I think fashion is finally waking up to it. It's long overdue."[28]

Endnotes

1. Focus Group, Lafayette, CA, July 7, 2005.

2. David Wolfe, interview by author, July 26, 2005.

3. Myrna Blyth, interview by author, July 20, 2005.

4. NOPWorld, *Mature Market*, Brand Loyalty/Purchase Behavior, 2002.

5. *Ibid.*

6. Hakuhodo Elder Development Division, *Jeans 50s: Japanese People in Their 50s*, 2003, 4, 10, http://www.h-hope.net/english/knowledge_box/02/.

7. Freedonia Group, *Anti-Aging Products to 2009*, http://www.freedoniagroup.com/medical.html.

8. Tony Margolis, interview by author, August 22, 2005.

9. Since 1999, Tommy Bahama has sponsored a racecar in the BF Goodrich Tires Trans-Am Series (a yellow Corvette painted with a green palm tree)—it was even the champion in 2000—and is the title sponsor of the award-winning Nemschoff power boat team.

10. Tony Margolis, interview by author, August 22, 2005.

11. Chico's FAS, Inc., *Chico's Annual Report*, http://www.chicos.com/store/pdf/Chicos_Annual_Report_2004.pdf.

12. Gap, Inc., "Forth and Towne Opens in New York, Chicago," August 23, 2005, http://www.gapinc.com/public/Media/Press_Releases/med_pr_ForthTowne Opening_Aug2305.shtml.

13. Jenn Abelson, "Hot Trend in Fashion: Maturity, Apparel Market Eyes Older Women," *Boston Globe*, March 5, 2006.

14. Untouched World, http://www.untouchedworld.com/en/uw/vision.htm.

15. Peri Drysdale, interview by author, March 20, 2005.

16. Lynn Madonna, interview by author, July 28, 2005.

17. RoperASW, *Mature Market: Beauty.* Fifty-two percent of working women express concern about growing older, while 44% of their nonworking counterparts express the same concern. *Ibid.*

18. Myrna Blyth, interview by author, July 20, 2005.

19. Dayle Haddon, interview by author, September 12, 2005.

20. Gino Chiodo, interview by author, July 7, 2005.

21. North Castle Partners, "Red Door Spa Holdings," http://www.northcastlepartners.com/portfolio/reddoor.php.
22. Gino Chiodo, interview by author, July 7, 2005.
23. Cynthia Robins, interview by Beth Witrogen McLeod, July 11, 2005.
24. Korky Vann, "High-Tech Clothing Helps Ease Hot Flashes," *Connecticut Courant*, June 8, 2005, http://www.hotcoolwear.com/index.php.
25. Uche Okonkwo, "Can the luxury fashion brand store atmosphere be transferred to the Internet?," Brandchannel.com, April 2005, http://www.brandchannel.com/images/papers/269_Lux_Goods_Online.pdf; "Dressing for Success on the Web," Cotton, Inc., March 9, 2000, http://www.cottoninc.com/lsmarticles/?articleID=211.
26. Kent Anderson, e-mail message to author.
27. Teresa Flatley, "Is Being Perfect Worth It?" EmptyNestMoms.com, http://www.emptynestmoms.com/pages/article16.html.
28. David Wolfe, interview by author, July 26, 2005.

7

GIMME SHELTER—AND A WHOLE LOT MORE

Introduction

One of my dearest childhood memories is of sitting on the front porch of my grandma's house in Virginia. It was the hub for the community. She lived across from Fonticello Park in Richmond, and every night there was a ballgame. The adults would rock on the glider cooling themselves with fans from the local funeral parlor and talk about the events of the day. There was a sense of community as neighbors stopped by to chat. The love that you felt on that front porch was special; it was "home" for me and for all our friends and family. That sense of Southern hospitality and community was very different from the suburbs in California. It has been a huge reason why community building has been a key part of my work for the past 25 years.

These days, as older baby boomers like me approach age 60, we're looking for housing that offers a sense of community, involvement, connection, and a reasonable lifestyle. Many boomers are cashing out of their homes and looking for places in Hot Springs, Arkansas; Austin, Texas; and Salem, Oregon where living is more reasonable and they can form a new sense of community and purpose.

This is a different vision of retirement than the one our parents had. David Schreiner, a vice president at Pulte Homes, Inc., wanted to investigate those generational differences and see how they might change the demand for retirement housing, so he dispatched staffers to interview 100 residents of the company's Del Webb developments from Florida to Minnesota.

Schreiner found that although the new generation of retirees wants to live in more relaxed communities, they don't equate "retirement" with "rest." One Florida resident had gone back to work driving a boat at Walt Disney World and had gotten married . . . at the amusement park. A former telephone company middle manager in Northern California described her life's mission as "teaching all the world to dance."[1]

Iconoculture, Inc., a leader in understanding cultural and consumer trends, says the slow-paced days of "shuffleboredom" in retirement are over. The ideal post-career housing choice for a baby boomer will depend heavily on that boomer's unique mix of needs and interests. But whether it's a 35-acre ranchette connected to equestrian paths or a single-bedroom apartment in center-city Philadelphia, many of the boomers will want what I was lucky enough to have in Richmond—a strong connection to family and community, as well as opportunities to stay engaged.

One of the key questions at midlife is where to live, and this question becomes acute after a life-changing event. Someone who loses a father usually feels an immediate and pressing need to be closer to Mom. The same sense of urgency passes over someone who loses a partner, retires, or whose children move away. The question is: How can developers and other businesses encourage a person going through these lifestage transitions to view them as aspirational opportunities? And what is the best way to find human connections in new communities that will satisfy an aging boomer's spirit and soul? How can developers capitalize on the many unique segments within the boomer housing market? And in a global and mobile world, how can businesses find ways to connect boomers to their children and grandchildren as the next generation takes jobs across the globe?"

In thinking about these questions and the trends outlined in this chapter, it is helpful to frame them in light of the three key points at the core of this book. First, baby boomers have more discretionary time and more discretionary money in midlife than any previous generation. Second, boomers are more educated than previous generations, so they tend to have more sophisticated tastes. Third, boomers love to be mobile.

Baby boomers won't move en masse toward any single housing trend. But they *will* use their attitudes, education, and affluence to create what they want. The search criteria the boomers will use in the housing market include price and location, of course, but also access to culture, education, and play. In this chapter, we take a look at the key trends driving boomers' housing decisions. These include the empty-nest phenomenon, the option to work at home, the desire for a wired "smart home," the need for community, and the purchase of second homes and timeshares to fulfill a passion for travel and relaxation.

Market Analysis
The Booming Housing Market

Over the past 35 years or so, boomers have purchased start-up homes, move-up homes, starting-over homes, and second homes at the beach, in the mountains, and at other favorite destinations. Today, boomers own nearly half of all homes in America.[2] And they are just getting started: according to the National Association of Home Builders, the 50-plus population is the fastest growing segment of the housing market. Americans age 55 and older bought nearly one-fifth of the 1.1 million new homes sold in 2003.[3]

Home ownership for Americans age 55 and older is the highest it has ever been. In 2000, an AARP study revealed that 86% of respondents stated they owned their home.[4] As boomers near retirement age, real estate is increasingly playing a more prominent role in investment planning than the stock market.

"Conditions in the housing market have been like the perfect storm," says David Hehman, former CEO of escapehomes.com. "We have had disappointing returns in the stock market, historically low interest rates, incredible appreciation with demand often outstripping supply, and the biggest transfer of wealth in American history."[5] Furthermore, many boomers' peak earning years have coincided with their last child graduating college or moving out on his or her own, providing additional means to buy a second, even a third, home.

Investment, Retirement, and Second Homes, Oh My!

Within the housing market, second home sales are booming. In 2005, second home sales occurred twice as fast as all new single-family home sales and almost four times as fast as resale homes.[6] The National Association of Realtors (NAR) estimates that in 2005, of all home sales, just under half (39.9%) were second homes—nearly one-third of these (27.7%) were bought for investment, while 12.2% were vacation homes.[7]

Indeed, one in four boomers in the United States has a second home. This is also true throughout Europe. In 2005, an English family could put down 100,000 pounds and get a second home on the coast of Spain or Portugal. The coast of Mexico is filled with boomers who want to capitalize on the reasonable prices, warmth, and sunshine. Alaska Airlines flies directly to Loretto, Mexico, so watch there for an uptick in development as boomers look for property near the beach at a reasonable price.

By all measures, it seems these trends will continue. At the 2006 convention of the National Association of Home Builders in Orlando, a new study released by consumer researchers at ProMatura LLC created quite the buzz. Based on a large survey of boomers, 52% of those between the ages of 45 and 54 years anticipate making some type of real estate investment—a second home, vacation property, or retirement property—over the next five years. Of those between ages 55 and 64, a slightly higher 57% said the same.[8]

Who are these buyers and where are they buying? In summing up a recent NAR report, "The 2006 National Association of Realtors Profile of Second Home Owners," Broderick Perkins from *Realty Times* noted the following trends:

- The typical 2005 vacation home buyer was 52 years old, earned $82,800, and purchased a property that was a median of 197 miles from his or her primary residence. Some 47% of vacation homes were less than 100 miles away and 43% were 500 miles or more away.

- Investment home buyers had a median age of 49, a median income of $81,400, and bought a home that was a median of 15 miles from their primary residence.

- The largest concentration of vacation home buyers (33%) are from the Midwest, although the property may be located in another region. Buyers in the South accounted for 30% of vacation home transactions, the West accounted for 20%, and the Northeast accounted for 17%.

- Most investment home buyers (38%) are in the South. Buyers in the Midwest and Western regions each purchased 24% of investment properties and Northeasterners purchased 15%.

- One in three vacation home buyers and 36% of investment home buyers said it was very likely that they would purchase another home, in addition to properties currently owned, within the next two years.[9]

When asked why they bought a second home, respondents to the NAR survey said they wanted to diversify their investments (30%), earn rental income (28%), or have a personal retreat (14%) or a place to vacation (6%). About 5% said they had bought a second home because they had the extra money.[10] Boomers also see a second home as a tangible legacy to pass on to their families—something that is more stable than stocks, more permanent than cash, and more meaningful than either.

This market is only going to get hotter, as recent revisions to tax laws have made it more attractive to buy a second home. These changes allow most sellers to exclude up to $500,000 in capital gains from taxation. As a result, boomers who've seen great appreciation in their primary residences are freed to use some of that windfall to purchase a second home with no tax penalty. Second homes are now easier to finance, as well. Most loans for second homes no longer require larger down payments and higher interest rates than primary residences.

Grandchildren are also fueling second home sales among boomers because homes in desirable areas can serve as magnets for far-flung family members. Boomers at midlife are all about building memories, and a house by the lake (or the beach, or in the mountains) is the perfect backdrop. Well-to-do boomer grandparents might add a separate guesthouse so the children can have a place of their own. The vacation house might need a large kitchen or great room solely because of the possibility of the family gathering for the holidays. Often the first home will get smaller—a condo or an apartment in the city will become the primary place of residence. In other words, the dream home of the future is actually the second home.

A person is most likely to buy a second home in a place where he or she has vacationed for several years. The second home is a respite from the everyday bustle, but it is neither exotic nor unknown. Its owner wants comfort and familiarity with fewer hassles. They want "lock-it-and-leave-it convenience" that allows a couple to get away whenever they want, without having to worry about taking care of their home. Look for red-hot growth in the getaway market wherever the boomers vacationed with their kids. Look also for places of serenity.

Some boomers are even buying a third home. According to the NAR, 51% of all vacation homes sold in 2004 went to buyers 55 and older, in a year when vacation home buying was up almost 20% in general from 2003.[24] Many of today's retirees not only have vast amounts of home equity, they have also accumulated wealth. Boomers are on the cusp of retiring even wealthier, so this trend is one to watch.

Should We Stay, or Should We Go?

Where boomers will go next is a topic of much speculation in the housing industry. Most boomers still live in the suburbs where they raised their families. Some vow to stay where they are and "age in place"— prepare themselves and their homes to live as long as possible right where they are. But as the children leave the nest and boomers approach retirement, the notion of rambling around a 3,000-square-foot home with a large yard to keep up loses its appeal to many.

Some plan to make a permanent move to their second homes at the beach, by the lake, or in the mountains. Others are being lured back to the cities where they are closer to work, recreation, the cultural arts, and entertainment. Some want to stay in the area where they currently live, but would like to downsize to something more manageable—but with all the perks and amenities, which can often be found in the burgeoning neighborhoods of 55+ active adult communities. Adventurous boomers are looking abroad to Mexico, Panama, and other exotic destinations where the views and lifestyle can't be beat, or at least found for a comparable price in the United States. Still others desire something else—a place that fosters community connectedness and vital living, intentionally nurtured in new models of communities, such as co-housing communities and the New Urbanist style of traditionally designed neighborhoods.

Not Everyone Is a Soccer Mom or a BBQ Dad

In analyzing the housing market for boomers, it is important to note that not all buyers are former soccer moms and BBQ dads fleeing the suburbs. In fact, less than one-quarter (23.5%) of all American households in 2000 were nuclear families—a married man and woman and their children 18 years old or younger—compared to nearly half (45%) of all households in 1960.[11]

Although some of this decline in traditional family households is due to boomers' children moving out or families breaking up, there is a significant number of boomers who have never married and/or never had children. For example, research conducted in 2000 by the Mature Market Institute found that more than 1 out of 10 (12.2%) boomers had never married, compared to only 3% of their parent's generation.[12] In addition, in 2000, nearly one out of five women in their early 40s, an age at which fertility markedly drops off, had never had children.[13]

Also contributing to an increasing number of single-person households is the high divorce rate among boomers, compared to previous generations. According to the U.S. Census, 14.2% of boomers are divorced, compared to 6.7% of people age 65 and older.[14] Because women tend to outlive their male partners and remarry less often, there is a significantly higher proportion of single-person households consisting of women and that proportion will increase as we get older. Today, of the 57 million American women age 45 and older, almost half—25 million—are unmarried.[15] By 2050, there will be almost 7 million more women than men alive in America.[16]

The number of Americans living alone, currently about 25%, is expected to continue rising. By 2010, 69% of the increase in the population living alone will be among people age 45 to 64.[17] These

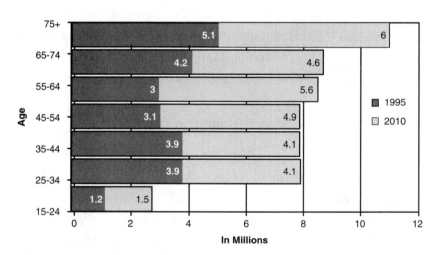

FIGURE 7.1 PROJECTED NUMBER OF PERSONS LIVING ALONE

Source: U.S. Department of Health and Human Services

demographic trends toward one-person households will significantly impact the type of housing boomers will be looking for in later life. Single boomers have a sense of adventure and opportunity as they age. Some are moving to Lincoln Center in New York, abandoning their former lifestyle to enjoy culture and entertainment that the city can offer. Some are taking apartments in world capitals for part of their time. And some find a place near their adult children and another in a community they call home.

Women Homeowners Setting Records

Make no mistake, boomer women are better educated, make more money, and are more financially savvy than previous generations of women. Women handle about 75% of the family finances, control half of the private wealth (about $14 trillion), and account for at least $2 trillion in annual consumer spending in the United States.[18] Boomer women are at the peak of their earning careers, and many don't expect to retire any time soon. Further, many are expected to be handling windfall inheritances from their parents and husbands over the next decade or two.

For many women, an increase in financial capital has been a passport to home ownership. According to several national studies, including studies by the National Association of Realtors, Fannie Mae, and Harvard University's Joint Center for Housing Studies, single women are the fastest growing segment of homebuyers today, buying one out of every five homes. They make up the second largest pool of homebuyers, following married couples who represent about 59% of home sales. Single women (21%) were more than twice as likely as single men (9%) to buy a single-family home in 2005, up from 15% and 7%, respectively, in 2001.[19] According to Fannie Mae, 17 million single women today own homes, and that number is projected to nearly double to 30 million in 2010.[20]

Housing Design Trends

Whether we are staying put or relocating to a new town, boomers like to make home improvements. According to Bill Apgar a senior scholar at Harvard's Joint Center for Housing Studies, "Boomers accounted for half of all remodeling expenditures as late as 2003. But the baby boom is not done. Even in their 50s, boomers are outspending their predecessors on remodeling."[21]

This is particularly true for boomers who choose to stay in the older homes in which they raised their children. The National Association of the Remodeling Industry (NARI) estimated in 2003 that remodeling in the United States was a $230 billion industry and was expected to experience significant growth. NARI also estimates that one million homes are remodeled per year in the United States.[22]

But don't mistake the boomers' home improvement ambitions as a desire to pick up a hammer and a power drill. As Home Depot CEO Robert Nardelli pointed out in a speech to alumni of the University of Georgia's Terry College of Business, "The baby boomers are moving from do-it-yourself to do-it-for-me."[23] This is why Home Depot offers complete installation services on most of their product lines, from flooring to kitchen remodeling. Through an innovative partnership with AARP, Home Depot cements the boomers' loyalty by making extra efforts to employ older workers in its stores.

So, what *are* boomers doing when they remodel and renovate? In this next section, we look at some of the hottest trends.

Interior Design

Square footage is no longer the Holy Grail. The average size of a new single-family home in the United States increased every year for 30 straight years until 2001, according to the NAHB. Since then, it has stabilized around 2,330 square feet.[24] Popular books, such as Sarah Susanka's *The Not So Big House* and Denise Sullivan Medved's *The Tiny Kitchen,* attest to the value that less is sometimes more. Allison

Arieff, former editor-in-chief of *Dwell* magazine, reports that a "small spaces" issue was the magazine's best-seller by far. She notes that "people just don't want to deal with all that unused space anymore."[25]

What boomers want instead is space that perfectly reflects their individual needs and personality, and something with quality, comfort, and class. Joszi Meskan, one of the country's leading interior designers, has guided many boomers toward this kind of design. Living in an increasingly fast-paced, high-tech world leaves us yearning for our own little sanctuary at the end of the day. Joszi helps clients create rooms for intimacy and quiet connection, private spaces for meditation, and rooms that are perfect for conversation and celebration. As the designer of The Lodge at Koelle, one of the top resorts in Hawaii, as well as the Royal Palms, Joszi thinks that what upscale, middle-aged people ultimately wish for is comfort. And comfort has different meanings, some taken from the present and some from when we were children.

" 'Comfortable' means we've gone back to our roots, to what we remembered as the most comfortable time in our lives," she says. "It has nothing to do with a sofa and two lounge chairs. It has to do with the memories of the places we've been most comfortable doing or being. So if it was the bathtub that made a kid comfortable, then as an adult, their bathroom might become their palace. It isn't the stuff; it's the *feeling*." Boomers want to be in a space that is welcoming and calm and that expresses who we are.[26]

Simplicity is another trend. Whether downsizing or rightsizing, boomers are intent on keeping the clutter at bay. Out is the fireplace mantle with 20 family photos, a handful of candlesticks, and other assorted knickknacks. In their place, one or two meaningful photos and a few well-appointed pieces are the new look. Simplicity is the current hallmark of elegance.

In the kitchen and bath, luxury reigns. High-end appliances, granite countertops, and custom tile floors remain popular. Kitchens that flow into the den also have great appeal because they allow homeowners to be part of the party while they cook and clean up. There are seven kitchen stores in my small community of Lafayette, California—more kitchen stores than coffee houses. It seems that the trigger to remodel the kitchen is when the last child finishes college. That is when the $36,000 per year tuition gets reassigned to the kitchen. My neighbors talk about how their last son will graduate in May and the remodel starts in September.

Gina Pais of Kohler knows what boomers want in their bathrooms. She emphasizes lighting, accessibility, and safety because more accidents occur in the bathroom than in any other room of the house. She predicts that the bathroom will become a "restorative place," almost like a personal spa, especially for women.[27] A bathroom featured in *Better Homes and Gardens'* May 2005 issue included vintage-style fixtures and overlooked a forest, pond, and farmland. The antique clawfoot tub was refinished, and designers added primitive-style cabinetry and a double-bowl vanity. And if the bathroom is for a man, technology will dominate: Envision a world in which you can have Internet access and video while you're seated on the toilet.

Universal Design

One of the biggest opportunities in the housing industry is renovation that accommodates the changing physical needs of boomers and other family members. When Mom moves in to be cared for by her loving son, he is going to want to get rid of the steps, put in a ramp, widen the hallways, and/or add an in-law unit if local zoning allows it. That's because injuries caused by falls are one of the biggest reasons older people enter nursing homes—and never leave. And thousands of people each year leave their homes for residential care facilities when they didn't need to because renovations that could have kept them at home weren't made.

A 2000 national housing survey by AARP found that given a choice, more than 8 in 10 respondents age 45 and over, and more than 9 in 10 of those 65 and older, said they would prefer to stay in their current residence for as long as possible. Even if they needed help caring for themselves, 82 percent said they would prefer to stay in their current homes. To enable aging in place in their own homes, many recognize the need to make modifications such as an entryway with no steps, a main floor bedroom and bathroom, and incorporating universal design features such as levered door handles and better lighting. More than two-thirds (67%) of those making such modifications said that doing so will enable them to live longer in their home than they would otherwise have been able.[28]

For those who want to age in place, universal design features are nearly a prerequisite. Unlike "handicapped accessible," universal design involves subtle changes that often blend into the décor so well that you wouldn't know they were there unless someone pointed them out as universal design features. This concept emphasizes the importance of designing a home or facility that is safe for all age groups to live in. Those who promote universal design say that features such as a main floor bathroom and bedroom, zero-step entry, open spaces, easy accessibility, and wider hallways are appreciated by disabled and non-disabled people alike.

With more discretionary income than any previous generation, boomers have the means to outfit their homes with all the latest modern conveniences. Home lighting is a big opportunity for new businesses. So are home elevators and stairway lifts—which help people stay in their homes and are also helpful with bringing in groceries and cases of wine. And as all new parents know, wheelchair accessibility is also stroller accessibility.

Making Space for Aging Parents

The rise in the number of adults who care for an aging parent or loved one is also bringing new demands to the marketplace. MarketWatch reports that builders of high-end homes say market demand is increasing for optional in-law suites, and modular-home builders have also seen increased demand for cottages that can be attached to existing homes.

"In the last 10 years, the demand has tripled," says Andy Gianino, president of The Home Store, which builds modular homes at its factory and installs them on customers' property. Andrew Kocehera, senior publicity advisor at AARP's Public Policy Institute, says in-low unites are one way of keeping people out of nursing homes and closer to independent living."[29]

"We design many of our homes with a suite over the garage . . . that can be used for an au pair, parents, returning child, or even a working office," says Cheryl O'Connor, vice president of sales and marketing for Warmington Homes. "A lot of baby boomers are going to want to have home offices, sometimes two, for consulting or telecommuting part time."[30]

Home Offices and Home-Based Businesses

Many are the baby boomers who can't wait to turn a child's former bedroom into a home office. Consequently, Joszi Meskan estimates that 20% of the pre-retirees she works with want to start a business after they turn 50,[31] and 40% of Americans who are in business for themselves are older than 50, according to an AARP survey. Home-based businesses account for roughly half of all U.S. businesses, and two out of three companies begin as home-based.[32]

According to a survey by AARP, 40% of Americans who are in business for themselves are older than 50, and that percentage has been rising.

This trend is also happening overseas: One survey of 1,000 people with a home office in Britain found that 46% of them were over age 45. An amazing 61% of adults older than 55 in the Netherlands are working from a home office space, compared with 59% in France and 30% in Italy.[33]

"Boomers are leading the way in this entrepreneurial wave," says Tony Lee, editor-in-chief of StartupJournal.com, a site for small businesses. "They have the resources and the built-in talents, and there are ways for them to work for themselves without starting from scratch."[34]

But it is one thing to carve out a home office and another thing to keep it organized. A lot of people don't know that you can pay someone to come into your home to help you get organized—but when they find out, they almost always want that person's phone number. This industry is relatively young as it was defined in 1988 by the National Association of Professional Organizers (NAPO).

"Overwhelmed" is the word Tiffany Mock, one of the leading personal organizers in the San Francisco Bay Area, hears most often. Sixty percent of her clients are boomers. "It takes courage to ask for help and open your home up to an outsider to go through your personal belongings," she says. "People are sometimes embarrassed that they need help, but the fact is that we were never taught organization in school. Some people are born with the skill, some are not, and most of us are somewhere in between."[35]

The Smart Home

Boomers appreciate and accept technology and will increasingly adapt its use to make their homes "smarter." Michael Sarfatti, managing director of the SmartSilvers Alliance in San Francisco, notes, "As boomers age, homes become centers for entertainment, work, commerce, learning, and wellness. It's the linkage among those activities that makes a higher quality of life possible."

Paraphrasing Joseph F. Coughlin, director of the MIT AgeLab, Michael emphasizes that a smart home will "fully leverage advances in information, communications, sensors, advanced materials, lighting, and other technologies." It will incorporate a variety of Internet-enabled technologies that can be programmed to communicate with each other to carry out complex functions that meet the evolving needs of the residents.[36]

Expect boomers to invest in home monitoring and response systems as well as those that enhance quality of life. These monitors will be embedded within the structure, furniture, plumbing, and appliances. Boomers will also buy assistive devices to perform housework and other chores, especially as more and more of them become functionally impaired. Companies like Intel and Lusora (see Chapter 10, "Financing Your Dream") are also beginning to produce communication devices for social contact, work, education, and entertainment. The Resource section has a list of smart home company providers.

Reverse Mortgages

Of course, all these home modifications come at a price. To finance major renovation work, some homeowners who are house rich and cash poor have discovered reverse mortgages. As the name implies, a reverse mortgage is the opposite of a forward mortgage; instead of the homeowner sending the lender mortgage payments, the lender pays the homeowner. Reverse mortgage funds are disbursed in several ways: an immediate lump sum payment, a tenure plan (monthly payments), a term plan (payments spread over a specified amount of time), a line of credit (with a credit line growth rate), or a combination of the above. Seniors may use the tax-free funds as they wish—to renovate or remodel their homes, supplement monthly income, travel, pay medical bills, or to simply enjoy an increased quality of life during the retirement years.

To be eligible, senior homeowners must be at least 62 years of age; the mortgaged property must be their primary residence; the current mortgage balance should be moderate to low compared to the value of the home; and the applicants must attend free, mandatory counseling by an outside, independent counselor. The loan becomes due and payable when the homeowner no longer occupies the home as primary residence. This could be due to death, illness, or purchasing a new home. For joint mortgages, the loan is not due until the last surviving borrower permanently leaves the residence.

Aging in Place in Suburbia

Boomers love the 'burbs—with their large homes and big backyards and where shopping, entertainment, and recreation are only a short drive away. Based on 2000 Census data, the Brookings Institute released a report mapping aging patterns in the suburbs. Accordingly, boomers accounted for 31% of the total surburban population, a steady climb from 26.6% in 1990. During the mid-1990s, the "middle-aged-plus" population outpaced growth of the 35-and-under population by a ratio of 4 to 1.[37]

The greatest concentration of boomers has been found outside high-end cities like San Francisco; Seattle; and Washington, D.C., while the fastest growing areas for the 55-plus population is mostly in the New Sunbelt metros in the Southeast and Southwest, such as Atlanta, Las Vegas, and Denver. Of those boomers planning to move, almost one-third (31%) said they would move only about three hours away from their current locations.[38] Within these states, the highest concentrations of baby boomers are in suburban areas where housing prices have risen beyond the budgets of most young adults.

Business opportunities abound to serve this suburban housing market, from lawn and home maintenance to real estate sales specializing in senior housing to the home renovation and remodel business. Products that ease the burdens of home maintenance and housekeeping, such as central vacuum and irrigation systems, will be in high demand.[39]

Affluent boomers also congregate in smaller towns that have great skiing, fishing, or other kinds of outdoor recreation. Areas with high concentrations of older boomers (ages 51 to 60 in 2006) contain clues about what will be most important to this group as it ages, says Brad Edmondson, whose website e-Podunk.com contains detailed profiles of 46,000 places in the United States and Canada.[40]

Several smaller metros on the list are also notable. Over the past decade, cities such as Denver and Nashville have attracted boomers to their fast-growing job markets. Metropolitan areas such as Minneapolis and Colorado Springs have enticed boomers with their cultural or natural attractions.

"Aging in place" regions, where many boomers are staying put in current homes, can be found in New England and the eastern seaboard, the upper Midwest, the upper Rocky Mountain west, and the Pacific Northwest. The largest share of baby boomers (more than 32% of each state's total population) can be found in Alaska, New Hampshire, Vermont, and Maine. Close behind, according to the 2000 Census, are Colorado, Connecticut, Maryland, and Virginia (surrounding the greater Washington, D.C. area). The midwestern states of Minnesota, Wisconsin, and Michigan have also retained a good share of their boomer populations.[41]

Although some boomers are staying put, and others are still moving up in multi-generational communities, some are moving over to the new "active adult communities"—age-restricted housing developments that offer single-family homes, townhouses, and occasionally, rental properties for financially secure and healthy adults age 55 and older (described in more detail in the next section). Empty nesters are attracted by the array of amenities, low maintenance, and resort-like lifestyle in the same geographic area where many still work, socialize, and play. Much of this growth is just outside of major metropolitan areas in the New Sunbelt—nine of the counties with the most growth in active-adult home construction are in the Southwest and Colorado, and one is in Florida.[42]

Big City Lights, Big City Style

Many cities are making a big comeback—this time as hip places to retire. Many empty nesters and new retirees are leaving the suburbs behind for the cafe-culture, pedestrian-friendly streets, and myriad cultural and recreation opportunities offered by urban living. For many, the move into the city eliminates a long commute to work, adding valuable time to take advantage of the cultural amenities and convenience of the 24-hour city. For others, it's a return to a lifestyle they enjoyed before marriage and family dictated a move to the suburbs, where the schools were better and the crime was less. What-ever the motivation, over the past 10 years, affluent boomers and re-tirees have been relocating to urban centers, spurring major growth in the downtown populations of several cities.

Luxury Condominiums

In mid-sized and large cities, a significant amount of the growth has been in upscale, luxury condominiums. Once thought of as a cheap alternative to the single-family home or a retirement or va-cation option, this new sumptuous condo version is looking to cash in on the boomers' desire to escape their spacious homes in the sub-urbs for something even better. Amenities define the word *luxury* and differentiate these homes from "just" a condo. In addition to quality architecture and top-tier interior design features, develop-ers have added such upscale elements as concierge service, boat dockage, 24-hour monitored security, maid service, five-star restau-rants, owners' lounges, business centers, dog parks on the roof, in-house movie theaters, wine cellars, and wine tasting and cigar rooms. All of this on top of the "standard" features of spectacular views, large decks, state-of-the art fitness centers, and resort-like spa and pool areas.

Let's take Seattle as an example. One cool spring morning in 2005, 38 people camped out in lawn chairs for a chance to buy one of 45 units at a downtown condo-and-hotel complex known simply as 2200. The project has 261 units total, ranging in price from $250,000 for a studio to upwards of $2 million for a penthouse. About 92% of the units sold—within a year after opening. Around the corner in the Belltown neighborhood, several other upscale developments are go-ing up and selling just as fast, with the strongest demand for luxury condos in the $400,000 range. Moreover, at least half a dozen condo projects are in the works from the Pike Place Market area to South Lake Union. According to the planning director for Seattle, 5,000 dwellings could be built downtown in the next five years.[43]

Seattle is not alone. Luxury condominiums are popping up from coast to coast. In California alone, condo sales in the $1 million dollar category reached 1,677 units in 2005—nearly double the sales in 2004.[44] But condos don't have to be luxurious to be desirable. Developers are retrofitting older apartment buildings to become condominium communities. National sales of "converters" more than doubled between 2004 and 2005, from $11 billion (77,193 units) in 2004 to $28 billion (182,742 units) in 2005.[45] Experts in housing believe this trend is being driven by a desire of empty nesters and retirees to move to affordable housing in the urban centers where they have less maintenance, more security, and all the advantages of being in town.

"Cities are great places to grow old," says John McIlwain, a senior fellow at the Urban Land Institute in Washington. "Why is that? It's easy to

TABLE 7.1 MEDIAN VALUE OF SINGLE-FAMILY HOMES VERSUS CONDOS

Year	Single Family	Change	Condo	Change
1990	$92,000	2.8%	$85,200	-0.9%
1991	$97,100	5.5%	$85,800	0.7%
1992	$99,700	2.7%	$86,000	0.2%
1993	$103,100	3.4%	$84,400	-1.9%
1994	$107,200	4.0%	$87,200	3.3%
1995	$110,500	3.1%	$87,400	0.2%
1996	$115,800	4.8%	$90,900	4.0%
1997	$121,800	5.2%	$95,500	5.1%
1998	$128,400	5.4%	$100,600	5.3%
1999	$133,300	3.8%	$108,000	7.4%
2000	$139,000	4.3%	$111,800	3.5%
2001	$147,800	6.3%	$123,200	10.2%
2002	$158,200	7.0%	$142,200	15.4%
2003	$170,000	7.5%	$165,400	16.3%
2004	$184,100	8.3%	$193,600	17%
Sept. 2005	$212,200	14.3%°	$213,600	9.0%°

°Compared to September 2004; Source: National Association of Realtors

get around—cities have great public transportation, and there's access to healthcare facilities, restaurants, and the symphony."[46]

The New Urbanism Movement

Who hasn't sat in a rush hour traffic jam and thought, "There has to be a better way to live!"? New Urbanists have—and they have come up with a plan. Actually, their plan is largely based on old plans, often referred to as "traditional neighborhood design." If you have ever been to an old New England colonial town or European village, you likely know intuitively what New Urbanism strives to achieve—walkable, people-friendly, vibrant, mixed-use communities, often formed around a public square that incorporates good use of green space and pedestrian pathways.

New Urbanism emerged two decades ago as a backlash against the burgeoning urban/suburban sprawl—the ever-expansive, rapid, and sometimes reckless growth of metropolitan areas that consumes green space, creates dependency on cars, causes traffic jams and air pollution, and contributes to the decline of civic life and social engagement.

Championed by planners, architects, city officials, community leaders, and citizens, the New Urbanist movement is centered on 27 key principles, such as having the town center as a public square or memorable cross street; mixed types of housing and income levels; and retail shops, a post office, and other businesses within walking distance.[47]

Since the first community, Seaside Village on the coast of northwest Florida, was built, there have been hundreds of New Urbanist projects, many within the infill areas of cities and first ring suburbs, including Haile Village Center in Gainesville, Florida; Harbor Town in Memphis, Tennessee; Kentlands in Gaithersburg, Maryland; Addison Circle in Addison, Texas; Orenco Station in Hillsboro, Oregon; Mashpee Commons in Mashpee, Massachusetts; and Celebration in Orlando, Florida.[48] Today, more than 600 new towns, villages, and neighborhoods are planned or under construction.

While these well-designed neighborhoods are attractive to all age groups, boomers are particularly drawn. New Urbanism offers that old-time feeling of community and comfort that so many of us are longing for in today's socially isolating, fast-paced, high-stress world. Our collective memory of and yearning for a simpler time comes alive in these neighborhoods with their wide sidewalks passing front porches complete with gliders, swings, and rockers. In our present lives, the ideals of New Urbanism feed into our generational consciousness of concern for the environment, healthier living, mindfulness, and personal growth. The Natural Marketing Institute, a research and consulting firm, estimates that about one-third of American adults (68 million) consist of the type of consumers who consider environmental, social, and health issues when they make consumer choices.[49]

As a housing trend, many believe New Urbanism will be *the* new style of development, offering a mainstream alternative to suburban, city, and country living lifestyles. It shares a unique mix of support, from city and regional planners to health advocates and environmentalists. For example, according to health officials, sprawl has increased the risks of respiratory and cardiovascular diseases, traffic accidents, and obesity, particularly among the elderly, children, and at-risk groups such as people with respiratory illnesses.[50] The New Urbanist model, with its emphasis on walkability and the diminished role of cars, provides an antidote to these health concerns. Likewise, environmentalists like the planning design because of its emphasis on wise use of green space and environmentally friendly design elements, such as reusing reclaimed water for irrigation and energy-efficient construction in buildings.

Exiled in Exurbia

Another hot area for development and growth is exurbia, the suburbs of suburbs. Located as far as a two-hour commute from the closest major city, these communities have sprouted up like mushrooms overnight across old farm fields and open spaces. Some of the fastest-growing counties in 2005 were on the outermost fringes of large metropolitan areas—in places such as King George and Caroline counties in Virginia, which are 40 to 60 miles from Richmond, and more than 90 miles from Washington, D.C.

Some new boomer arrivals to exurbia are motivated by the opportunity to find more affordable housing, bigger yards, and a better place to raise their families. Others are lured by the increasing number of active adult communities and waterfront properties.[51]

It's easy to understand the allure when passing through rolling hills and farmland in the surrounding countryside outside of many metropolitan areas. Vast, open space; clean air; less traffic; and a slower pace of life—and it all comes with twice the house and property one could afford closer in to the city. And to sweeten the deal, many of the exurbs have appreciated at a much higher rate than other homes in the area.

So what's not to like? Some disgruntled newcomers and old-timers complain that the problem is that everyone else has the same idea! Areas like Loudoun, one county in from King George County in

TABLE 7.2 WHERE THE GROWTH IS—THE USA'S FASTEST-GROWING COUNTIES WITH POPULATIONS GREATER THAN 10,000 IN 2004–2005, WITH THEIR PERCENTAGE OF GROWTH AND THE DRIVING DISTANCE FROM THE COUNTY SEAT TO THE NEAREST MAJOR CITY.

Rank/County	Growth	Distance
1. Flagler, Fla.	10.7%	25 miles to Daytona Beach
2. Lyon, Nev.	9.6%	80 miles to Reno
3. Kendall, Ill.	9.4%	50 miles to Chicago
4. Rockwall, Texas	7.7%	20 miles to Dallas
5. Washington, Utah	7.7%	120 miles to Las Vegas
6. Nye, Nev.	7.4%	210 miles to Las Vegas
7. Pinal, Ariz.	6.9%	60 miles to Phoenix
8. Loudoun, Va.	6.8%	35 miles to Washington
9. King George, Va.	6.7%	60 miles to Richmond
10. Caroline, Va.	6.5%	40 miles to Richmond

Sources: Census Bureau, *USA Today* research

Virginia, grew 41% in four years between 2000 and 2004, making it the fastest-growing county in America.[52] The infrastructure needed for this kind of growth—roads, electricity, sewer, water, schools, police and fire departments, and so on—cannot keep up with growth this fast. And it takes money—resulting in spiraling property taxes, special fees, and assessments. The commute traffic—what many were hoping to escape from—compounds the problem.

So, will exurbia become a retirement mecca? Only time will tell. One vision is that we will build homes and communities that will help facilitate our connection to one another. There could be local business incubator spaces, new forms of political meet-ups, and a renaissance in clubs of all kinds. SeniorNet-type community centers would be part of every town. There would be ways to engage online and in real life. There would be a new call to action for volunteerism and lots of other ways to engage. And, of course, we would go back to designs with a front porch with that same sense of warmth and love that existed across from Fonticello Park.

Endnotes

1. David Schreiner, "Love those Boomers," *BusinessWeek*, October 17, 2005.
2. "What Builders Should Know about Boomers," *Nations Building News Online*, 2004, http://www.nbnnews.com/NBN/issues/2004-11-29/Seniors+Housing/index.html.
3. International Council on Active Aging, *2006 Media Planner*, August 1, 2005, http://www.icaa.cc/Marketingopportunities/2006mediakit.pdf (accessed April 12, 2006).
4. AARP, *Fixing to Stay: A National Survey on Housing and Home Modification Issues* (May 2000).
5. David Hehman, interview by Julie Penfold, August 10, 2005.
6. Broderick Perkins, "Record Second Home Sales Protect Housing Market," *RealtyTimes*, April 6, 2006.
7. *Ibid.*
8. Kenneth R. Harney, "Baby Boomers Planning Big Splashes in Next 60 Months," *RealtyTimes*, January 23, 2006, http://realtytimes.com/rtcpages/20060123_boomers.htm.
9. Broderick Perkins, "Record Second Home Sales Protect Housing Market," *RealtyTimes*, April 6, 2006.

10. *Ibid.*

11. Population Resource Center, "Executive Summary: The Changing American Family," 2001, http://www.prcdc.org/summaries/family/family.html.

12. Mature Market Institute, *Demographic Profile: American Baby Boomers* (2005), http://www.metlife.com/WPSAssets/22807472301113318349V1FBoomer%20Pr ofile%202005.pdf.

13. Karen S. Peterson, "Many Boomers May Face Old Age Alone," *USA Today,* December 12, 2000, http://www.globalaging.org/elderrights/us/12dec2000-1.htm.

14. Mature Market Institute, *Demographic Profile: American Baby Boomers* (2005), http://www.metlife.com/WPSAssets/22807472301113318349V1FBoomer%20Pr ofile%202005.pdf.

15. Sarah Mahoney, "The Secret Lives of Single Women," *AARP Magazine,* May/June 2006, http://www.aarpmagazine.org/lifestyle/single_women.html.

16. Blanche Evans, "Oldest Boomers Turn Sixty," *RealtyTimes,* January 16, 2006, http://realtytimes.com/rtapages/20060116_boomers.htm.

17. Population Resource Center, "Executive Summary: The Changing American Family," 2001, http://www.prcdc.org/summaries/family/family.html.

18. "The New Women's Market," *Growth Strategies,* February 2005, http://www. findarticles.com/p/articles/mi_qa3908/is_200502/ai_n9521514.

19. Steve McLinden, "Women Become a Force in Home Buying," Bankrate.com, July 1, 2003, http://www.bankrate.com/brm/news/real-estate/women-buyers1.asp.

20. Laura Hnatow, "Sisters Are Doin' It for Themselves," *Imago Creative,* February 7, 2005, http://www.imagocreative.com/about/imago_news.php?NewsID=000023.

21. Tom Kelly, "Boomers take center stage in housing picture," *The Sacramento Bee,* February 4, 2006, M2.

22. National Association of the Remodeling Industry, "Start Planning for that Summer Remodel: May Is National Home Improvement Month." http://www.nari.org/ level2/pressroom/index.cfm?fuseaction5viewarticle& rowid=13500000000000032.

23. Nardelli, Robert. Lecture, Terry College of Business, August 15, 2005.

24. National Association of Home Builders, http://www.nahb.org.

25. Allison Arieff, interview by Julie Penfold, 2005.

26. Jozi Meskan, interview by author, August 2005.

27. Gina Pais, interview by author, October 11, 2005.

28. AARP, *Fixing to Stay: A National Survey on Housing and Home Modification Issues* (May 2000).

29. Andrea Coombes, "Relative Proximity: As Boomers' Parents Age, 'In-law' Living Options Grow," *MarketWatch, Inc.,* October 7, 2004.

30. Susan Fornoff, "Whither Boomers," *San Francisco Chronicle,* September 18, 2004.

31. Joszi Meskan, interview by author, August 2005.

32. Michael J. McDermott, "There's No Place Like Home for Starting Your Own Business," Busop1.com, http://www.busop1.com/homebus.html.

33. Paul Edwards and Sarah Edwards, "Home-Based Business 101," HomeOffice Mag.com, February 2002, http://www.entrepreneur.com/mag/article/0,1539, 296891,00.html.

34. Michael J. Martinez, "Taking Ownership: Boomers Are Leading the New Wave of Entrepreneurship," *Cincinnati Post,* May 4, 2004.

35. Tiffany Mock, interview by author, August 2005.

36. Michael Sarfatti, interview by author, 2005. Michael paraphrased Joseph F. Coughlin's "Technology Needs of Aging Boomers," *Issues in Science and Technology Online,* Fall 1999, http://bob.nap.edu/issues/16.1/coughlin.htm.

37. William H. Frey, *Boomers and Seniors in the Suburbs: Aging Patterns in Census 2000* (The Brookings Institution, Center on Urban and Metropolitan Policy, January 2003), http://www.brookings.org/es/urban/publications/freyboomers.pdf.

38. Del Webb, "Baby Boomer Report: Annual Opinion Survey," 2003, http://www.pulte.com/PressRoom/BabyBoomer2003Summary.pdf.

39. Susan Fornoff, "Whither Boomers," San Francisco Chronicle, September 18, 2004, www.sfgate.com/cgi-bin/article.cgi?f=/c/a/2004/09/18/HOG198P1871.DTL.

40. Brad Edmonson, "Where Are the Boomers?" Lecture, What's Next I, San Francisco, CA, April 13, 2004.

41. U.S. Census Bureau, *Census 2000.*

42. Al Heavens, "Active-Adult Boomers Still Favor Suburbs," *RealtyTimes,* October 14, 2004, http://realtytimes.com/rtcpages/20041014_boomers.htm.

43. Tom Boyer, "Hot Market for High-End Condos Fuels Downtown Building Boom," *Seattle Times,* June 6, 2005, http://www.vulcanrealestate.com/content/Docs/SeattleTimes060905_BuildingBoom.htm; Henry Springs, "Seattle's Luxury Condo Market," *International Real Estate Digest,* June 2005, http://www.ired.com/news/ springs/seattleluxcondo.htm.

44. Michelle Hofmann, "Finding Success in the Condo Craze," *Realtor Magazine Online,* February 1, 2006, http://www.realtor.org/rmnomag.NSF/pages/Feat22006 02?OpenDocument.

45. *Ibid.*

46. Angelica Pence, "Back to the Bright Lights," *San Francisco Chronicle,* Sept. 18, 2004.

47. Robert Steuteville, "The New Urbanism: An Alternative to Modern, Automobile-Oriented Planning and Development," *New Urban News,* July 8, 2004, http://www.newurbannews.com/AboutNewUrbanism.html.

48. Ibid.

49. Amy Cortese, "America's 50 Million Cultural Creatives Impact the Marketplace," *New York Times,* July 20, 2003, http://www.organicconsumers.org/organic/cultural_creatives.cfm.

50. Steve Kemme, "Suburban Sprawl Spawns Concern." *Cincinnati Enquirer,* July 9, 2003, http://www.enquirer.com/editions/2003/07/09/loc_sprawlhealth09.html.

51. Haya El Nasser and Paul Overberg, "Metro Area 'Fringes' Are Booming," *USA Today,* March 15, 2006, http://www.usatoday.com/news/nation/census/2006-03-15-census-growth_x.htm.

52. Mark Morrison, "Living too Large in Exurbia," *BusinessWeek Online,* October 17, 2005, http://www.businessweek.com/magazine/content/05_42/b3955060.htm.

8

A FAMILY OF OUR OWN CHOOSING

Introduction

You know who your real friends are as you age because their pictures end up on your refrigerator. For a person in midlife or older, friends *are* family. As people age, they seek the company of people they care about, focusing their attention on those with whom they have honest and reciprocal relationships. After you lose your parents to illness and your kids to college, your family is the person you walk your dogs with. They are the people programmed into your cell phone.

I call this phenomenon "the family of our own choosing." Having a closely held circle of friends is of major importance to boomers who aren't always geographically—or psychologically—close to their kin. The global economy has spread families around the world, so people who outlive their partners and parents often find themselves without nearby blood relations. Yet we all still want to love and to be loved by people who are trusted friends.

The family of our own choosing is also the community a person builds during his or her life transitions. As empty nesters and retirees plan for the next 30 years, they are often surprised by how lonely their new lives are; after the desk is cleared out at work and the kids have left home, many of the institutions a person has counted on for companionship are shut down. Marriages sometimes collapse because the structure of the family changes. Divorce can send two people reeling into the unknown, and many valued friendships that were bound up with the marriage vanish. Anne Morrow Lindbergh, in her book *Gift from the Sea*, talks about this stage of life as "an abandoned shell," using the metaphor of a series of shells to represent the shifting shapes of relationships in marriage. Originally written in 1955 as a groundbreaking, best-selling work, *Gift from the Sea* was recently re-released in a 50th anniversary edition to help the boomers navigate between the "oyster bed" and the "abandoned shell" phases and find peace and solace in the outcome. Anne Morrow Lindbergh's meditations on love and marriage and aging provide inspiration for boomer women.

One of the biggest losses boomers face is that of their parents. Most boomers have two parents at age 40, but many only have one parent by age 50. Family dynamics change, often with an adult daughter assuming a caregiver role for her remaining parent. The adult child faces two profound changes: one is the loss of a treasured parent and the second is the new responsibility in caring for the other. For many, this means the president of the fan club is gone, along with irreplaceable connections to youth and a buffer against life's harder lessons. I lost my father to a heart attack when he was on his way to play golf with my two sons. Later that afternoon my mother had a sympathy heart attack. Luckily she survived and we've had the joy of having her around for the past seven years, but my life has never been the same.

People in midlife really need the comfort that friendships provide. So they ask themselves, "How can I build a new set of friends? With whom do I want to play? Work? Travel? Grow older? Who will help me navigate life's changes and celebrate the holidays? Where is my new community?" The answers are triggers for business opportunity.

Researchers at the University of Michigan have found that the most powerful predictor of life satisfaction after retirement is the size of a person's social support network. Those who were more satisfied with life had networks of at least 16 people. Those who were less satisfied had fewer than 10 in their circle of friends.[1] Friendship also supports health: a recent UCLA study revealed that women who had the most friends over a nine-year period cut their risk of death by more than 60%.[2] A Japanese study found that adults over 65 who have strong relationships with family or friends experience better self-esteem, less depression, a positive estimation of personal health, and better life satisfaction.[3] Clearly, boomers should be paying as much attention to their social lives as they do to their financial portfolios.

The need for connection is especially acute for men. Women have always linked up with other women for support. They make friends while standing in line at the supermarket or for the ladies' room at the symphony. But many men who retire or whose kids move out find themselves not knowing how to make human connections in the absence of structure. With social organizations like the Elks Club on the wane, there is a great need to create communities that can give people at midlife a sense of connection and worthiness, particularly if these people are men.

Fortunately for aging boomers, the Internet has changed the way friendships and family work. We no longer live in a world where human connection depends solely on geography. Electronic greeting cards are one of the most popular online applications today, along with email and photos. This is especially true for older people. When I was running SeniorNet, I met a gentleman who hosted a popular online chat room he called the "talking after midnight room." Joining this chat room meant you didn't have to put your head down next to a vacant pillow at midnight. This virtual room was as soothing and comfortable as a cup of hot tea. It became a popular place.

This is what family means now. Businesses that understand the need to combat loneliness in aging will win. The companies profiled in this chapter show us the depth of the baby boom generation's desire to connect and reconnect with family and friends.

Market Analysis

In the year 2000, for the first time, fewer than 25% of U.S. households were made up of a husband, a wife, and their children. The nuclear family's share of all U.S. households has declined from 40% in 1970, according to the Census Bureau.[4] Meanwhile, the percentage of all unmarried partner households increased from less than 1% in 1970 to 3.7% in 2000, when there were 5.5 million unmarried partner households. In 2000, 41% of unmarried partner households had children.[5] In 2002, single parents accounted for 28% of family households with children under 18 and about 5.6 million children were living with one or both of their grandparents.[6]

The bottom line is that most Americans have been, are, or will be in a stepfamily household at some point during their lives. In 2000, more than 600,000 gay and lesbian families declared themselves to the Census Bureau. Thirty-three percent of these lesbian households and 20% of gay male households had children.[7] There are also more than 4.5 million married and unmarried couples in the United States who are mixed racially or ethnically.[8] And this redefinition of family is not just happening in the United States. In Australia, for example, the traditional nuclear family will make up barely 28% of all households by 2011.[9]

Entrepreneurs should pay attention to three factors that will dictate how and where boomers build their communities: loneliness, empty nesting, and grandparenting. Friendship can be a business. Families are the axis on which the world turns, and people will spend freely to create and nurture their families. Following are the major trends that underpin the most successful businesses in the family space.

Loneliness

One of the most difficult issues facing our society is the marginalization of older adults, and the isolation of family caregivers. Mother Teresa understood that loneliness is today's true cultural illness. She returned to her work in India because she came to believe that poverty was an easier problem to solve than loneliness.

Many gerontologists are predicting that the baby boom generation is headed for a crisis of loneliness. Boomers have the highest divorce rate of any generation in history: Not only do they divorce more often, they also divorce earlier. The most dramatic growth in single-person households over then next decade will occur among those between ages 45 and 64 as baby boomers move into middle age. The number of these households is expected to increase by 42%.[10]

One of the greatest services a business can provide is to find solutions to the loneliness of older people. The desire to connect, meet new friends, and find intimacy and care was illustrated by the large number of people who visited articles on these subjects at ThirdAge.com. It was also a leading reason that people joined SeniorNet and attended its national gatherings. These encounters have been the inspirational force behind my efforts to provide community-based solutions that provide social engagement and connection through technology. As an increasing number of older people live alone, there will be great needs for entrepreneurs to provide everything from winter transportation services to compelling interactive websites.

What are the kinds of social structures that can be put in place to combat loneliness? SeniorNet is one example of a structure. Another is Elderhostel and its new boomer brand Road Scholar. Look around you, listen to the elders, and see what good products and services you can create that will make a real difference.

Empty Nests

The wife of a leading business executive shared this story of her husband's coming to terms with his own midlife transitions. During a cross-country trip back home after a meeting, her husband called her and said, "Honey, I want to spend more time with the kids." She said, "Bob, they're gone."

However, the empty nest isn't all sniffles and regrets. It is also new beginnings. A recent television ad shows a father packing up a Jeep Cherokee with his son's belongings. His son asks, "Where's mom?"

thinking she must be upstairs crying. Instead, she is taking measurements for the new home office. This is why Home Depot has forged a deal with AARP to hire older workers:[11] it wants to be the first place boomers go to make a new start after the kids leave home.

Most baby boomer parents will go through the empty nest transition in this decade.[12] By 2009, there will be 181 million empty nesters in Europe and the United States, according to *American Demographics*. In 2004, empty nesters in the United States and Europe spent $698 billion on food, drinks, and personal care, and these expenditures are expected to grow by 2.5% a year over the next five years.[13]

Although an empty nest can bring out troubles in a marriage, a 2004 survey revealed that boomers are embracing the idea of empty nesting.[14] Most of them look forward to getting back to their own lives—doing the home repairs, travel, and leisurely breakfasts that were put aside during the years of soccer games and sleepovers.

Grandparenting

Grandchildren, someone once said, are "the dessert of life." And the baby boom generation is redefining grandparenthood by adding an active, adventurous style.

Three-quarters of Americans over the age of 65 have grandchildren, and most become grandparents between the ages of 49 and 53.[15] And as the populations of other affluent countries grow older, grandparenting is becoming more common there as well. According to *The Times*, more than one in five people in Britain were grandparents in 2005.[16]

In our interviews with baby boomers, Mary Furlong & Associates has consistently heard that they are choosing retirement housing locations near amenities that will encourage children and grandchildren to visit often. Grandparent travel is becoming a large opportunity in the travel industry. These are early signs of major market change.

Grandparents spend an average of 35 years in their relationships with grandchildren; compare this with an average of 22 years people spend as a parent with children living at home, 14 years as an adult with no children, and 15 years as a child.[17]

Grandparents spend more than $30 billion each year on their grandchildren, including an estimated 17%[18] of the $21 billion per year spent on toys in the United States.[19] Adults age 55 to 64 spend more per capita on toys than do adults age 25 to 44.[20] Retailers say boomers are transferring their own purchasing habits, which reflect a focus on health, education, and trendiness, onto what they buy their grandchildren.

Wachovia has targeted its 529 college savings account specifically to grandparents.[21] Expect to see purchases in financial services, tutoring, college education, fashion and clothes, books, games, and travel in the grandparent marketplace.

Elephant Entrepreneur: Myfamily.com

Tools that connect family are more important today because families don't all live in the same neighborhood anymore. When families look for ways to stay connected in meaningful and fun ways, storytelling is one of the keys. Two decades of research has found that when people share stories of their deepest life experiences, they gain a better sense of well-being, greater feelings of community, and an important awareness of their contributions to others. Reminiscing can actually lower one's heart rate and increase a sense of overall physical well-being, according to psychologists Howard Thorsheim and Bruce Roberts.[22]

David Moon is chairman and CEO of MyFamily.com, one of the five leading online subscription-based businesses and the market leader for family history research. Before coming to MyFamily.com, he was a computer software developer and chief technology officer for WordPerfect. Since then, his focus has been on helping to build technology companies that are oriented around software. MyFamily.com was attractive, says

David, because the company had an underdeveloped core business of selling subscriptions to people researching their family ancestors.

MyFamily.com identified a growing appetite for genealogical information and it provides a way for people to access this information easily. Using MyFamily.com, a person can answer a question like "Where did my great grandfather live, and when did he die?" without leaving home. Users can search billions of digitized family history records from a home computer, including census forms; birth, marriage, and death certificates; military and immigration forms; and even historical newspapers.

MyFamily.com evolved out of Ancestry.com, which will soon celebrate its 20th year in business. In its first few years, the company published genealogy-related magazines and books. Then it moved into CDs containing family history content records. Under David's guidance, MyFamily.com has zoomed to $140 million in sales, growing from 100,000 paid subscriptions in 2002 to 1.5 million today. Subscriptions cost $7.95 for the first month, then $239 per year. The company's network of websites includes MyFamily.com, Ancestry.com, Genealogy.com, and RootsWeb.com.

The vision behind the current company came from founder Paul Allen, who purchased Ancestry.com with a group of investors and began making genealogy records searchable online. The Internet brought huge value into this business equation. Genealogy is the category with the highest percentage of Internet users over 65. MyFamily.com is heavily oriented to older visitors, with the "sweet spot" around ages 45 to 65. Six in ten customers are women. David says that MyFamily.com grows in value over time because it combines content and community. "The idea of being able to connect people who share common resources or relatives is a powerful part of our business. So it's not just content that makes for a valuable subscription business, it's how content and community feed off each other."

Cell phones are already a central device for family communication; David sees their applications expanding as they become capable of linking to the Web and recording or storing videos. He also sees a wide-open market for digital photography as a way of passing on family history. Customers also use MyFamily.com as the site to share photos, coordinate calendars, and communicate with other family members.

MyFamily.com also has a direct marketing division that helps people create self-published family history books. "Because of the high touch component, people can convey their emotions," says David. "Most of our customers are women, so they respond well to a social experience, such as Pampered Chef or Tupperware, in marketing."

David says that baby boomers will buy genealogy products because they have disposable income and spare time, which means they are spending more time on hobbies and learning. Family.com speaks to the desire to connect with one's roots and return to a safe place. Says David, "When we remember where we have come from, and what our forbearers have done for us, it fills us with gratitude. When we are feeling gratitude, we are more likely to do good things. Part of the vision of this company is helping improve society by helping people remember their legacy."[23]

Emerging Entrepreneur: Telling Stories

Seth Socolow finished business school and moved to San Francisco in the late 1990s. He had already had a career in consumer software, so he renewed his Silicon Valley contacts when he decided to start a new company. Seth is only in his 30s, but his vision is clear. With a brilliant idea, the tenacity to go after funding, and clear marketing and PR, he has built Telling Stories into an emerging enterprise.

Seth sells software and websites that make it easier for people to tell their stories. His business is anchored in the major themes of midlife: making family connections, leaving a sustainable legacy, mentoring, and creating life-affirming experiences.

A few years ago Seth was looking at a thumb drive, which is a thumb-sized storage device that plugs into a computer's USB port.

He decided to make it into a time capsule for important memories. How would the average person do that? Thus, Telling Stories was hatched as a software program to help people create a record of their major life events. The customer base is mostly age 45 and older, and mostly women.

Seth based his company on what his customers want. So for boomers, there is a list of music—hits from every year through 1955. The music plugs into the stories in interesting ways. For example, when Seth put the story of his mother's life together for her new granddaughter—the only girl she'd ever had, after raising nothing but sons—one of the songs he used was Maurice Chevalier's "Thank Heaven for Little Girls."

Telling Stories software was distributed through Fry's and CompUSA, but the product is now offered as a limited free trial from the company's website at www.tellingstories.com. Seth uses a lot of PR to drive people to his website to download the product; he hired a freelance agent to get him written up in the *Wall Street Journal* and *USA Today*, and to get a spot on CNBC's *Power Lunch*. That attracted the attention of a software publisher. Then it was time to seek funding.

"Venture capitalists have a very clear idea of what they want," says Seth. "They're looking to invest $5 million in a company and get $50 million back in three to five years. We didn't feel we were ready for them. Our strategy has always been to build this up to a level where we can be acquired, which is much lower than $50 million."

So Seth went to the Silicon Valley Association of Software Entrepreneurs (SVASE), an association of start-up entrepreneurs, and also talked with the Band of Angels, who taught him how to value the deal and how to price it. Then he hooked up with the Keiretsu Forum, a global organization of investors who screen business plans. If you make it through various stages, Keiretsu invites you to present for 15 minutes in front of several investors. Seth's first pitch received interest from 30 investors out of 150 in the audience.

Keiretsu was a lesson in the number of people in the room and the average size check they write. "In these professional angel organizations, generally you're looking at people writing checks from between $25,000 and $100,000. If you take an average of $50,000, you have to figure out, how many of those people in the room do I need to write checks for $50,000? That was how we needed to think in order to get the deal done."

What advice does Seth offer aspiring entrepreneurs? "Persistence. It's an incredible struggle and nothing happens overnight." He also advises finding out what kind of support investors can lend an entrepreneur. How actively involved will they be? Will they be micromanaging? Can they make important introductions? Networking with other entrepreneurs is also critical because the journey can be lonely at times.

Seth says that the real business opportunity is to move his technology into a cell phone-based service, so that people can use their phones to watch their grandchildren in a school play or a baseball game. "The Web is one of the greatest connection tools we've ever had. We want to leverage that power to help people share their stories and collaborate on the writing of their stories.

"Anyone who has lost someone and has been left behind with boxes of photographs in the attic knows the need I'm addressing," he says. "You can never ask that question afterward: 'Where did you buy that dress? Where was that picture taken? Why was it taken? Who else is in the photograph?' Telling Stories gives people a chance to answer those questions, organize that information, and have something really cohesive that will live beyond the individual."[24]

Connecting Through Media

Mike Perlis has been a publishing executive with Playboy, Rodale, and Ziff Davis. He is now a venture capitalist and an insightful leader on the needs of male baby boomers. In preparation for his speech on what men want at midlife at the What's Next? conference in 2004, Mike put together a focus group in the basement of his house in

Connecticut. It took a few beers to get his friends to reveal what was on their minds, but eventually the men in Mike's group opened up. And now he has a wealth of information on how boomer men think about health, safety, family, financial security, companionship-love-sex, time and the lack of it, peace, spirituality, and community.

Mike says that one of the main things that distinguishes boomer men from their fathers is that family is now front and center. "I was in the delivery room when my children were born," he says. "I delivered my kids to college. I delivered the family on vacations, and when my parents die, I'll be right there too."[25] Belonging, whether it is to a health club, a charitable organization, an alumni group, or even a weekly pickup basketball game, is meaningful. Mike talked about the spiritual journey of the second half of life, as reflected by the men in his group. There has not been a media property developed (to date) that speaks to these issues of men at midlife. But there has been a media success at serving women at midlife—*MORE* magazine.

Myrna Blyth created *MORE* in 1996 and had a rare success in the women's magazine market by targeting women over 40. She knew that family relationships and connections would be big issues for midlife women, and she wanted to create a magazine that would capture this sensibility. She also knew it was important that women wanted to look better, not younger, and that they wanted to feel good about the lifestage they were in. She peppered the magazine with real stories about the issues that women face and photos of models who were over 40. Advertisers followed her to reach customers who spend a lot on skincare, beauty, and pharmaceutical products.

There is still a need for media products for men and women at midlife, but several other projects are in the works. WomenSage, for example, is a popular website established by Jane Haas, an award-winning journalist based in Southern California. After receiving 3,500 responses to a survey question she posted online a few years ago—"How is your life different from your mother's?"—she learned that boomer women want a sense of inclusiveness they've never felt they had.

"Our mothers had women's clubs and neighborhoods to give them a sense of community and purpose," Jane says. "When boomer women said they were not going to do that kind of thing, they threw the baby out with the bathwater. Now we're older and the children are gone, and suddenly we have this awareness that our lives are not as full as we want them to be. It is also a time when women can think about themselves in a positive way. Boomer women can ask, 'What do I want to do with the rest of my life?' instead of, 'What do I need to do to get through the day or keep the family happy at this point?'"

WomenSage meets in women's circles because personal contact is what Jane learned was most missing from women's lives. The circles meet online and in person to talk about what they want in life. Unlike their mothers, says Jane, boomer women "want to share what they're doing with other women and get support from that. And so they're jamming into these monthly meetings. They love to hear about relationships and transitions, but they have also filled up meetings on why diets don't work. The energy in the room is astonishing. We have about 200 women sitting at tables, talking about these things."

WomenSage has about 1,000 members worldwide, mostly between the ages of 50 and 70. According to Jane, the difference in how this generation builds community and friendships, Jane says, comes from having more education, which creates opportunities and choices. Some boomer women even want to do typical retirement things like golf, tennis, and horseback riding. At WomanSage, they can build friendships around that—or anything else.

"They also really want to get into community work," Jane says. "They volunteer at the library. They volunteer at the hospital. There's a new wave of energy out there that business can tap or the community can tap, but these women want something more challenging than what their mothers had."[26]

Scrapbooking

Making elaborate scrapbooks is the third most popular craft activity in the United States, according to the Hobby Industry Association. People spent $2.5 billion on scrapbooks and supplies in 2004, a 28% increase from 2002. Almost one in four households keep a scrapbook, with Western states showing the highest proportion of households involved.[27]

Baby boomers want to leave something of themselves behind for later generations, and scrapbooking is the perfect legacy-maker. The market was overlooked by national retailers until a few years ago, but it is now being embraced by discount, hobby, and craft stores nationwide. Big players are drug stores (film and cameras) and chains that do photo processing. There are about 2,500 independent scrapbooking stores, but many other retailers are eyeing business opportunities in this sector.[28]

In 2001, 33% of scrapbook enthusiasts purchased products online. The top themes for scrapbooks are family life, birthdays, holidays, vacations, business, babies, and friends. The most popular supplies include decorative sheets, tape and ribbons, stickers, cutters, and different types of scissors for cropping and displaying photos. The trend has also spurred consumers to buy photo printers and scrapbooking software.

Wal-Mart, Target, Michael's Stores, Inc., Rose Art, and Hobby Lobby are all cashing in on the trend. Creative Memories, a direct-selling organization that has 60,000 consultants worldwide who advise their customers on how keep their photos safe, helped push the movement. The organization, started in 1987, sponsors events and seminars across the country and sells its own exclusive line of products, which includes bleed- and fade-resistant pens, through consultants.

End-of-Life Issues

Boomers broke the mold when they stayed wide awake and present at the birth of their children. They will also be there when it is time for the intimate journey of helping loved ones through the final phases of life. And the best-known model for building community around illness and death is the hospice movement.

In medieval times, a *hospice* was a way station for weary pilgrims. Today it is a network of services and residences that provide supportive, quality care for those at the end of life. A hospice is often the only family that a terminally ill person has. More often, hospice team members become family because they can talk openly about death and grief.

Hospice is a Medicare benefit that involves a team of physicians, nurses, aides, volunteers, social workers, and clergy. The team creates and monitors a treatment plan, including emotional and spiritual support along with medical and palliative care. Hospice workers also answer questions about such things as insurance, funeral plans, and death certificates. Services can be delivered at home or in an institution, but they always involve building community and helping people through their fears.

The hospice industry has grown steadily since its inception in the 1970s in England. There were about 3,300 hospice programs in the United States in 2003,[29] with large numbers also in the United Kingdom, Australia, New Zealand, and Japan. China also has entered the field.

No one wishes to add end-of-life care to their personal agenda, but the day will inevitably come for most boomers—and there are plenty of opportunities for those who can provide practical, caring solutions. The right model for a boomer-based business around end-of-life issues might be a trusted adviser who comes to a person's home to explain the range of issues he or she will face in the last stages of life—advance directives, power of attorney, living will, trusts, and transfer of assets. Maybe boomers could host gatherings and invite their friends, along with people who can help us make smart decisions and feel well cared for.

As more boomers face the reality of death, the industry will undergo huge changes. Although most hospice care is in the home, many services are also given in institutions and residential care settings. There is room for hospice to follow the lead of the Eden Alternative and others who are interested in changing institutional culture so that an elder's last months are more homelike and family-oriented.

Voices of Civil Rights

The family of our own choosing can also be our national family. Rick Bowers, a pioneer in media for older adults who is now director of digital media for AARP Publications, is rising to this opportunity with a program called Voices of Civil Rights, which includes collecting oral history interviews of people who were involved in the Civil Rights movement. AARP CEO Bill Novelli is an enthusiastic champion of the idea because AARP wants to grow its membership from 36 million to 50 million, and one of their membership goals is more racial and ethnic diversity.

Rick launched the first Hispanic newsletter for AARP members. His vision for Voices of Civil Rights is to create a multimedia initiative designed to save important—and vanishing—pieces of Civil Rights history. The initiative began with clear goals and objectives, moved through distinct phases, and culminated with the installation of materials in the Library of Congress on February 24, 2005. The collection continues to expand, and it is already the world's largest archive of firsthand accounts of the Civil Rights movement, with thousands of personal remembrances from men and women who took part in the struggle for equality.

The Voices of Civil Rights website contains a searchable database of hundreds of interviews in text, audio, and video formats, plus a news section to keep visitors updated on the project. The third component of the project is a book filled with powerful Civil Rights stories published under a new partnership between AARP and Sterling, a subsidiary of Barnes and Noble.

AARP has also formed a partnership with the Leadership Conference on Civil Rights, which represents 180 civil rights groups. Rick also arranged for a bus tour to go to cities throughout the South. People went on the bus and saw some of the exhibits, which inspired their writing. Reporters throughout the South covered the story. Today, awards for the project hang in Bill's office.

Summary

Whose picture will be on your refrigerator door? Where will you celebrate the holidays? Who will be the members of the "family of your own choosing"? What business ideas will be there to support you and your friends? What technologies, products, and services should be invented to help you stay more connected to those you love?

As you address these questions, keep in mind that family and friends are crucial to our sense of happiness and joy. For example, women have always linked up with other women for support. We make intimate friends while standing in line at the supermarket or in the ladies' room at the symphony. But for many men of our generation, when they retire or the kids move out, they are at a loss for how to connect in the absence of structure. Same-sex organizations overall are on the wane, so there is a great need to create the kinds of communities at midlife that can give us this sense of connection and worthiness.

Endnotes

1. Diane Swanbrow, "To Retire Well, Invest in Making Friends," *The University Record*, September 16, 1998, http://www.umich.edu/~urecord/9899/Sep16_98/friend.htm.

2. Gale Berkowitz, "UCLA Study on Friendship Among Women: An Alternative to Fight or Flight," 2002, http://www.anapsid.org/cnd/gender/tendfend.html.

3. "Patterns of Social Relationships and Psychological Well-being among the Elderly," *International Journal of Behavioral Development* 21, no. 3 (September 1, 1997): 417-30.

4. U.S. Census Bureau, "Living Together, Living Alone: Families and Living Arrangements, 2000," in *Population Profile of the United States: 2000 (Internet Release)*, 5-2, http://www.census.gov/population/pop-profile/2000/chap05.pdf.

5. Laurie Schwede, *Complex Households and Relationships in the Decennial Census and in Ethnographic Studies of Six Race/Ethnic Groups* (U.S. Census Bureau, 2003), 5, http://www.census.gov/pred/www/rpts/Complex%20House holds%20 Final%20Report.pdf.

6. Jason Fields, *Children's Living Arrangements and Characteristics: March 2002*, (U.S. Census Bureau, 2003), 5-6, http://www.census.gov/prod/2003pubs/p20-547.pdf.

7. Tavia Simmons and Martin O'Connell, *Married Couple and Unmarried-Partner Households: 2000* (U.S. Census Bureau, 2003), 2, 10, http://www.census.gov/prod/2003pubs/censr-5.pdf.

8. Women's Educational Media, "That's a Family! Statistics on U.S. Families," http://www.womedia.org/taf_statistics.htm.

9. Bernard Salt, "Nuclear Family Gets Nuked by the Gen-Xers," *The Australian*, September 15, 2005, 26.

10. Kerby Anderson, "Loneliness," http://www.leaderu.com/orgs/probe/docs/lonely.html.

11. AARP, "Home Depot and AARP Launch National Hiring Partnership," February 6, 2004, http://www.aarp.org/research/press-center/presscurrentnews/a2004-02-06-homedepot.html.

12. Joan Raymond, "The Joy of Empty Nesting," *American Demographics*, May 2000.

13. Datamonitor, *Empty Nesters 2005*(2005).

14. "Baby Boomers Reclaim Independence in the Empty Nest but Many Expect Parents to Move In or Kids to Come Back," SeniorJournal.com, June 29, 2004, http://www.seniorjournal.com/NEWS/Housing/4-06-29Survey.htm.

15. Sharon L. Mader, "Benefits of Grandparenting," Ohio State University Extension Factsheet, http://ohioline.osu.edu/hyg-fact/5000/5313.html.

16. Alexandra Frean, "Grandparents Awake to New Spirit of Adventure," *The Times*, July 28, 2005, Home News Section, 27.

17. Sarah Womack, "Average Age of the First-time Grandparent Is Now Under 50," *The Daily Telegraph*, July 28, 2005, 008.

18. Tina Dhamija, "Grandparents Offer an Expanding Market Niche," *TD Monthly*, August 2003, http://www.toydirectory.com/monthly/Aug2003/Special_Grandparents.asp.

19. NPD Funworld, "The NPD Group Reports on 2005 Toy Industry Sales," February 13, 2006, http://www.npd.com/dynamic/releases/press_060213.html.

20. Cheryl Russell, "The Ungraying of America; Older Americans Are the Biggest Spenders, and Their Importance to the Consumer Marketplace Is Growing," *American Demographics*, July 1997, 12.

21. Sue Stock, "Retailers Target Grandparent Buyers," *Raleigh News and Observer*, July 8, 2005.

22. David Demko, "Family Storytelling Boosts Health," http://www.demko.com/cs000 311.htm.

23. David Moon, interview by author, September 21, 2005.

24. Seth Socolow, interview by author, August 30, 2005.

25. Mike Perlis, interview by author, July 8, 2005.

26. Jane Glenn Haas, interview by Beth Witrogen McLeod, July 23, 2005.

27. Scrapbook Industry Trends, "Results from the 2004 'Scrapbooking in America' (SIA) Survey," http://www.scrapbookartistry.biz/Scrapbooking%20Industry%20Stats.htm.

28. Barbara White-Sax, "Baby Boomer Fad Has Drug Eyeing Burgeoning Scrapbook Business," *Drug Store News*, October 20, 2003.

29. National Hospice and Palliative Care Organization, "NHPCO's 2004 Facts and Figures," http://www.nhpco.org/files/public/Facts_Figures_for2004data.pdf.

9

ELDERCARE: THE NEW MIDLIFE CRISIS

Introduction

When a child is born, you have nine months to prepare. When a parent has a health care crisis, the changes in your life can be almost as great, but the news can come without any warning. Greater longevity is a great blessing, but it also means that an increasing number of elderly Americans are living with serious conditions that range from diabetes to Alzheimer's disease. As they pass through midlife, boomers will be called upon in massive numbers to care for their loved ones.

Eldercare is one of the biggest issues facing boomers today. MetLife's Mature Market Institute predicts that 40% of people over age 65 will require long-term care at some point in their lives.[1] This kind of care most often falls to families, who must scramble to muster the resources for a job that can last years. In fact, many adult children will take care of their parents for as long as they took care of their own children.

Eldercare is the new midlife crisis. Innovative products and services will be needed as we move into the longevity economy. The opportunities range widely, from housing and reverse mortgages to travel, assistive devices, durable medical supplies, in-home care, self-care, caregiver training, estate planning, end-of-life care, relocation help, gift packages, and drugs.

People who provide eldercare are often frustrated and anxious. One reason for their discomfort is that the network of home- and community-based eldercare services is complex, and there is often no number they can call to arrange for everything. Families can enter the world of long-term care through medical, legal, financial, work, or housing issues, and most of them don't know enough about what they will need before they are engaged in it. There are dozens of questions. Should Mom move into her daughter's house, or should she go to an assisted living facility or a nursing home? Does she need a reverse mortgage or long-term care insurance? How long will someone need to provide care for her? How can you get her to share her fears and needs with you?[2] The answers to these questions are insights that inspire entrepreneurs.

Eldercare is one of the key business opportunities over the next several decades. Chip Baird of North Castle Partners sets the current size of the market at $71 billion, and he doesn't even include ancillary services like respite care.[3] This chapter outlines some of the opportunities and businesses now exploring them. It describes the strategies of successful players, from business-to-business health care services to consumer products. We'll see how entrepreneurs have created entirely new fields to address social issues, and we'll visit businesses that have carved new niches by relaunching an existing brand.

Market Analysis

More than 44 million people provide unpaid care to an adult in the United States.[4] Compare this with the more than 100 million Americans who have chronic health conditions. Multiply these numbers by global demographics, and you will see why Jay Greenberg says that the marketplace for eldercare products and services is almost unimaginable. One projection says that U.S. spending on home- and community-based long-term care will increase from $41 billion today to $193 billion in 2030. Total national expenditures for nursing home care could reach $330 billion—equal to today's entire Social Security budget. Medicaid's annual nursing home expenditures are projected to rise from $29 billion today to $134 billion by 2030, an increase of 360%.[5] An analysis by the American Institute of Certified Public Accountants (AICPA) identifies financial services for the elderly as a major area of growth, but only if the service is "reasonably priced, independent, and objective."[6] As executive vice president with the National Council on Aging (NCOA), Jay says that in order to succeed in this market, businesses are going to have to answer one key question: who will pay for long-term care?

Jay says there are five major sources of money for long-term care. First, some corporations offer eldercare benefits. Employees for the most part can't afford these services, he says, but executives can. Second, some people will pay cash for non-medicare-covered services. But again, you have to be fairly well-to-do to pay for nursing homes or assisted living out of pocket, as costs can run upwards of $50,000 per year. Third, some expenses are covered by home equity loans and reverse mortgages. Fourth, wise planners will have purchased long-term care insurance. But the biggest burden for payment, says Jay, will fall on federal and state assistance programs for the elderly. Tens of millions of elders will be turning to the government in coming decades for help with the cost of prescription drugs, health care, utilities, and food. "We've had a million screenings on NCOA's Benefits Checkup," he says. "Over 33% of them were eligible for at least one significant public program."

Jay calls for a more holistic approach to solving the challenges of eldercare. For example, smart companies will combine a number of products and services, such as technology and home care, rather than just focusing on one or the other. "Our cities are going to have to become friendly places to elderly people. That will have implications for transportation and other services, for the nature of housing, and on and on. Automakers will need to make passenger seats that pivot so that seniors can get in and out more easily. These changes are not going to come because of any political movement—it's going to be an economic imperative. There is real power in the numbers."[7]

The Demographics of Aging

As they age, boomers are learning how to juggle work and family in new ways. Twenty-one percent of U.S. households have at least one caregiver, according to a 2004 survey by AARP and the National Alliance for Caregiving.[8] A study in Canada showed that 30% of parents with children at home are also caring for an elderly person. Among this group, 80% also work outside the home.[9]

Aging is a global phenomenon. When the youngest baby boomer celebrates her 65th birthday in 2029, the United States will have twice as many people age 65 and older as it does now.[10] Over the next quarter century, the elderly population is projected to grow faster than any other segment of the population worldwide,[11] especially in Europe and other developed countries. By 2050, about one third of the elderly in the United States will be other than non-Hispanic white. Among some ethnic minorities, the 65-plus population will more than triple.[12]

While the population is aging, another demographic megatrend— declining fertility—means there will be fewer family caregivers to take care of older people. The bottom line is that a growing share of household budgets will be devoted to caring for aging loved ones.

The emotional issues surrounding eldercare are just as dramatic as the demographics. Providing care for a parent until the end of life can be an overwhelming experience. It can sidetrack a career or upset family dynamics. Loved ones prefer to age in place, but their caregivers may not know how to do that. Adult children want to give their best to their parents, but they also have to juggle their own family, work, and self-care needs.

Caring for an elderly person can increase stress for all concerned. Caregivers feel isolated and have less leisure time; they are more likely than the general population to suffer from depression, sleeplessness, and back pain.[13] Those who care for someone with dementia have the most difficult jobs, and a global surge in Alzheimer's disease is forecast in the years to come. Australia is anticipating that dementia will cost its health care system $6 billion per year over the next decade.[14] By easing the anxiety and frustration surrounding these lifestage issues, businesses can do well by doing good.

Emerging Entrepreneur: Lusora

More than 5 million U.S. baby boomers live more than an hour's drive away from the loved ones for whom they are caregivers,[15] so electronic home monitoring is becoming a huge business opportunity. And in the U.K., almost one third of older people have no relatives living within 5 miles, and many are dependent on their neighbors for daily social contact. This is in stark contrast to the Britain of 25 years ago, in which most people lived close to where they were born.[16] One solution, developed by a British group called Age Concern, is a telephone campaign called Someone to Talk To.

Richard Jones, fresh from a successful IPO for his last company in Europe, decided to take a deeper look into how technology can help older adults stay independent. So in 2003 he co-founded Lusora Limited, a privately held company headquartered in London that provides wireless security and surveillance services. Lusora's remote sensing technology, which helps families know their elders are safe at home, attracted major venture capital interest because its technology is leading edge, the data are undeniable, and it addresses a deep social issue: staying connected.

Richard's previous venture, Fortunecity.com, attracted more than one million older visitors per day from Britain, Spain, Germany, and Scandinavia. They chatted, met, dated, and married online. "Building senior communities across Europe and in the United States has given me a privileged perspective on what seniors are actually looking for," he says, "How they're approaching old age, how they cope with loneliness, and how they interact with governments and health organizations. I learned that the overwhelming majority of seniors want to stay in their own homes for as long as possible, even if they don't know they need help."

Richard is also a pioneer in the field of embedded visual security, and he holds several patents in security technology. What inspired him to address the need for sensor monitoring is seeing the lonely lives many caregivers lead. He envisioned inexpensive wireless sensors combined with web access, packaged and sold to boomers as a way to keep tabs on their parents. "It's a hugely powerful communication tool, especially when you turn it into a combination of community building and health monitoring," Richard says.

Lusora sensors can be controlled from the company's website. Its first product, called Lusora Intelligent Sensory Architecture (LISA), provides nonstop images and data describing where and how a person is getting about. The monitoring is configured according to a person's normal daily patterns, so observers can be alerted when something unusual occurs. For example, if Mom has always arisen at 6 a.m. but now is getting out of bed progressively later in the morning, the sensor will track this change in habit and the caregiver can follow up to find out why. The sensors can also detect when a refrigerator is opened and when the front door is locked. If Mom falls, the sensors will track the acceleration of the fall, pinpoint where it happened, and send an alarm.

Lusora understands both the demographics of aging and the psychology of caregiving. It allows frail elderly people to remain independent and retain a sense of purpose. It keeps seniors hooked into the community. And it relieves some anxiety for caregivers. The value proposition is compelling, and Lusora is seeking partnerships with financial services companies and other major players in eldercare.

Unlike traditional monitoring services, which require the use of a dedicated call center and expensive equipment, Lusora uses a VoIP gateway and home-based agents to minimize both the initial capital cost and the ongoing cost of communications. Lusora envisions uses other than homecare monitoring, including home security, nannies, delivery people, and surveillance.

The systems might be installed by local companies that specialize in alarm and security systems, or they could be sold directly to institutions such as hospitals, housing authorities, and senior-living programs.

Lusora plans to invest heavily in marketing and training programs. It expects to sell 18,000 box units the first year and more than 200,000 units per year by 2008. "The demand is real," Richard says. "This is the next wave of community."[17]

Emerging Entrepreneurs: TLContact and Moving Solutions

Eldercare is a major concern for many companies with aging workforces because many of their employees provide it. Entrepreneurs are developing products aimed at this niche. TLContact is a consumer-driven startup that was founded—as many of the best businesses are—when a smart person found a new way to cope with a personal crisis. Eric Langshur's son Matthew was diagnosed with a rare congenital heart defect five days after he was born, and he required three open heart surgeries over the next 18 months. The family lived in the hospital and created a website, called a CarePage, to help keep their friends and family abreast of what was going on.

Matthew recovered, and the family was impressed with how well the CarePage had allowed so many people to get involved. Eric saw an unmet need for patients and their families to stay connected with family and friends, so he created TLContact by pooling personal money with investor friends. Based in Chicago, TLContact offers CarePages, a free, private website service that enables people to share health news and photos and receive messages of encouragement and support. Founded in 2000, the company now offers customized CarePages to over 500 healthcare providers across the healthcare spectrum, including hospitals, cancer treatment centers, rehabilitation hospitals, hospices, and long-term care facilities.

Bryan Preston, vice president for long term care at TLContact,, explains, "For aging boomers who are faced with caring for an elder, CarePages provided by a long-term care facility offers a new way to find peace of mind. CarePages allows family members to exchange private messages with staff members at any time, from anywhere. This direct communication assures the spouse or adult child that they are up-to-date and involved in their loved one's care—even if they live across the country. The opportunity to include extended family through updates, photos, and community messages makes communication and family involvement more manageable." Nearly 50% of all Americans who reach age 65 will spend some time in a skilled nursing facility, according to an AARP study. Communication is one of the top priorities for families with a loved one in a nursing home, and the service is seeing great progress in the extended care market.[18]

After spending two decades on the corporate side of health care, Margit Novack decided she wanted "something different. I don't want on my tombstone, 'She kept surgical overhead at 45%.'"

At 46, Margit took a course on how to write a business plan and visited retirement communities to talk about their needs and operations. She also spoke with movers and to gerontologists. She found that moving an older person to a new residence is a daunting challenge, and that many people could use help. The stress of relocation, leaving a familiar neighborhood, making new friends, managing health conditions, and paying for the move create a lot of anxiety. So she founded Moving Solutions in 1996 to help solve this problem. Soon after, Margit saw enough other people doing what she had done to start a trade association, the National Association of Senior Move Managers (NASMM).

Serving metro in Philadelphia, in 2005 Moving Solutions expanded its services to include baby boomers. Margit says, "The working boomer is a perfect target population because, one, they have a lot of disposable income; and two, they are accustomed to buying services to make their life easier."

Margit's business addresses particularly difficult questions of eldercare, such as: How does a woman who has outlived both her children get help when she decides to move? How does a boomer daughter decrease her mother's apprehensions about moving while allowing her mother to remain in control? Where does a 65-year-old hoarder, who is afraid of being evicted from her condo due to clutter, get assistance?

In 2000, Margit developed a marketing and training program to help would-be entrepreneurs start similar businesses in their own territories, and during the next four years, helped 20 licensees in 14 states develop successful businesses. In 2005, Moving Solutions launched a new franchising model called Moving Solutions Franchise LLC. Today, Moving Solutions is a network of independently owned businesses encompassing seven locations in six states. Margit says that one reason for her success is that self-employment and franchising is popular with boomers: 40% of all people in business for themselves in the United States are older than 50, according to AARP. "Boomers have acquired resources and business skills over two decades," says Margit. "Through franchising, they can work for themselves without starting from scratch."

"I am clear on what my brand is and how to grow it," says Margit. "The people who own my franchises want to provide a wonderfully caring service to their client, and it's my job to get them this knowledge. I have to provide the kind of support they need so they can be what I want the brand to represent. You can't just say it; you have to be it."[19]

Corporate Programs

U.S. companies lead the world in work/family programs. Diane Piktialis, senior product manager at Ceridian, has been in the field of work/life services for more than 20 years. In the 1980s and 1990s, she helped guide Work/Family Directions (WFD) to the top of the field in eldercare.

WFD began as an information and referral company for childcare. Its first client, in 1983, was IBM. In 1987, when the company had annual revenues of about $2 million, IBM asked it to do a feasibility study on the need for eldercare services and also to develop an infrastructure of programs for employees caring for older relatives that would be similar to the programs offered for childcare. In 1988, WFD was the provider when IBM launched the world's first corporate eldercare program.

Minneapolis-based Ceridian, which bought WFD in 1998, now provides benefit packages, including eldercare, to 8,000 companies and 8 million employees. "What's on a caregiver's mind is not solutions, but questions," says Diane. "What's going to happen as Mom's dementia increases? Will the building throw her out? How will we afford $40,000 a year for the nursing home and still put the kids through college?' There is no one-size-fits-all solution to questions like these. The more we learn about caregiving, the more we evolve different kinds of solutions because people don't need the same things."

Diane targets what Ceridian calls "the inner customer," paying attention to the emotional struggles that are not always apparent in caregiver-employees: anxiety, embarrassment, pressure, guilt, and financial issues. In response, Ceridian offers work-life and employee assistance services to help employees manage these personal demands that impact work performance. "In the next five to ten years," Diane predicts, "eldercare is going to become a very mainstream issue. People will be buying a lot of products and services."[20]

Forecasting and market research is something that IBM does well. The need for both childcare and eldercare products and services emerged in its first survey on work/life sent out to employees in 1986. Ted Childs, who now oversees workforce diversity at IBM, says that market research also showed that a lot of employees were struggling with long distance care for parents. That was a signal to create corporate programs and policies like flex-time hours, which give employees more control over their time and allow for extended leaves of absence for family needs.

Eldercare is such a huge employee issue that IBM now offers a work/life initiative program to its employees worldwide. More than one quarter of IBM employees reported having eldercare issues in 2001, which was triple the percentage of those who reported having them in 1986. Forty-five percent of IBM's Asia/Pacific employees have elderly dependents, as do 41% of their employees in Latin America.

"Eldercare is not at a stage of maturity," Ted says. "The prominence of the eldercare needs over childcare needs will increase in the years to come. Strategies of aging and the businesses related to that will be the social issue of the next century." He also predicts that labor shortages will encourage companies to create innovative ways of using the talents of an aging population—and to be more creative in the use of technology and services to support them.[21]

Intel: Technology and Aging

Helping elders age in place is the biggest trend driving the home health market, according to Steve Agritelley, manager of Intel Corporation's Home Health Innovation Lab. However, the United States is falling behind other countries in preparing for the age wave, he says.[22] For example, South Korea is giving each citizen broadband Internet access, partly because it is building an infrastructure for home health services. Other Asian countries are using cell phone technologies to monitor heart disease and diabetes. European countries are funding telemedicine, smart homes, and personal health technologies.

Intel has joined with the American Association of Homes and Services for the Aging to create the Center for Aging Service Technologies (CAST), a national coalition of 300 technology companies, universities, and long-term care providers that will develop solutions for the continuum of care. CAST was inspired by a study revealing that boomers are willing to pay up to $100 monthly for technology that improves monitoring for family caregivers and for more accurate medical records.

"Caregiver burnout is a huge problem we're trying to address through technology," says Eric Dishman, manager of Intel's Proactive Health Strategic Research Project. "One avenue we're exploring is how sensor networks can provide a level of monitoring so that the caregiver would know it's safe to take a nap for an hour or pursue some other activity."

Intel is also exploring how technologies might help someone care for another person via long distance. How can you check in via technology to see that Mom is OK? How can technology help her develop a social network that keeps her engaged? Caregiver isolation is also a huge issue, so Intel is exploring technology mechanisms, such as online support groups, that caregivers could access without having to leave home.[23]

Wells Fargo: Private Client Elder Services

Seven years ago, Norwest trust officers Sandra Anderson and Bill Sanden realized they had a significant number of elderly clients who kept asking about personal care services. Sandra says that in meetings with elderly clients, many were not asking about investment return. They were far more concerned about whether they could find someone to take them to the doctor or clean their house once a week.

Private Client Elder Services has grown since Norwest merged with Wells Fargo. Today, it operates in 21 cities, and plans are to make it available in any market that Wells Fargo serves. Sandra and Bill operate as 24-hour on-call care coordinators for the elderly, a rare position among bank employees. Their services range from geriatric care to estate planning for clients who typically have at least $500,000 to $1 million portfolios.

Sandra says that this mix is a top growth market that serves both Wells' elderly clients and their boomer children. "This business is very focused on life events," she says. "People don't just say 'Let's go find somebody to help.' Something has to happen—a fall, or a mishap that happens to a neighbor, or a bad doctor's appointment. It takes an event, or it takes a plan."[24]

Reverse Mortgages

One of the biggest problems in eldercare is that frail elderly people are often struggling to age in place, choosing between food and prescription drugs. Yet, this same group owns more than $2 trillion in untapped housing wealth.[25] If frail elders had liquidity, they could buy the services and products that would allow them to remain independent. A reverse mortgage is one way to do that.

Reverse mortgages are specialized loans that allow adults age 62 and older to convert some of that equity into cash they can use to live in their homes. The loans help pay for long-term care services like home care and home modifications. Of the 21 million U.S. homeowner households over the age of 62, 71% are estimated to meet eligibility requirements.

Reverse mortgages have been around since the 1960s, but today they are experiencing a dramatic increase. Jay Greenberg says an NCOA study of home ownership among the elderly shows that reverse mortgages are a huge opportunity. "There's going to be an opening for companies that work with reverse mortgage lenders to put the package of services together," Jay says. "Most seniors are going to want to have access to services with some semblance of quality assurance and pricing. We think there is a big opportunity to bring together a financing mechanism like reverse mortgages with the providers of care. A lot of seniors do not want to 'go on the dole.' They are nervous about using the assets in their house. Like any social transformation, this is not going to happen overnight."[26]

Reverse mortgages were a $6 billion industry in 2004.[27] They could become a $74 billion industry by 2015, according to Wells Fargo projections.[28]

Some visionaries have created entirely new fields to address social issues. In 1977, Rona Bartelstone had two grandmothers suffering from dementia. "I saw the disruption, the confusion, and the conflict that this caused my family," she says. After a colleague solved some of their eldercare problems, Rona had her insight. She learned grant writing, quit her day job, and started a business she called "care management." She spoke at churches and seminars, began to get referrals, and birthed one of the first such firms in the nation. In the mid-'80s she helped form the National Association of Private Geriatric Care Managers, creating a field that is now indispensable to the aging network and to work/family programs. Rona Bartlestone & Associates' annual revenues now exceed $3 million.[29]

Summary

We can describe the products and services that will make money in eldercare, but the questions on caregivers' minds do not have to do with money. They are about what experiences the caregiver will be having: the gifts they will give from their hearts, the time they will take for themselves, and what the future holds.

Our society needs to be more creative about how we care for others. A boomer facing 20 years of parent care has a compelling personal challenge. Perhaps he or she needs a day at a spa, gift packages, respite services, or holistic hospices. Opportunities abound for businesses that support caregivers and enable them to have the richest experiences possible.

"When you look at it from a market perspective, you want to go after boomers because they're the biggest caregivers other than spouses," says Jay Greenberg of NCOA. "The first thing you must focus on is meeting their caregiving needs."

When you think about the products and services that will help solve these critical social issues, keep in mind that caregiving is not a linear process. We need to be more creative about how we care for others when many elders will need help for decades, not years. The market for making this a sustainable journey is wide open.

Endnotes

1. MetLife Mature Market Institute, *MetLife Market Survey on Nursing Homes and Home Care Costs* (Metropolitan Life Insurance Company, 2002), 1, http://www.metlife.com/WPSAssets/17157088621027365380V1FPDF1.pdf.
2. A survey by AARP of seniors 65 and older with children 35 and older revealed that 67% had not talked with their children about what their future needs might be. Linda Barrett, *Independent Living: Do Older Parents and Adult Children See It the Same Way?* (AARP, 1998).
3. Chip Baird (panel discussion, Silicon Valley Boomer Venture Summit, Santa Clara, CA, June 21, 2005).
4. National Alliance for Caregiving and AARP, *Caregiving in the U.S.* (National Alliance for Caregiving and AARP, 2004). Most (52%) are between ages 35 and 64; 39% are men. 28% of those receiving care are mothers, 8% are fathers; 9% are

mother-in-laws; 9% are grandmothers; 5% are siblings; and 17% are unrelated friends. *Ibid.*

5. David J. Demko, "Can Aging Boomers Avoid Nursing Home Care?" AgeVenture News Service, May 24, 2000, http://www.demko.com/m000522c. htm.

6. Ann Elizabeth Sammon, Karen Duggan, and Paul Pethick, "Assisting the Elderly," *CAmagazine*, December 1999, http://www.camagazine.com/index.cfm/ci_id/5989/la_id/1.htm.

7. Jay Greenberg, interview by Beth Witrogen McLeod, June 28, 2005.

8. National Alliance for Caregiving and AARP, *Caregiving in the U.S.* (National Alliance for Caregiving and AARP, 2004).

9. "The Sandwich Generation Has to Care for Their Children and Elderly Parents," Seniorscopie.com, December 13, 2004.

10. Administration on Aging, "A Profile of Older Americans: 2002, Future Growth," http://www.aoa.gov/prof/Statistics/profile/2.asp. By 2050, the world median age will be 38, up from 24 in 1950; Italy will have the oldest median at 53, although France, Germany, the U.K., China, India, and the United States will all be above the world average. "IDB Population Pyramids," U.S. Census Bureau, http://www.census.gov/ipc/www/idbpyr.html.

11. United Nations Population Fund, "Fast Facts," http://www.unfpa.org/pds/facts. htm.

12. Administration on Aging, "Statistics: Aging into the 21st Century," http://www.aoa.gov/prof/Statistics/future_growth/aging21/demography.asp.

13. National Family Caregivers Association, *Family Caregiving Demands Recognition: Caregiving across the Lifecycle* (National Family Caregivers Association, 1998).

14. Judy Skatssoon, "Dementia Epidemic as Baby Boomers Age," *The Advertiser*, May 28, 2003, 23.

15. MetLife Mature Market Institute, *Miles Away: The MetLife Study of Long-Distance Caregiving* (MetLife Mature Market Institute, 2004), 3.

16. "Loneliness Report Highlights Plight," *The Scotsman*, June 23, 2005.

17. Richard Jones, interview by Beth Witrogen McLeod, July 22, 2005.

18. Bryan Preston, email message to author, April 17, 2006.

19. Margit Novack, interview by Beth Witrogen McLeod, June 17, 2005.

20. Diane Piktialis, interview by Beth Witrogen McLeod, April 12, 2005.

21. Ted Childs, interview by author, September 1, 2005.

22. Steve Agritelley (panel discussion, Silicon Valley Boomer Venture Summit, Santa Clara, CA, June 21, 2005).

23. Intel, "Interview with Eric Dishman," http://www.intel.com/research/print/one_on_one_dishman.htm.

24. Sandra Anderson, interview by Beth Witrogen McLeod, July 19, 2005.

25. The National Council on Aging, *Use Your Home to Stay at Home: Expanding the Use of Reverse Mortgages for Long-Term Care: A Blueprint for Action* (The National Council on Aging, 2005), 1, http://www.ncoa.org/attachments/Reverse MortgageReport3.pdf.

26. Jay Greenberg, interview by Beth Witrogen McLeod, June 28, 2005.

27. The National Council on Aging, *Use Your Home to Stay at Home: Expanding the Use of Reverse Mortgages for Long-Term Care: A Blueprint for Action* (The National Council on Aging, 2005), 24, http://www.ncoa.org/attachments/Reverse MortgageReport3.pdf.

28. Tom Kelly, "Reverse Mortgage Companies Battle Misleading Perceptions" (Seattle Financial Group, 2004), October 8, 2003, http://www.seattlesavings-bank.com/ pr_revb.html.

29. Rona Bartelstone, interview by Beth Witrogen McLeod, June 28, 2005.

10

FINANCING YOUR DREAM

Introduction

The boomer generation is changing "business as usual" in two significant ways. First, they are the customers for the visionary businesses that we have explored throughout this book. But they are also creating these businesses and making the products and services they want so they can age well.

If you've been thinking about leaving the corporate grind or starting a business aimed at this juicy market, you're not alone. A study by Challenger, Gray, and Christmas, a leading outplacing company, says that unlike the dot.com era, "This time around . . . the burst in entrepreneurial activity will not be led by 20-somethings, but by baby boomers and would-be retirees in their 40s, 50s, 60s, and even 70s, who are better educated, healthier, and more tech-savvy than their predecessors." The number of self-employed Americans age 55 to 64 has increased 29% in the last five years, according to the Bureau of Labor Statistics, while the number of self-employed people age 65 and older has increased 18%. "All told," the study says, "the boomer-and-older [cohorts] now account for 54% of self-employed workers."[1]

The inevitability of a traditional retirement is eroding. Most boomers intend to work all their lives, and many will have to because they need the income. Some boomers are challenged by adult children who still need financial help; others lack confidence in the solvency of Social Security; and many never funded their own retirement plans. But few boomers who keep working will settle for just any job. Millions of them seek creativity and passion in their work lives. They are more likely than previous generations to want work that reflects their values and identity; they want to make a difference and have fun while doing it.

Boomer-run businesses are also erasing the difference between for-profit and nonprofit companies. In a nonprofit, value is measured by the ability to make a positive difference in society. In a for-profit institution, success is measured by financial returns. Increasingly, we find that businesses can succeed on both fronts. They can do well by doing good.

Throughout the book, you've seen profiles of entrepreneurs who have started their businesses in a variety of ways. But regardless of your motive, or whether your company is a franchise, nonprofit, venture-capital-backed business, or something else, you're going to need startup money. Recruiting is at the heart of building a company, and your ability to attract and retain a top-level team is directly correlated to your financial position. This chapter is a toolkit for making your dream a reality. It shares insights and resources from these entrepreneurs and also basic business sense in funding a company or enterprise.

Becoming an Entrepreneur

Before taking the first step to becoming an entrepreneur, ask yourself these questions. Are you a self-starter? Are you tenacious? Are you passionate? Are you a good listener?

Do you have the stamina to run your own business? Do you have the ability to put in the work necessary to make your idea grow? And what impact will all of this work have on your family?

Most people don't realize the exhilaration of starting a new business until they are doing it. And, once you take the step, you are likely to take it more than once. Entrepreneurs often apply the experience they have gained from past successes or failures to refine the launch of their next enterprise.

Start with a Business Plan

Although the first phase of planning a business is often a chat with a friend over lunch and a sketch on the back of a napkin, you will eventually need to write a business plan. This will be your guide for growing your idea into the marketplace. "Entrepreneurs have passion, vision, and drive, but often they don't have a plan for their business," says Cheryl Mills, associate deputy administrator of the Small Business Administration. "Their innovative spirit needs discipline. They need a roadmap to success and extensive due diligence before investing time and capital."[2]

Careful preparation is important. In these early stages, you should decide how much risk you're willing to tolerate to get your business off the ground. Recently, an older entrepreneur wrote that his son-in-law wanted to go into business with him. He asked us, "How much of our savings should we risk on the venture?" Our answer was, "Less than 20%. For one thing, who knows if your son-in-law is going to be an asset to the business?"

As you put your business plan together, you may discover that there is too much competition or not enough demand. If you persist with an idea that isn't carefully researched, you will risk losing your capital and even going bankrupt. According to Cheryl, "baby boomers are at a wonderful stage in life where they are free to move, because their children are probably grown and they may have already downsized their home. They have savings that can provide seed capital. What could be a challenge is that they are at a stage in life where they are becoming risk adverse, as their productive years appear to be diminishing. Due diligence and having a solid business plan are the key to reducing the risk of failure. Entrepreneurs in their 50s and 60s will have fewer years to recover from failure, so every effort should be made to front load all of the research and competitive analysis."[3]

A good business plan defines your business, sets your goals, and sets your enterprise apart from the competition. It is especially important to spend time on market research so you can define your niche. The more energy you spend in the early planning stages, the better prepared you will be to make good business decisions and handle unforeseen complications.

Bob Hendershott, a venture capital and private equity consultant and professor of entrepreneurship and finance at Santa Clara University's Leavey School of Business, makes sure that all of his students consider the following questions (and be able to communicate credible answers):

- What is the market opportunity?
- What is your product or service, and what is your potential revenue?
- Who will be your customers, and why will they purchase your product or service instead of your competitor's?
- How will you reach your customers?
- How will you calibrate the lifetime value of a customer?
- How will operations be handled, and what is the planned gross margin?
- What are the product development/service development costs?
- Do you need to develop a recognizable brand?
- What is the sales strategy?
- What is the sales pipeline?
- How much financing do you need to start and maintain your business, and where will you get this capital?[4]

You should ask lots of questions having to do with banking, insurance, and other financial matters, and you should consider how the answers relate to your particular business. Remember, every time you tell your story, explain your idea, or share your business plan, you'll actually refine and improve it in the process. You should develop one page of talking points that defines the market opportunity, the problem your business solves, the "value proposition" (what makes you different from competitors), and three supporting points. You should be able to identify the competition—it is almost always naive to assume there isn't any. You should know why your product or service is going to win.

One of the most important abilities is learning how to tell the story of why you will win and why you need financial support. You need to be able to pitch the idea in less than three minutes; this boiled-down version is known as the *elevator speech*. You also need a *pitch deck*, which is a summary of what you are trying to do that you can send around to investors or foundation officers.

The best pitch person we know is Guy Kawasaki. He has not only delivered many pitches, but he has listened to thousands of them. Table 10.1 contains his ideas. If it inspires you, read his bestselling book *The Art of the Start*.

TABLE 10.1 INVESTOR PITCH (FOR BOTH PROFITS AND NOT-FOR-PROFITS)

Slide	Content	Comments
Chapter 1, "Title"	Organization name; your name and title; contact information.	This is where you explain what your organization does. ("We sell software." "We are a church." "We protect the environment.") Cut to the chase!
Chapter 2, "Problem"	Describe the pain that you're alleviating. The goal is to get everyone nodding and "buying in."	Avoid looking like a solution searching for a problem. Minimize or eliminate citations of consulting studies about the future size of your market.
Solution	Explain how you alleviate this pain and the meaning that you make. Ensure that the audience clearly understands what you sell and your value proposition.	This is not the place for an in-depth technical explanation. Provide just the gist of how you fix the pain—for example, "We are a discount travel website. We have written software that searches all other travel sites and collates their price quotes into one report."

Slide	Content	Comments
Chapter 3, "Business Model"	Explain how you make money: who pays you, your channels of distribution, and your gross margins.	Generally, a unique, untested business model is a scary proposition. If you truly have a revolutionary business model, explain it in terms of familiar ones. This is your opportunity to drop the names of organizations that are already using your product or service.
Underlying Magic	Describe the technology, secret sauce, or magic behind your product or service.	The less text and the more diagrams, schematics, and flowcharts on this slide, the better. White papers and objective proofs of concepts are helpful here.
Chapter 4, "Marketing AND Sales"	Explain how you are going to reach your customer and your marketing leverage points.	Convince the audience that you have an effective go-to-market strategy that won't break the bank.
Chapter 5, "Competition"	Provide a complete view of the competitive landscape. Too much is better than too little.	Never dismiss your competition. Customers, investors, and employees want to hear why you're good, not why the competition is bad.
Chapter 6, "Management Team"	Describe the key players of your management team, board of directors, and board of advisors, as well as your major investors.	Don't be afraid to show up with less than a perfect team. All startups have holes in their team—what's truly important is whether you understand that there are holes and are willing to fix them.
Financial Projections and Key Metrics	Provide a five-year forecast containing not only dollars, but also key metrics, such as numbers of customers and conversion rate.	Do a bottom-up forecast. Take into account long sales cycles and seasonality. Making people understand the underlying assumptions of your forecast is as important as the numbers you forecasted.
Current Status, Accomplishments to Date, Timeline, and Use of Funds	Explain the current status of your product or service, what the near future looks like, and how you'll use the money you're trying to raise.	Share the details of your positive momentum and traction. Then use this slide to close with a bias toward action.

The first time my colleagues and I did a pitch for ThirdAge Media, one of the key questions from potential investors was how could we build a media company from the West Coast when so much of the talent (and the advertising base) was located on the East Coast.

We should have listened closer. ThirdAge should have been created as a bi-coastal entity with the sales team headquartered in New Brunswick, New Jersey. This is because we needed our sales force to be near many of the pharmaceutical brands that would eventually provide funding, and much of the media writing talent is based in New York.

It is crucial for entrepreneurs to find out as much as possible in advance about the venture capitalists who support their category. During the pitch, make sure you are *listening carefully,* and write down every question that is asked. The answers can help guide your strategy.

Capital to Make Your Business Grow

There are several ways to finance your business. Often the first source of capital is your own savings, home equity, pension plans, and even credit cards. Millions of entrepreneurs go out on a high-interest limb to pay for materials. It's risky and expensive, but many businesses actually do get launched on Visa and MasterCard.

During this early stage of business ownership, a self-funded entrepreneur is growing the business to show potential investors or supporters that the concept is viable. This first phase is often the one that presents the most challenges and tests your mettle. However, the experiences gained during this time will enable you to make a good case to investors or foundation officers who can step in and provide the capital needed to help the business rise to the next level.

If your business is for-profit, funders will look for you to build revenue—actual paying customers—or they will need to see that you have had previous success in building another business. The first question a for-profit investor will ask is how much revenue do you have, and how consistent is that revenue base? If your business is a nonprofit, a foundation officer will look for two to three years of evidence that you've built something worth funding.

Another source of capital is private loans, often from friends and family. It might be easier to get a loan from your closest friends than it is to get a loan from a bank, but that doesn't mean it's a particularly good idea. Money changes relationships, even the sturdiest ones. You and the person investing need to be clear with each other about expectations and risk. If you choose to accept money from someone you know personally, spend the time and money to work with an attorney and get everything spelled out in writing. Is it a loan or a gift? What does the other person expect from you in return?

There are also other significant drawbacks to self-financing. Without sufficient capital, your business may never reach its full potential. And as the owner and CEO of a self-funded business, it will be up to you to create your own contacts and networks. You won't have access to the robust network of contacts that professional investors have. You may want to join a professional association so you can create relationships that benefit your business.

Small Business Loans

After your credit cards are charged to the max, and perhaps even after you've dipped into your savings as much as you dare, where can you go next? For many, the next logical step is the Small Business Administration. The SBA does not make direct loans to small businesses; instead, it provides loan guarantees to lending institutions, which then make the loan to the business owner.

Another source of government-backed money is small business investment companies (SBICs), which are federally funded, private venture capital firms that mainly offer money to small businesses in risky or high-tech fields. You can often find people who have a lot of business experience at SBICs, and they are usually eager to share their wisdom with young entrepreneurs. You can also turn to the SBA's

Surety Bond Guarantee Program, which includes subgroups such as Minority Small Business Investment Companies.

It is not always easy to get a business loan. The bigger banks often have a hard time making significant returns on these loans, and the interest rates might be prohibitive. But some bank divisions do help small business owners. Local banks and credit unions may court startups, especially for their cash business. Some banks and lending institutions have divisions that specialize in lending to women and minorities. You never know where you may encounter someone who has the right knowledge for your situation. So keep presenting your business plan; even if you don't get the loan, you will benefit from the experience.

Angel Investors

Individual private investors who invest in entrepreneurial companies are commonly known as "angel investors." They make investments with their own money, often in the $200,000 to $1 million range. Angels usually fund companies that are in the startup or first stage of development. But a good angel offers much more than just capital. He or she may also bring successful experience to the table, as well as a wealth of contacts and emotional support.

Greg Chabrier is an angel investor in Silicon Valley. He is a technology sales whiz who made his fortune, as he says, "on the bubble of the bubble of the tech boom." He finds investing in startups thrilling, and it is also his way to give back. Greg has guest lectured at the University of Santa Clara, where the students treat him like a business rock star. Their eyes widen as he shares how he got stock options in his first job as a sales executive with Sun Microsystems. Their eyes grow even wider when he tells of the long hours he put in and how he arrived at work every day at 4:30 in the morning so his car would be in its parking space before the COO arrived.

Greg and potential investments find each other through "friends of friends." They are almost always fledgling enterprises, and the entrepreneur usually still has a day job. "Usually they need the angel money to get out of the garage," he says. There are distinct qualities Greg looks for in ideas and the people who propose them. "I ask four questions: about technical risk, market risk, financial risk, and team risk. In other words, are the specific individuals involved good individuals, and are they going to be able to take this thing and make it go?"

"If I've resolved all the risk issues, if I believe in the team, if I believe there is a financial exit, if I believe in the technology, if I believe in the market, and I have said I am going to put this kind of money aside—after I have all that stuff in my head and I've referenced as much as I can and I can't think of anything else that I really need to investigate—then I'll write a check."

In Chapter 8, "A Family of Our Own Choosing," we introduced you to Seth Socolow, whose Telling Stories software company was able to secure angel financing. He has a small market, but he defined his niche well and he combined a great idea with his technical expertise to create a successful company. He is the type of entrepreneur that angel investors like to bet on.

Angels offer equity capital, which means that they buy part of your company. So if you choose to seek angel investment, you must be prepared to give up some control. Also, your company must be able to provide an "exit" to these investors. They will eventually want to get their investment back, in the form of a public stock offering or a buyout from a larger firm.

Venture Capitalists

Many entrepreneurs seek venture capital only after they know they cannot get a bank loan. That is because there is a big difference between getting a loan and selling equity in your business. If you're trying to decide whether to pursue the venture capital (VC) route, ask yourself if you are you willing to sell equity in your business. Then ask yourself, "Am I prepared to have a partner who will put controls on my organization or take some responsibility in setting up my management team? Can I handle having my business management scrutinized? Am I comfortable with someone looking over my shoulder asking, 'Have you made your numbers this quarter?'"[5]

Not every entrepreneur can say yes to these questions. If you would prefer to remain smaller and in control, then you shouldn't seek venture capital. "The good entrepreneurs put an idea out there and test it with friends," says Jon Staenberg, managing director of Staenberg Venture Partners. "They ask, 'Is this fundable? Would you put money into it? What do I have to do to make it fundable?'"[6]

What VCs have most is prescience, informed by their own long experience as well as reports, success and failure stories, and data for analysis. Once they've invested, most VC firms take an active role in the growth of their companies. They guide the process. They recruit the best and brightest to build the team. They analyze partnership activities. And they seek other financing partners for later rounds of capitalization. The best VCs develop reputations for seeing trends before the rest of us do. Their reputations attract billions of dollars from investors, who are willing to take risks that could result in big payoffs when a company goes public or is acquired.

"We're the counselor, the father confessor, and the coach," says Dick Kramlich, founder and general partner of New Enterprise Associates. "We're equity partners with the entrepreneurs. We do a lot of recruiting for all our companies. If they're needed, we put people on the management team. We put someone on the board."[7]

Before you start negotiating with a VC firm, you should have a solid idea of how much capital your business needs to meet certain milestones. This will help you get exactly the amount of investment capital you need, and no more. Remember, the more investment you receive from VCs, the more control they will have over your company. You don't want to dilute your ownership so much that you're unable to realize your vision.

A venture capitalist may look at hundreds or even thousands of investment opportunities in a year. How do they choose which ones to bet on?

We have seen this process in action by hosting an annual Baby Boomer Business Plan Competition in partnership with Santa Clara University and the American Society on Aging. We invite some of the country's leading venture capitalists, as well as angel investors and business school educators, to judge business plans submitted by entrepreneurs from the United States and a dozen or so other countries. Everyone who enters gets at least one shot at having their plan evaluated by an expert in the field (see the list of judges in Figure 10.1).

The first thing VCs look for in a business plan is whether there is growth potential. David Yarnell says, "The industry has to be large and growing enough and have a structure where a player can grow. That's probably the first screen."[8]

The next screen is whether the goods or services offered by the entrepreneur are really innovative and add value. Jon Staenberg says, "We ask what problem are they solving or what customer need are they serving that isn't being solved or met today. And are they doing it in a way that makes good, logical sense? And if so, how are they doing it so that others can't just copy it? If you can answer that, then we should have a conversation."[9]

Frank Batten adds, "There's very little that's truly unique. How does this idea stand out from the rest? The number-one thing is how are they going to differentiate themselves from their competitors. Warren Buffet has written a lot about this. You want somebody with a large castle and a deep moat around it. The large castle is something that's going to be big enough to be material and worth the trouble of working on it. And then the moat is going to be what keeps the competitors from getting in. What you want is something that's at least partially insulated from competition. Does it have some competitive differentiator or moat around it that keeps the competitive edge?"[10]

"The [boomer] market has requirements that don't exist in any other market," says Greg Chabrier. "They have opportunities that don't exist anywhere else. That's why they are interesting."[11]

Frank Batten, Jr., Chairman and CEO, Landmark Communications
(finalist judge, 2005)

Laura Rossman, VP, Lifestage Products and Integrated Marketing,
AARP Services, Inc. (finalist judge, 2004, 2005)

David Yarnell, General Partner, Brand Equity Ventures
(finalist judge, 2005)

Ilya Oshman, VP, General Manager, Pfizer Strategic Investments
Group (finalist judge, 2004, 2005)

Jon Staenberg, Partner, Rustic Canyon Partners (finalist judge,
2005, 2006)

Dick Kramlich, General Partner, New Enterprise Associates
(finalist judge, 2004)

Ellen Marram, Partner, North Castle Partners (finalist judge, 2004)

Barry Posner, Dean of the Leavey School of Business at Santa Clara
University (finalist judge, 2004)

Richard Rosenberg, Chairman and CEO (Retired), Bank of America
(screening and finalist judge, 2004)

Jennifer Fonstad, Managing Director, Draper, Fisher, Jurvetson
(finalist judge, 2006)

Michael Goldberg, General Partner, Mohr Davidow Ventures
(finalist judge, 2006)

Nancy Kamei, Senior Director, Digital Health, Intel Capital
(finalist judge, 2006)

Emilio Pardo, Chief Brand Officer, AARP (finalist judge, 2006)

Brad Vale, Vice President, Johnson & Johnson Development
Corporation

FIGURE 10.1 BOOMER BUSINESS PLAN COMPETITION JUDGES

What Do VCs Look for in an Entrepreneur?

VCs look for knowledge, experience, good business ethics, and a record for assembling a good team. An entrepreneur should have good strategic sense, know what to do with the big decisions that need to be made, and be equally adept at running the day-to-day details of the business. David Yarnell says of his investment group, "We're looking to talk to entrepreneurs who have built something before. I'd prefer that their experience not be within a large organization, but they could have been running a division of a decent-sized organization. Have they put some sweat equity into it? I want to know that they have a real proof of concept. I like it when they have really worked hard to get where they are."[12]

Laura Rossman emphasizes the importance of presenting yourself in the most professional manner possible so you'll be taken seriously. Laura's ability to listen to the pitch and recognize value helped AARP grow a revenue stream that now equals about half of the budget of the organization. "Be crisp and clear and to the point," she says. "It's important to say, 'Here's the market, here's why my product will meet the needs of the market, here's how I'd start it, here's how I'd scale it.' Investors want to know your growth strategy and that you understand what the potential is."

Laura is now out on her own; her firm Outside Insite helps companies develop and implement product development and marketing strategies for the 50+ market. "The people who are most successful, and those I always took most seriously, are the ones who had really done the market research, who had looked at what is the potential for this kind of product. Where most people go wrong is in thinking that all people over the age of 50 are one market. The more serious proposals have narrowed it down to say, 'These are the kinds of people who might want this and this is how many of them there are.' It is a very *segmented* market—it is not one lump. So within that marketplace, you've got to figure out where your target is and who are the people who are most likely to be interested in your product. You have to be realistic about whether enough people will be interested to actually scale the product to a reasonable level."[13]

"The passion of an entrepreneur is that of never giving up," says Jon Staenberg. "We often see someone who comes in with an idea and we say no. Three months later they're back and say, 'We've refined the idea and here it is.' And we say, 'that's more interesting, let's take another look at it.'"[14]

Entrepreneurs must have stamina, the ability to change direction quickly, and tenacity. "I consider all forms of athleticism—a mental athlete, an emotional athlete, as well as a physical athlete—to be a plus," says Dick Kramlich. "You see some athletes who flame out; they just don't have the discipline to do it all the time. An entrepreneur who's an athlete has the ability to endure."[15]

What Does a VC Expect in Return for the Investment?

If an investor puts in $1 million today, what would he or she think is a reasonable return in five years? "It depends on how much risk there is," says Frank Batten. "If it's a company with a proven business and established cash flows, we would look for 15% over a period of time. If it's an unproven business model, you'd want 25 to 30% because there's always the chance it could be minus 100%. Whenever there's a chance you could lose all your money, you want the upside to be pretty good."[16]

David Yarnell's group has similar expectations. "As a venture capitalist, the General Partners get a piece of the profits they make for their investors." Yarnell generally looks for a 40 to 55% internal rate of return (IRR)—this is the interest rate that makes net present value of all cash flow equal zero. This often translates to four to seven times his initial investment, depending on how long his firm stays in the deal. "Overall, our fund looks for top quartile returns in the industry," he says. "In the long run, this is an IRR over the life of the fund of at least 20%."[17]

Venture capitalists enjoy rewards that go beyond cash. "Since I've started in this business, I've averaged a return of ten times on my invested capital," says Dick Kramlich. "Beyond that, what I actually receive is tremendous psychic rewards. We have created over one-half million jobs. I regard what we're doing as the headwaters of the capital allocation process, and that is tremendously satisfying."[18]

Finding the Right VC for Your Enterprise

When seeking venture capital investment, get advice from your attorney, accountant, consultant, or other entrepreneurs who have previously raised venture capital. VC seminars and panel discussions, such as the Silicon Valley Boomer Venture Summit, are another good arena in which to gain exposure and make contact with investors and entrepreneurs with experience in fundraising. The National Venture Capital Association is one of the best sources on the Web. It has a trove of information and a wealth of links. Venture Wire is terrific for research as well.

It is a big advantage to work with a VC who is near you geographically because you are likely to have lots of meetings about building the team, reviewing progress, and making deals. You need someone who can go to lunch with the CEO or the partner and find out why they are making their numbers or missing them. The National Venture Capital Association site also includes a listing of venture capital investment companies arranged by geographical location.

On the other hand, VCs specialize in industries in which they believe they can be a market leader. It is always a good idea to find a VC who knows the kind of business you are in. For example, North Castle Partners specializes in businesses that are dedicated to healthy living and aging. The firm can match up different companies that are within their portfolio, and it can open doors to other firms.

Succeeding On Your Own

Some companies are not the type that attracts investors. Todd Healy is a prime example of someone who took a personal passion and turned it into an occupation. In the early 1980s he was an airline baggage handler working the night shift. During the slow times, he made beautiful sketches of historic homes and scenes of Old Town Alexandria, Virginia. His painstaking renderings of each brick and ornament were eventually published as a series of limited edition prints.

Todd founded his company, Historic Cards and Prints, in 1987. He would get up at 5 in the morning and set up a booth at the Alexandria

Farmer's Market. He sold a calendar; offered special original artwork to homeowners; and even had items for sale that children could afford, such as magnets and napkins. He learned a lot by listening to his customers.

"I never had a career. I had jobs," Todd says. "I always did art on the side. I was making $50,000 a year working for the airline, but I was always an artist. Things changed when I had a daughter and wanted to be home at night. With a young child at home and a day job, my art went on hold for a few years."

Todd lost his airline job during the 1990 recession and did not know how to make a living. He decided to pursue his art full time and rented studio space at a friend's art gallery. He thought that if he could make $10,000 a year from the sale of his calendar, he could get by. "The first year, I sold 3,000 calendars. Now, I sell 25,000 calendars."

Todd learned some deep lessons about the patience and perseverance it takes to be a success. "You're not an entrepreneur until you're close to losing everything, and then you find a way to make it work. You really don't know you are an entrepreneur until everything can crumble. That's when you find out you are made of steel on the inside, and that is what carries you through."

Todd ended his relationship with a souvenir company when they took all the profits from the sale of his coffee mugs. He went directly to the manufacturers, adding a product each year and convincing the manufacturer to make smaller lots. Later, he started wholesaling. His wife Laraine is the product manager and comes up with new ideas, such as the linens in their gift shop.

Todd says that building relationships is key to success. Every Monday he writes a personal note on good stationery to every customer who made a purchase the week before. He views this as the best thing that he does to market his business. His customers are loyal and trust him to choose the kinds of frames they will appreciate on the prints; he even sends them elsewhere if he doesn't have a frame they want. Todd does something that is important for every businessperson to do. He views the business as a gift, each customer as a treasure, and the challenge as an invigorating opportunity.[19]

Creating a Not-for-Profit Organization

If you have an idea about the boomer/senior market and you believe you can make a social contribution, a nonprofit organization may be the best path. If you go down this road, you will need to incorporate as a 501(c) 3, and you will need to find a board of directors who can provide direction and financial oversight.

There are several avenues for funding your nonprofit. Twenty-six federal grant-making agencies and over 900 individual grant programs award over $400 billion in grants to nonprofits each year.[20] Websites such as grants.gov and foundationcenter.org are good spots to begin your search.

You have to be tenacious when you look for foundation funding. Grantors receive countless proposals for every idea that is funded. It can take years and a hundred doors that do not open. You have to do your homework researching foundations and program officers and then patiently build your network until you find the right contact. You cannot start and run a nonprofit if you do not have an aptitude for fundraising.

Some foundations that have targeted aging as a key priority include the Archstone Foundation, the Retirement Research Foundation, the MetLife Foundation, the Robert Wood Johnson Foundation, and Atlantic Philanthropies. One benefit of obtaining funding from groups like these is the guidance you will receive from program officers. They act as social venture advisors and can assist with team recruitment, strategic partnering, and market opportunity. One of the challenges of nonprofit funding is the pace at which foundations make decisions—they usually hold only one or two board meetings each year. Program officers also come and go, and foundations can change directions when leadership changes.

First and foremost, a nonprofit organization needs to focus on its social mission. Second, it needs to create a business model that will allow the institution to grow and thrive. Today, many nonprofits are establishing multiple revenue streams with some earned income from sales of publications, research initiatives, and events. A continuing revenue stream of membership sales and retention can help sustain a nonprofit. No one has done this better than AARP, an organization with more than 35 million members over 50. For that reason, many for-profits try to partner with AARP. With more than 35 million members over 50,[21] it just makes sense to cultivate and develop a relationship with AARP.

There are many reasons to form a nonprofit, and the most obvious is to build something great and make a contribution to the lives of many people. This endeavor brings many psychic rewards. A nonprofit organization must have social goals as well as business goals. It is wise to clarify the success metrics for each at six month intervals. It is also wise to manage your nonprofit budget in a fiscally conservative way. Foundations usually make their decisions on a quarterly basis. So if you miss a quarterly deadline, you could miss the funding opportunity until the next quarter. That delay could break a fledgling organization. Or the foundation that funds your nonprofit could hire a new director who could change its priorities and cut your group loose. The bottom line for building a nonprofit is the same as it is for a regular business: you have to believe in your dream and be tenacious. You also need to have a strong and realistic business model. A board with fundraising capability as well as sound governance can be a giant help.

Creating a Franchise

Margit Novack's Moving Solutions (see Chapter 9, " Eldercare: The New Midlife Crisis") and Thomas Peeks' Fitness Together (see Chapter 2, "The Business of Health") are good examples of franchise businesses targeted at aging boomers. For entrepreneurs, the advantage of a franchise is that there is a blueprint and a starter kit. You can also benefit from experience, having a brand, and working with a network of other franchise owners. The downside is that you have to play by the franchise's rules. And if one member of the franchise network doesn't keep his or her service working well, it will reflect poorly on your brand.

Many boomers are taking on franchise opportunities as a way to supplement their retirement income. But once again, driving a successful franchise means doing your homework. Experts recommend doing demographic research and planning aggressive marketing to create a solid customer base. Remember that boomers will use and pay for many kinds of services that their parents deemed unnecessary, such as food deliveries, home cleaning services, and other concierge services. They will also pay for romance: The Right One is now the largest franchised dating service in the country, with 100,000 members and 100 locations.

To learn more, plan to attend a franchise expo. There are many available, from the West Coast Franchise Expo to the International Franchise Expo and the International Mexican Franchise Fair. These conferences showcase hundreds of franchise concepts and cover a vast array of industries at all investment levels.

Owning your own business offers no guarantee of success. But planning and foresight (and a little luck) will serve you well as you pursue your goals. Many new business owners underestimate the time and difficulty it takes to launch an enterprise. Those who've been there will tell you that hard work, patience, and good planning can bring great rewards. There is nothing more thrilling than to make an idea come to life. The thrill of the ride and the lives that are touched can make all of the challenges worthwhile.

Opportunities to Learn More: Resources for Entrepreneurs

There are many resources available to entrepreneurs. Several are featured on Mary Furlong & Associates website at www.maryfurlong.com.

Another worthwhile resource is the Service Corps of Retired Executives (SCORE), a nonprofit organization of volunteers—working or retired business owners, executives, and corporate leaders—who offer free counsel to small businesses. Local SCORE chapters are located throughout the country. SCORE is a partner of the SBA.

The SBA offers many helpful guides for small business owners, from how to create a business plan to how to handle the business finances. You can find its guide at www.sba.gov/starting_business/index.html.

Entrepreneurial magazines, such as *Entrepreneur* and *Forbes*, are another good source of information. The more knowledgeable you are about entrepreneurship and the market conditions for your product or service, the better able you'll be to guide your business to success.

There are more than 1,200 entrepreneurship programs in business schools across the United States, and you can learn about some of the best by visiting the website of the Kauffman Foundation. Another good way to learn more is to attend small business classes or seminars, such as the collaborative program between Cisco Systems and the SBA at Cisco's Entrepreneur Center in San Jose, California.

On the nonprofit side, Grantmakers in Aging (www.giaging.org), an organization dedicated to promoting grant-making for an aging society, has a more complete list of organizations that fund in the field.

Summary

The best ideas need capital to make them grow. There are many business opportunities in the boomer marketplace. And, there are many different ways to fund those opportunities. This chapter provided a blueprint to help you get started. Be realistic about the kind of business you want to build. If you have a big idea and expect to build a global business, you will likely need outside funding. If you want to have a smaller, niche-oriented business, you can choose from a franchise model or learn from some of the emerging entrepreneurs who have self funded or raised angel funding for their enterprise. And, you can also try the nonprofit path and work with some of the foundations that are providing support for good ideas. Being an entrepreneur is a wonderful opportunity; it is more like riding the rollercoaster than the Ferris wheel. You will have giant ups and you will navigate through more than just a few challenges. Whatever path you take, having a successful funding strategy is a key to success.

Endnotes

1. "US: Start-Up Explosion on the Horizon with the Baby Boomers," the Mature Market.com, http://www.thematuremarket.com/SeniorStrategic/Start_Up_Explosion_On_The_Horizon_Baby_boomers-5348-5.html.
2. Cheryl Mills, interview by Lori Covington, July 28, 2005.
3. *Ibid.*
4. Bob Hendershott, interview by Helen Gray, April 2005.
5. Greg Chabrier, interview by Helen Gray, June 1, 2005.
6. Jon Staenberg, interview by Helen Gray, June 25, 2005.
7. Dick Kramlich, interview by Helen Gray, May 6, 2005.
8. David Yarnell, interview by Helen Gray and author, May 26, 2005.
9. Jon Staenberg, interview by Helen Gray, June 25, 2005.
10. Frank Batten, interview by Helen Gray and author, July 1, 2005.
11. Greg Chabrier, interview by Helen Gray, June 1, 2005.
12. David Yarnell, interview by Helen Gray and author, May 26, 2005.
13. Laura Rossman, interview by Helen Gray, June 20, 2005.
14. Jon Staenberg, interview by Helen Gray, June 25, 2005.
15. Dick Kramlich, interview by Helen Gray, May 6, 2005.
16. Frank Batten, interview by Helen Gray and author, July 1, 2005.
17. David Yarnell, interview by Helen Gray and author, May 26, 2005.
18. Dick Kramlich, interview by Helen Gray, May 6, 2005.
19. Todd Healy, interview by author, April 20, 2006.
20. grants.gov, "About Us," grants.gov, http://www.grants.gov/aboutus.
21. AARP, http://www.aarp.org.

11

ON THE AGE BEAT: THE MEDIA AND THE MESSAGE

Introduction

Everyone talks about the media, but not enough business leaders pay attention to it. The power of media became clear to me back in 1985, when a positive article about SeniorNet appeared in *InfoWorld*, the widely read computer magazine, and led us to our first funder, the Markle Foundation. Articles on SeniorNet also appeared in *The Wall Street Journal, The New York Times*, and *Time* that first year, which helped establish the credibility of the idea. I quickly learned the value of meeting reporters who cover aging, knowing their beats and perspectives, and learning how to pitch a story.

In January 1987, a five-line item about us in *USA Today* brought SeniorNet more than 1,000 letters from older adults. This response helped make the case for growing SeniorNet from a university research project into a nonprofit organization. What made the story important was that it was real. Seniors had been bypassed by the computer world, and SeniorNet.org was one of the first groups to provide access to the technology and show the power of creating a vibrant community of older adults. The media liked the story because they could visit a SeniorNet Center, take a photo, talk to the members, and illustrate the impact technology could have on quality of life.

Sharing an authentic story is key. Sharing a product or service that can enhance and change lives is important. And knowing how and to whom to pitch an idea is vital. These are the topics of this chapter.

Posit Science Corporation (see Chapter 2, "The Business of Health") provides a great example of effective media relations. In his first public presentations, CEO Jeff Zimman often started with a detailed video about his San Francisco-based firm, which identifies its product as "a cutting-edge mental training program . . . offering new hope of a vibrant retirement for seniors and the baby boomers not far behind them." Posit Science did not spend a dime to create this slick video—it was produced by CNBC-MSNBC as a regular news item in early 2005 and aired on February 18, 2005. Now that the company has been covered on several national and local TV news programs, Jeff selects his clips based on his audience. These televised pieces, along with a seemingly endless stream of articles about the company in leading magazines and newspapers, including Forbes, Reader's Digest, BusinessWeek, Science, and The Wall Street Journal, can be found on the company's website.[1]

This great publicity didn't materialize out of thin air, however. Posit Science's media relations staff developed a strong list of contacts and worked with reporters and producers to produce these stories. An appealing product, good media relations, and excellent follow-through are axiomatic for a business's success when the subject is the baby boom.

Doing Your Homework

When you ask reporters why businesses don't get publicity, the most common answer, in the words of Wall Street Journal editor Glenn Ruffenach, is, "They don't do their homework."[2] With a helping hand from writer Elizabeth Pope, we asked a number of reporters how businesses can better work with them. Here's what they said:

- **Make sure a reporter is interested in your topic area.** When targeting a selected list of reporters, review articles they have recently written and try to draw a connection between your product or service and these stories. If you don't know whom to contact, search the news organization's website for stories about topics, products, or companies similar to yours and then approach those authors.

- **State the facts.** Journalism's essential five Ws and the H are *who, what, why, where, when,* and *how.*

- **What the heck is it?** Make sure any press release translates technical or industry jargon into plain English.

- **Cut the fluff.** Every line, including the obligatory quotes from company executives, must provide reporters information they might use.

- **Prove it.** Include credible sources a reporter can contact.

- **Don't be greedy.** The reporter may not find your product or service interesting enough to sustain an entire story. But there are many other ways you can get some press exposure. For example, you can develop your CEO or another executive, such as the chief scientific officer, as a quotable source for stories in your field. If you're going this route, be specific about the person's expertise. Reporters sneer at generic announcements that a company's executive is available for interviews.

    Smart company spokespeople share information such as background data from market surveys or new reports about your industry. Reporters remember people who are knowledgeable and generous with their knowledge, and those are the people who tend to get quoted.

- **Be aware of deadlines.** Before you start pitching a story, ask the reporter if he or she is on deadline. Keep a list of deadlines for each person contacted.

- **Consider other media options.** Target local media, not just national. Depending on your business offering, you might start local to generate press that will help pitch larger placements. Other ways to get noticed are editorial opinion pieces, a letter to the editor, event sponsorships, and direct communication with reporters on other articles.

A Difficult Relationship

Aging and the news media have a difficult relationship. The generation born after the baby boom, which is known variously as Generation X, the baby bust, or people born between 1965 and the late 1970s, is only about half the size of the boomer generation. Yet television, radio, and newspapers continue to be obsessed with audiences age 18 to 34 or 18 to 49, mostly because these groups command considerably higher ad rates than do midlife and older consumers. These differences in ad rates have a subtle but pervasive effect on editorial content in the mass media. Rather than struggling against the bias, entrepreneurs might get further faster if they focus their PR budgets on the many varieties of online media that are generating new ways to identify and reach targeted audiences.

The Age Beat

One of the most important developments in targeted communications for the mature market since the late 1980s has been the creation of The Journalists Exchange on Aging (JEoA). The 900 "age beat" journalists in this group do not routinely pop up on standard public relations contact lists, and they are ready to listen. The following is a list of reporters who were full time on the age beat in the spring of 2006:

> Betty Booker, *Richmond Times Dispatch*
> Kelly Greene, *Wall Street Journal*
> Susan Jaffe, *Cleveland Plain Dealer*
> Marsha King, *Seattle Times*

Janet Kornblum, *USA Today*

Diane Lade, *The Sun-Sentinel* (south Florida)

Bob Moos, *Dallas Morning News*

Sean Mussenden, Media General, Washington Bureau

Stephen Nohlgren, *St. Petersburg Times*

Glenn Ruffenach, writer and *Encore* editor, *Wall Street Journal*

Marsha Kay Seff, *San Diego Union-Tribune*

Connie Sexton, *Arizona Republic*

Nancy Weaver Teichert, *Sacramento Bee*

Suzanne Travers, *Herald-News* (northern New Jersey)

Warren Wolfe, *Minneapolis Star Tribune*

The group's national coordinator is Paul Kleyman, who is also the editor of *Aging Today*, the newspaper of the American Society on Aging (ASA). "The specialized focus on aging had been brewing for years," he says. "Reporters discovered this rich vein of untold stories and then wanted to talk shop and compare notes with other writers. Enough of us found each other in 1993, while attending the ASA conference in Chicago, to gather over a dinner of Polish dumplings at a cafe on Michigan Avenue. This is where we hatched the Journalists Exchange."

Paul calls boomers and longevity "the revolution that's been televised all along. Television grew up with the boomers, but it might not outlive them as a mass medium unless it stops pushing us away once we turn 50. The same goes for newspapers."[3]

The age beat has evolved despite the prevailing youth-focused business models in media because reporters keep forcing stories about aging into the news. Paul has learned from reporters over the years that their passion for this enormous field of stories usually begins with a personal experience; often it is caring for a parent or in-law.

One of the best examples is Michael Vitez of the *Philadelphia Inquirer*, who won the Pulitzer Prize in 1997 for his series on death and dying. Michael told Paul that he'd originally proposed a modest two-article piece, but Max King, then the paper's executive editor, gave the age-beat reporter carte blanche with staff resources to spend six months developing what became a weeklong series. Why? King had recently joined his family in surrounding his favorite aunt during her final days. He responded enthusiastically when one of his top reporters proposed informing the community about how seniors and their families can find better ways to meet life's greatest challenge.

More recently, in 2004 Nancy Weaver Teichert, award-winning reporter on aging for the *The Sacramento Bee*, stressed the importance of targeted coverage about issues in aging in an article for *Age Beat*. "Without a special column, section, or other guaranteed niche, news reporters who cover issues in aging for the main news sections of a publication have to compete with celebrities, recall elections, and state budget deficits for space to get news on aging issues into the newspaper," she says. "It's not uncommon to hear an editor who does not deal with stories about aging say at a news meeting, 'Well, we've written about bad nursing homes already,' or 'Haven't we already covered aging baby boomers enough?'"[4]

The simplest way for businesses to counter ageism in U.S. news management is to feed reporters newsworthy stories that will appeal to their editors. Age beat reporters do not follow the medical model of reporting on aging—the disease-of-the-week approach. They might cover health and aging, but they will also write about housing, Medicare, Medicaid, personal finance, lifestyle issues, and other stories that might end up in different parts of the newspaper.

Some age beat writers on retirement-finance issues might be anchored to the business desk, but they will inevitably branch out when they learn about the broader movement to redefine retirement. Other reporters on aging are on news desks, science units, the features section, general assignment, and elsewhere.

Paul has conducted three national surveys of journalists on aging since 1994. The latest survey, in 2001, showed that only half the stories written or planned by reporters on aging were about health. The rest were all over the map. "The age beat is not the kind of assignment that boosts a career up the newsroom ladder—at least not yet," Paul says. He estimates that 50 to 60 newspapers in the United States have reporters assigned to cover aging on a part-time basis. He found that the assignment was most often proposed by the reporter and approved by an editor, both of whom often had personal experience with the world of aging.[5]

Sixty percent of the 152 age beat reporters surveyed in 2001 were women, and the reporters had an average of 22 years of experience as professional journalists, with eight years on the age beat. Most of the reporters are baby boomers, and virtually all of them had experienced aspects of issues in aging themselves or through their families.[6] The reporters have a passion and a deep desire to bring helpful resources to the reader. They also have a uniquely helpful relationship with one another, in marked contrast to the competitive world of other media groups.

Many age beat journalists have a long-term commitment to issues in aging and are continually looking for fresh angles, including "unretirement" possibilities for boomers and the effects of population aging on schools and prisons. Because age beat reporters tend to weave these threads together over time, they and their articles can be among the best sources the world of business can find about developments in the field, especially trends that might affect the climate for certain products and services.

The aging of the population is also a global interest. For example, most Japanese newspapers began an age beat when the government made a major commitment to old age security in 1990. Journalist Ritsuko Inokuma says that the media in her rapidly aging country—one of the oldest national populations in the world—has tagged the issues as the "2007 problem," for the year when the first Japanese baby boomers retire. In 2000, Inokuma's newspaper, *The Yomiuri Shimbun*, with a circulation of 10 million, became the first Japanese daily to establish a special age beat called "the social security news department," with 11 staff members. The rival national daily, *Asahi*, and the Kyodo news agency soon followed with their own social security news departments.[7]

Diversity Media

AARP's *Segunda Juventud* is a Spanish-language bimonthly magazine for the huge, expanding—and aging—Latino market in the United States. The magazine's growth has been rapid, and in 2005, AARP launched a radio version.[8] The rapidly growing ethnic and racial diversity of the older population suggests that many product areas might well be targeted to these groups.

Another media segment to watch is publications for older people who are lesbian, gay, bisexual, and transgender (LGBT)—nowadays, this is the preferred term to *gay and lesbian*. Gerard Koskovich, staff coordinator of ASA's Lesbian and Gay Aging Issues Network (LGAIN) and editor of its OutWord Online newsletter, told me, "The LGBT media have had a spotty record for reporting aging-related stories, although many outlets have been improving."[9] He recommends checking OutWord Online periodically for its Media Watch column.

Media Relations: The Basics

To make sure your business takes full advantage of media opportunities, watch the specialized news and features outlets carefully. One helpful resource is the *Senior Media Directory* published by Mature Market Resource Center. Its 2004-2005 edition includes 285 pages of media listings, 77 pages more than the 2002 version. The industry newsletter *Selling to Seniors* is also a great resource. It recently launched two new publications for boomers: *Satisfaction*, aimed at affluent boomers in the Chicago area (Chicagoland Publishing Company, owned by Tribune Media Services), and *NYCPlus*, a tabloid for the 50-plus market that hit New York City streets in the spring of 2005. Another market entry is *GeezerJock*, for athletes age 40 and older. In 2005, this Chicago-based independent magazine claimed 45,000 subscribers. Another 2004 entry was *Grand Magazine*, based in St. Petersburg, Florida, for grandparents age 45 and older.

Focusing on age beat reporters can save you time and money. The rule of thumb is that 10% of a marketing budget should be spent on public relations. Reserve more for a digital marketing strategy—such as convocations where you meet potential customers and invite repeat customers to live events on your website—and then do some print and radio.

You also should develop a media background document with facts, figures, and clear explanations about the market you are trying to reach and how your product or service meets particular needs. Besides offering your own expertise, you might suggest contacting gerontologists not affiliated with your firm who can provide reporters with an overview of the social concerns your company is addressing. Keep in mind that journalists usually have specific assignments and are looking for people who can help them. If you provide them with a solid story and sources they can use, you'll hear from them again.

One of the new tricks in media relations is linking old media, such as print, to the new electronic outlets. "We've found that readers really like some kind of interactivity to relate a story to themselves," says Carolyn Said, who recently covered the age beat for *The San Francisco Chronicle*. "For example, when I wrote about Posit Science, we asked the company to provide a brief memory test that readers could administer to themselves. We ran this as a box accompanying the story. It drew tremendous interest." Posit Science could have generated even greater public response, she adds, "had the company provided an online interactive test, or a brief online demonstration of their software exercises." In general, companies in today's media markets need to invest in their own media capability in order to take advantage of press coverage when they generate it, such as by creating game-like interactive demonstrations or other ways to engage Internet visitors.

"Working with journalists to maximum effect means building relationships," says Carolyn.[10] *Wall Street Journal* editor Glenn

Ruffenach noted that relationships with sources begin with a good story. "The best pitches are those in which a product or service is put in context—something that's part of a larger story, or that highlights a broader theme or a significant trend."[11] Some examples are services that help older adults grapple with rising health costs, financial products or strategies that help older consumers manage a fragile nest egg, companies or organizations that are responding to older consumers' growing appetite for educational services or educational travel, and intergenerational travel.

Encore: Developing a Niche

Glenn has guided *The Wall Street Journal's* "Encore: A Guide to Retirement Planning and Living" almost as a new product line at the newspaper. In 1997, the paper decided to devote a special report to retirement. "We assumed this would be a one-time look at retirement," Glenn recalls. "But as we started assigning and writing articles, we found that the people we were interviewing—primarily age 50-plus— had dozens and dozens of questions about aging and retirement, questions about money and health and travel and estate planning and inheritance and working in later life and generational issues." He queried his editors about possibly developing a series of reports.

"I felt very strongly that there was a huge appetite for information about navigating life after 50," he says. "As it turned out, my bosses were thinking along the same lines."

In 1998, *WSJ* began publishing Encore as a quarterly special section mailed to the newspaper's 400,000 subscribers who were age 50 or older. Six issues will be published in 2006. Starting in 2002, *WSJ* ceased publishing Encore as a targeted special mailing—and began inserting it into every issue of the paper. "A big part of that decision was a perceived interest among all readers (not just those age 50-plus) in preparing for, and navigating, later life," Glenn says. More than 2 million people now see Encore.

Glenn's bosses at *WSJ* felt so confident in the future of regular retirement coverage that they had him start a biweekly column for *WSJ's* Sunday edition, which is included as a supplement in almost 90 newspapers across the United States. They assigned staff reporter Kelly Greene to work on both the quarterly report and the Sunday feature, which eventually turned into a weekly column. "The Sunday column gives us exposure to an audience of about 10 million people across the country," Glenn says. "One of the best measures of our success has been reader response. We get hundreds of emails and letters each year asking for additional advice and information."

Glenn hopes to publish 10 or 12 issues of Encore per year as boomers begin retiring. "In some ways, I feel as if our coverage about later life is just getting started," he says.[12]

Why Not More Coverage?

Why isn't there more advertising support for the coverage of an area of social change that affects so many people and every aspect of twenty-first century life? And why are there so few outlets for organizations and businesses reaching out to the rapidly aging population? "My biggest ax to grind," says Steve Slon, editor of *AARP The Magazine*, "is simply that most companies neglect this huge market."[13]

In his book *Advertising to Boomers*, Chuck Nyren observes, "We're the elephant in the room that everybody ignores. Actually, we're the cash cow everybody ignores. This is a big mistake." The primary victims are "tens of thousands of companies, large and small, who have products and services for the consumer market. When a company hires an advertising agency, it's a good bet that they are *not* getting their money's worth."[14]

Even products designed for older audiences continue to be "targeted young," such as Buick's use of Tiger Woods. In fact, according to an article printed in *American Demographics*, Buick stands 8th in sales to those 50 or older—and 25th among younger consumers. The article notes that even though annual household spending on goods and services is about 10% lower in 50-plus homes than in younger house-holds, per capita spending by those age 50 or older is 30% higher.[15]

One of the main models being touted in newspaper management is the "Experience Paper," the daily that attracts new readers by couching editorial content in terms relating to their own experiences. These efforts are almost entirely focused on generating more reader-ship among young adults. Relatively few newspapers—and fewer other news outlets—are paying much attention to the experiences of aging boomers and their parents.

The attitude of benign neglect toward older readers—counting on their steady business while ignoring coverage of stories that affect them the most—pervades the newspaper industry. This attitude was expressed by Mary Nesbitt, managing director of Northwestern University's Readership Institute, which is conducting a large news-paper readership study. She explained that newspapers need to pur-sue younger readers because "the current framework continues to serve older, more loyal readers at the expense of younger, less fre-quent readers. Younger adult readers continue to erode at a frighten-ing pace; older readers much less so."[16]

In fact, newspapers are losing everyday readers at every age. Paul says, "It's as if Macy's ordered their sales staff to ignore the regular older costumers standing at the counters and to run outside to beckon in the younger people walking by. Aging boomers and their parents need information about health, finance, and other areas to help them navigate their later years. The newspaper industry needs to wake up and smell the demographics."[17]

New Media, New Opportunities

The real competition is for reader attention, not age groups. Podcasts, webcasts, blogs, wikis, and other media converging around Internet ac-cess are reforesting the media and marketing landscapes. The cross-fertilization of media technologies might well deactivate old advertising models and open new opportunities for both marketers and journalists to serve our aging society.

Dick Lee, a marketing consultant who owns High Yield Methods, Inc., sees hope for reaching the boomer market: "The demographic of Internet users is getting older by the year. It certainly feels like Internet content is much more responsive to participant profiles than is the case for other media. Health information sites, for example, are proliferating to meet user demand. Also, advertising agencies have precious little impact on web content, which frees the Internet of agency age skew and allows Internet content providers to find their own audiences without agency interference."[18]

Exactly how the current technology explosion will offer new opportunities to effectively target audiences remains to be seen. Marketing executives will be watching new media with the rest of us, and they too will be experimenting with it. Some marketing executives are already working to get their products mentioned in respected blogs and online newsletters. But whatever direction media and technology take, it will be important to follow the reporters who write with passion about aging.

Endnotes

1. Jeff Zimman, email message to author, September 18, 2008. The Posit Science video is available at http://www.msnbc.msn.com/id/6974765/, and ongoing news coverage of Posit Science can be found at http://www.positscience.com/newsroom/news/.

2. Glenn Ruffenach, email message to Paul Kleyman, September 29, 2005.

3. Paul Kleyman, interview by author, March 29, 2006.

4. Nancy Weaver Teichert, "The Age Beat's Hard-News Challenge," *Age Beat*, Fall 2004, 2.

5. Paul Kleyman, interview by author, March 29, 2006.

6. Paul Kleyman, "The Journalists' Exchange on Aging Third National Survey: The Agebeat's Heartbeat Steady, Despite Ageist Media Economics," *Age Beat*, Fall 2001.

7. John Cutter, "On the Age Blog," Age Beat Online/The Blog, http://agebeat.blogspot.com/2005/10/age-beat-online-oct-18-2005-continued.html   (quoting Ritsuko Inokuma).

8. AARP, "AARP's Original Spanish-Language Radio Program Hits the Airwaves," December 15, 2004, http://www.aarp.org/research/press-center/presscurrent-news/a2005-01-12-radio.html.

9. Gerard Koskovich, email message to Paul Kleyman, August 1, 2005.

10. Carolyn Said, email message to Paul Kleyman.

11. Glenn Ruffenach, email message to Paul Kleyman, September 29, 2005.

12. *Ibid.*

13. Steve Slon, email message to Paul Kleyman.

14. Chuck Nyren, *Advertising to Baby Boomers* (Ithaca, NY: Paramount Marketing Publishing, 2005), 8.

15. Bradley Johnson, "Implications of Latest Baby Boomer Milestone/50-Plus Age Group Accounts for Half of U.S. Auto Sales," *American Demographics*, July 4, 2005.

16. Mary Nesbitt, email message to Paul Kleyman, July 20, 2005.

17. Paul Kleyman, interview by author, March 29, 2006.

18. Dick Lee, email message to Paul Kleyman, May 31, 2005.

12

GROWING THE BOOMER BUSINESS: SALES AND MARKETING STRATEGIES THAT REALLY WORK

Introduction

One of the key points of this book is that life transitions create business opportunities. In previous pages, you've seen how the transitions in baby boomers' lives are creating underserved markets ripe with potential. This chapter shows how to bring commercial innovations to consumers using new sales and marketing tools that have developed in recent years.

As more businesses become aware of the unprecedented number of people around the world who are approaching 60, they are getting serious about reaching boomers. Call it the new Silver and Gold Rush. Smart businesses understand that the old media—print, radio, and television—won't be enough to reach this market. To communicate with boomers, your business will need to evaluate and choose among a wide variety of online and offline marketing methods. And you will need to go beyond marketing to the sale, which is the critical function that will allow you to build a sustainable business.

Alan Rothenberg, a co-founder of ThirdAge Media, used to say, "Revenue is what keeps the doors open." This chapter is about setting a sales strategy, building a revenue pipeline, and managing the sales process. The best businesses have strong and deep sales pipelines. They are careful to honor the length of the sales process, and they never forget how to qualify a prospect. This chapter also explains why technology, making connections, and thinking global are three of the biggest themes to remember when targeting boomers.

Entrepreneurs often focus on product and service development and forget about tracking the progress of the company. But the best executives—like Mike Bloomberg, the media-mogul-turned-mayor-of-New York—manage to the numbers. If you master the new technologies for sales and marketing, you can harvest the information they generate to get a better sense of how you're doing.

There are many reasons why online marketing is a must for reaching boomers. This chapter will review the best practices for creating a winning website, the first of several touch points when you're building customer relationships. It will describe new technologies, including blogs, podcasts, and RSS feeds, as well as more basic subjects such as how to write good copy. Finally, this chapter will give you some basic rules to follow when working with government contracts, and it will show you how to manage a profitable sales effort.

Reaching the Wired Boomer

The cheapest way to get insights about your customer is to gather information online. The information you get from a website, web log, or email campaign can make your spending on print, radio, and television much more efficient. Or you might be better off ignoring traditional media altogether. At least one successful company aimed at boomers spends 10% of its marketing budget on its website and the other 90% on improving the website's position in the results of web search engines, such as Google.

Most boomers have vivid memories of television: their first black-and-white set, the birth of color, and the arrival of cable. Television's ability to reach a mass audience has had a profound influence on this generation. But the most profound media innovation of the baby boom era wasn't television—it was the Internet.

The Internet now drives the connection between brands and consumers, and it also drives social connections between people. As Internet access has become ubiquitous and its capabilities have evolved, communications have become democratized and decentralized, giving an entirely new meaning to the old expression "power to the people." Consumers decide what they want to receive, when they will get it, and in what format it will arrive. If you're marketing a company in the twenty-first century, you need to understand this shift.

We are entering what some observers have called Web 2.0, thanks to a number of new tools that make the Internet more collaborative and participatory. This technology is spawning a huge amount of consumer-generated content. Web logs, or *blogs*, are web-based journals that have periodic posts by one or many contributors. There are also video web logs, or *vlogs*; downloadable audio files known as *podcasts*; and collaborative web projects called *wikis* that all represent new forms of individual expression. One of the best examples of a wiki is Wikipedia (www.wikipedia.org), a free content encyclopedia to which anyone can contribute. You may have even contributed content to the Web yourself by posting family photos on sites such as Flickr or reviewing a product you purchased on BizRate, Epinions, eBay, or Amazon.

The growth in user-generated content sites and social networking sites has been phenomenal. Among the fastest-growing websites from February 2005 to February 2006, measured by site traffic increase, were Blogger.com (528%), MySpace.com (318%), Wikipedia.org (275%), and Citysearch.com (185%).[1]

Recognizing the unmet need for a social networking website for the 50-plus audience, Jeff Taylor, founder of Monster.com, launched Eons.com in July, 2006. Eons.com content includes health, money, entertainment, love, home, and interactive tools. The site also has a nationwide database of obituaries to which Eons.com members can add photos and videos. Members can also receive region-specific death alerts.

Safa Rashtchy, managing director and senior analyst of Internet research with Piper Jaffray & Co., cites five major Internet growth areas: 1) online communities and content (social networking, viral, photo sharing, blogs); 2) local search; 3) wireless media and services; 4) web applications; and 5) online entertainment. Safa indicates that communications, commerce, and entertainment will be the fastest-growing areas for web applications. Search will continue to grow as a critical means for exploring information and as a gateway for commerce. The Internet has changed our lives already and there are bigger changes to come, as the Internet will be integrated into our lives.[2]

Advertisers realize that, because of the Internet, they have much less control over their brand and the consumer opinions surrounding it than they once did. Everyone who has web access can make their opinions known through public forums. It is also significant that advances in technology have been exceeding the mainstream adoption of those technologies. This means that marketers will benefit from watching closely and experimenting with new tools as they emerge.

Why You Should Have an Online Marketing Strategy

Older adults are going online in record numbers. People over age 50 now account for about one quarter of all U.S. Internet users, according to eMarketer, and their numbers are growing at 7 to 8% each year, compared with 2 to 3% for overall Internet user growth.[3] In 2005, almost two thirds of U.S. adults age 50 to 64, and 25% of those age 65 and older used the Internet, according to the Pew Internet and American Life Project.[4] Boomers are also enthusiastic about high-speed Internet connections, as 44% of Internet users age 50 to 64 have this service. Broadband users tend to stay online longer,[5] which means they are more likely to see online marketing. And broadband connections give marketers more options—they can add audio files to websites, and they can give visitors more opportunities to interact with their databases.

Boomers are such a large group that their behavior online is much like that of the general Internet audience. They send and read email, look up health and medical information, research products prior to purchase, get financial data, view maps, and check the weather. Seventy-five percent of boomer Internet users get news online, 55% research jobs, and 31% use instant messaging, according to the Pew study.[6] But baby boomers spend more money online than average online users do; according to a study from Jupiter Research, 37% of boomers who bought products or services on the Web said they spent more than $250 in the last three months, compared with 32% of all online users. Three out of four baby boomers say they have made online purchases of products or services at some point.[7]

Online Marketing Today—Best Practices and New Technologies

"Let the marketplace drive the marketing," says Anne Holland. She is president of MarketingSherpa, Inc., a research firm on marketing tactics. "The key thing that most people get wrong is to start by looking at what their competition is doing. They build their marketing tactics in reaction to their competition. But this is me-too marketing. Merely advertising in the same places, using the same tactics, usually doesn't work well."

Anne brings a unique perspective to the world of online marketing, which can be overwhelming to newcomers. She worked for a large business-to-business company before founding MarketingSherpa in 2000. The firm publishes case studies twice weekly to keep readers informed about what's working and what isn't in web marketing. "Search marketing is still a strong trend," she says. "Brand awareness can be built through online search and also purchase intent. It can make a tremendous difference."[8]

Internet shoppers rely on search engines more than anything else when they're looking for something. If you're new to the Web, a search engine is a website such as Google.com that allows you to type in a word, phrase, or name for free and almost instantly get leads to websites that are closely related to what you typed. If your goal is to drive traffic to your website, it is prudent to include your website's address (also known as a uniform resource locator, or URL) in all your promotional efforts.

When asked how they typically found websites in the past month, 83% of respondents said they used search engines, 54% linked from another website, 49% clicked on an email from family or friends, 47% typed in the web address, and 43% linked from a source heard by word of mouth, according to Forrester Research. Thirty-six percent of respondents saw the URL in a print advertisement, 34% saw it in a television advertisement, 33% picked it up from a news story, and 32% linked from a promotional email. Only 16% had clicked on an ad in another website (known in the trade as a *banner ad*).[9]

The top search engine and directory sites in terms of searches are Google, Yahoo! Search, MSN Search, AOL Search, and Ask.[10] Most commercial search engines sell guaranteed placement—in other words, a site that pays them is guaranteed to show up in the first page of results for certain keywords. Paid search is based on keywords, or words that may be used by people who are seeking information on the Internet. However, a good marketing strategy will include ways to get a higher ranking in both paid and unpaid returns. For those wanting to try paid search, there are many online resources available. Google and Yahoo! Search have excellent tutorials, tools, and tips. Another website, Wordtracker.com, helps you settle on the best keywords for your site.

The most common way to pay for a search engine listing is called *pay per click*, or *PPC*. As more advertisers use paid search services, the cost of each click has risen. The best way to manage this rising cost is to understand what you're selling and buy very specific keyword phrases. For example, if you sell health insurance, use phrases such as "group health insurance," rather than just "insurance." Your website's ad is more likely to appear on searches when the keywords are highly relevant to the viewer's query. Another important principle is to actively manage your online ad campaign by testing the headline, the description, the offer, and which keywords get good levels of response. Track your results by creating a separate website for each campaign, and make sure you track both click-through (people who visit your site) and conversion (people who buy). A strong call to action encourages click-through.

Email Marketing

In the world of email, *spam* refers to unsolicited commercial messages sent via email. Spammers usually send out thousands or millions of messages indiscriminately. But email marketing continues to grow at an explosive pace, despite the public's hatred of spam, for one simple reason: It's inexpensive. And if you do it correctly, email marketing won't even annoy your customers.

If unsolicited email is spam, house email lists are filet mignon. A house list is composed of people who already have some awareness of and interaction with you, and they have given permission for you to contact them. "The key," says Anne, "is to grow house lists and target within those lists. This means that you need a heck of a database."[11] You can always go out and buy that database—you can rent a commercial email list of people who have given their permission to be contacted (in industry parlance, they have *opted in*)—but this is much more expensive and less effective than doing it yourself.

Smart online marketers tie their email database to their order database, their in-store or e-couponing programs, and perhaps a newspaper insert program as well. "All the ways I'm touching people tie in," says Anne. "I can measure what works and how many times I've touched that person, how I'm interacting. When you're considering a CRM [customer relationship management] system, ask yourself, 'How am I going to tie this all together and understand the relationship with the customer? How did the email campaign affect sales, store traffic, and catalog sales?'"[12]

Batch and blast is the industry's term for mass, untargeted email campaigns, which are becoming less and less effective. More companies are using segmented lists, personalized messages, and offers they know are relevant to the lives of recipients. The campaign must be designed to encourage an ongoing customer relationship. Send relevant information to selected people who are most likely to be interested in your offer and will want to stay in touch with you.

Email campaigns are generally more successful in retaining customers than they are in acquiring new ones. Offering online coupons is one exception to this rule. However, email is most often used to distribute newsletters, value-added information, and special offers to existing customers. It creates an implied relationship between the company and the reader and provides another touch point with the consumer.

Anne says that co-registration is effective when a consumer requires a significant amount of education before making a purchase decision.[13] Co-registration takes place at the point of registration or order confirmation on a website. Users are given the opportunity to request information from their choice of the site's named partners (each partner must have a separate checkbox for opt-in). If they click Yes, their contact information becomes a lead that is sent to the partner. This opt-in process is called *co-registration*. Each lead costs the advertiser between $0.50 and $5 per name, depending on the quality of the name and brand and the amount of data transmitted. Financial services, insurance, time shares, technical products, and high-ticket products do well with co-registration.

"Co-registration leads work best when you offer something special and educational, like an insurance university tutorial if you're in that business," says Anne. "This reinforces your reputation as a trusted adviser. Don't be sales-y when you contact leads, but do be sexy and interesting. Send two messages a week for the next couple of weeks, and maybe seven or eight messages in all. Include a link to the opportunity to purchase each time. The key is to not just grab names from co-registration, dump them into the house file, and send regular sales information. These are newbies. Give them something special. Then measure how many people take advantage of your offer by signing up for something or buying something from you. That's the conversion rate. This will work with boomers because boomers have the patience and interest to learn something that's educational."[14]

Your Website as the First Touch Point

Your company's website is the cornerstone of a sound online marketing strategy. These days, when you speak to a potential client on the phone, they are typing your website's keywords into Google while you are talking to them (a process known as *Googling*). Prospective customers expect your website to teach them about you and your product or service. They also want to use the website to interact with you, learn how to purchase, and receive responsive customer service. Your website needs to provide so much valuable information that clients will want to sign up for your email newsletter and bookmark your site.

A site's branding should be consistent with the company's marketing materials. Both should be designed for readability and usability—remember that boomers have aging eyes. The navigation should be straightforward. The content must be excellent and refreshed often. The text should be easy to read and have high contrast against its background. Avoid small, light gray copy. Use plenty of white space. Use images to tell a story, but be conservative in the number of images you use and prudent in the length of text. Primary messages should be "above the fold"—that is, what the viewer sees on the first page of your website—but boomers will scroll down the page if what they see up top is valuable. Make sure to include your telephone and email contact information, postal mail address, and perhaps a toll-free number throughout your website.

Your website should contain a strong call to action if you want it to generate leads. Make a special offer—encourage visitors to sign up for a regularly published newsletter, a free information download, or an opt-in to receive email and/or snail mail communications. This is how you build a house list. Your content should include useful interactive tools such as dealer locators, personalized assessments and quizzes, daily updates, and features. Give visitors a reason to return often.

Anyone who is targeting older adults needs to keep the special needs of disabled readers in mind. You will want to consult the National Institute on Aging and the National Library of Medicine's web usability guide.[15] You should also test your site with WebXact, a free online service that tests web pages for quality, accessibility, and privacy issues.[16]

Blogs, Podcasting, RSS Feeds—Should You Use the New Technologies?

Web logs are growing at a meteoric rate, with a new blog being created at the rate of one per second, says David Sifry, the founder and CEO of Technorati.com. David's company tracks millions of websites devoted to every conceivable topic, from "what I did today" to interviews with prisoners at the U.S. military facility at Guantanamo Bay.[17]

Visitors to the Technorati site can search for a topic that interests them and explore blogs on that topic. Those who are interested in publishing a blog themselves can go to sites such as Bloglines.com or Blogger.com and follow easy instructions to get started.

Anne Holland of MarketingSherpa says that blogging is "vanity publishing." She adds, "Journalists pay more attention to blogs than anyone else. Fifty-three percent of journalists read blogs daily to look for stories. What they used to find in press releases isn't exclusive anymore. It's on all the news feeds. They read blogs because it's fun, not because they need to, and that is the critical difference. They're passionate, special, personable, quirky, and cool. They probably don't have a great impact. But to a corporate marketer, blogs could be effective if you're willing to take on a fair amount of liability. People regularly lose their jobs because of blogs. But ads on blogs work, if they're specific to the blog audience. For instance, the last presidential race had ads on blogs for fundraising. It worked well because boomers give to presidential races."[18]

A blog can tell people about a new product, new uses for an existing product, and upcoming events. They are a tool for online instruction. If your idea for a blog serves a business purpose and its benefits can be measured, test it. Keep in mind that blogging has its roots in social networking, so its readers value authenticity and quality content. It's another way of building community.

Another new way of distributing content online also bears close watching. RSS, which stands for *really simple syndication,* allows consumers to build their own customized information packages by delivering automatically updated content from multiple websites. Popular RSS "feeds" include news headlines, industry or company news, stock prices, weather reports, sports and entertainment news, and special offers. These feeds can be received on a computer or through a PDA—that's web jargon for a personal digital assistant, a handheld device that is an organizer, a computer, and a cell phone.

One of the easiest and most popular ways to subscribe to RSS feeds is to go to www.my.yahoo.com and set up a free account. The key to using RSS feeds for marketing is to publish fresh, high-quality content frequently. But no one has real data yet on RSS feeds, says Anne; it isn't known yet how many people actually use this new device. Information overload is a common malaise these days, making it critical for marketers to carefully segment, target, and provide relevant, meaningful content.

Podcasting means publishing audio broadcasts via the Internet. Listeners can subscribe to feeds and receive periodic, self-selected audio programs. Sound files are usually delivered in the audio format known as MP3, downloaded by podcatching software, and played through speakers by a free program such as iTunes, QuickTime, or Windows Media Player. Podcasts can be created by using readily available software and hardware. The steps include recording the sound file, finding someone to host it, and notifying listeners of its availability. If you want your podcast to be studio-quality, professional producers have stepped into this market to help. Although not completely user friendly now, podcasting will become easier. As we gather more case studies, podcasting will become another marketing tool.

Although it is important to experiment with these new technologies, it is equally important not to divert any of your marketing budget away from proven tactics. The most critical element is how to measure success. What makes a campaign successful? For an online campaign, it goes beyond the number of people who visit your site. How are you going to track the leads that convert to sales? How will you determine the campaign's ROI (return on investment)?

How you measure success depends upon your marketing objectives and your budget. For instance, you may want to generate a specific number of leads by offering a free booklet. Set your goals at the beginning of the campaign based on that objective and how much you are willing to spend per lead. You will want to track both the *click-through rate*, which is the number of clicks divided by the number of times the ad was served up, and also the *conversion rate*, which compares the number of people who clicked though with the number of people who actually signed up. The number of conversions divided by the media dollars you've spent is one measure of performance—the cost per lead. By continually improving and testing the ad, and keeping track of how each change affects the cost per lead, you can learn what works best for you.

What You May Not Know About Radio: Boomers Are Big Listeners

Music defined the generation of boomers, and radio has always been a great way to reach this generation. "Radio listening increases with age, and radio is a great way to accomplish remarkable goals, especially branding," says B. Eric Rhoads, the chairman of Streamline Publishing, founder of *Radio Ink* magazine, and a startup veteran of three radio networks.[19]

Radio reaches more than 95% of Americans age 35 to 64 each week.[20] Oldies and classic rock appeal to baby boomers age 45 to 54, and so does smooth jazz. Classical is very popular among adults age 55 to 64, as is smooth jazz and talk radio. Adults age 65 and older are the majority of the audience for adult standards.[21]

"The key to use of radio is to not do it like television or print," says Eric. "The message needs to be well written. It should not be an audio version of a television ad. And the message must be played often and for a long period of time. Short campaigns can work, but long consistent campaigns build deep customer relationships and brand preference."

Your radio strategy should be based on what kind of customer you want to attract. If you are trying to make an immediate sale, you'll want to use short-term, quick attention-getting methods. If you want long-term relationships, you'll want to plant mental triggers and build awareness over time. "Radio can drive instant results," says Eric. "It can drive brand results, and it can motivate brand preferences. But most people don't know how to use radio properly, and many radio advertisers throw their dollars away because they will copy someone else's strategy even though it is not right for their needs. All strategy boils down to four equally important elements: message, frequency, placement, and time."[22]

A well-placed strategy with a poor message is a waste, as is a great message with poor frequency or placement. If you have a great radio marketing campaign driving customers to a website, but that site is poorly designed so that orders are difficult to place, your spending is wasted. Radio is great for direct response, but only if you're selling a direct-response kind of product.

If you don't know the industry, it is usually wise to hire a radio commercial producer and work with radio ad agencies that can help you create a campaign strategy. A local station should be willing to check the most recent Arbitron ratings to learn the stations that do the best job of reaching your target audience. The key to success, Eric suggests, is stability and consistency. "Buy 13 spots a day, seven days a week, for one year. Do this on as many stations as you can afford. Dominate only one if that is all you can afford. If you cannot afford this frequency, do 13 spots a day for six months instead of buying fewer spots over the course of a year. If you do this for two to four years, you will own the market."[23]

How do you measure the effectiveness of a radio campaign? If your goal is to establish long-term relationships, you can't test it quickly. Start by setting your expectations, and then design a campaign that will reach the audience you will need to get the returns you expect. You can test response rates by putting toll-free numbers or website addresses in the ads.

Internet radio looms on the horizon, but so far it cannot compete with the old-fashioned version. Internet-delivered stations only had about 6 million listeners per week in 2005.[24] Again, this is a technology to watch, but don't jump into it until you can test it.

The Meaning in the Message

Marketing to boomers is an arena in which trust, legitimacy, and authenticity are the watchwords. Most consumers have become numbed by hyperbole, and deception will produce a lasting negative impression.

You can learn a lot about the verbal and visual cues that get boomers' attention by talking to Susan Hoffman. She directs San Francisco State University's Osher Lifelong Learning Institute, whose mission is to help older learners navigate the future and find ways to make a difference in their communities. The Institute defines its audience as "cultural creatives," or people who align their time and money with their values. The typical student is a well-educated woman with a progressive social agenda who places a high value on self-expression.

"Our students are thinking about life after 50, the people they've known, making sense of their lives, and leaving a legacy," says Susan. "We have learned that you must be very careful with your language when you're talking to people over 50. There are actually three generations of Americans over age 50. Each has different needs and expectations around time and money, and they respond to the world differently. Boomers are more emotional. Seniors are very rational."

The Institute's marketing copy is primarily for boomers, so it emphasizes energy, animation, and emotion. Every word and image is carefully selected—nothing is accidental. It avoids using the words *senior, older*, and *elderly*. It makes its points with strong quotes and short references that add credibility. And it makes extensive use of photographs. "Image is inspiration," Susan says. "People want to see people who are younger than they are and they want to see them doing things and learning." Though stock photography has its place, Susan advises building your own archive and testing responsiveness to the images. "If you're marketing to people aged 50 to 75, most of the images should show people aged 45 to 50. We typically put at least two dozen photographs in a brochure."

Susan's marketing tactics include large direct mail mailings, email campaigns, online marketing, pledge drives, public relations efforts, and placing four-color brochures at venues such as libraries and community centers. Her secret weapon is building high-value partnerships with like-minded nonprofit organizations. "This has been instrumental to getting established," Susan reveals. "It creates word-of-mouth and enables cross-marketing, both of which are helpful."[25]

Washington, Medicare, and Marketing

The Internet isn't the only locus of power for baby boomers. Another crucial place is Washington, D.C., where there are numerous groups that influence spending on medical care, pensions, and other things of key importance to adults age 50 and older. Veterans' groups; the National Association of Federal Retired Employees (NAFRE); AARP; and niche groups like the Older Women's League, the Gray Panthers, and the Visiting Nurses Association are all based in Washington or maintain a presence there. When you're doing business with these groups, the name of the game is forming connections.

When Pfizer announced its ShareCard in conjunction with the National Council on Aging and the American Society on Aging last year, it was following an "association strategy." Another company that understands this strategy well is The SCOOTER Store, which makes high-quality power wheelchairs and scooters. It now has approximately 1,100 employees and 23 retail stores throughout the United States. Its average customer is age 78 and typically suffers from chronic conditions such as arthritis, cardiopulmonary disease, and diabetes.

"Baby boomers will be our customer base 10 years from now," says president Mike Pfister. "Between now and then, society must accept what it means to get older. It doesn't mean going to nursing homes. It's important to go to church and the grocery store on your own, and to have fun shopping as if it were 20 years ago. The SCOOTER Store helps restore freedom and independence to those with limited mobility. By doing that, we create a better society for everyone."

The SCOOTER Store is a durable medical equipment supplier, and most of its customers' power wheelchair and scooters are covered by Medicare. To earn a Medicare supplier number, a company must meet 23 standards and undergo a regular federal audit. Mike says that if you are considering a Medicare strategy, there are three crucial issues: "risk profile, patience, and passion." Medicare is a complex federal agency, so patience is important. Because coverage criteria can be complex, it can sometimes take years to get paid on disputed claims. The Scooter Store has a group that works to understand the federal government's direction and influence nascent policies before they are finalized.

Mike says that the springboard for The SCOOTER Store's success was its decision to advertise directly to consumers. It wants people to understand the Medicare benefits available to them and the characteristics of the equipment so they can make informed choices. The SCOOTER Store's marketing includes several million direct mail pieces dropped each month. Television and Internet-based advertising has also been effective. Targeting influential people with face-to-face visits is another key: 80 account managers call on doctors and clinical groups that can prescribe a power chair or scooter. The latest push is to partner The SCOOTER Store with other organizations, such as Visiting Angels and Meals on Wheels.[26]

Creating a World-Class Sales Campaign—Best Practices

Recruiting a great sales team is essential to the success of any business, but great salespeople are not easy to find. You need sales leaders who are hungry enough to make 10 sales calls per week, diligent enough to write up detailed reports on each call, and mature enough to deliver on their promises. When you have to ask yourself, "Do I have the right sales person?," you don't. It's best to say goodbye and upgrade.

Vince Thompson, author of *Ignited*, wanted to make a change from television advertising sales to Internet sales when he left CBS. He quickly created a prospect list, sourced accounts, developed a team to support his efforts, and created rapport with the client services group. Every sales call with Vince was successful and fun, which is how sales works best. Here is his story.

As regional vice president for America Online Networks Sales and Solutions, Vince led teams responsible for selling millions of dollars per week in online media. Vince also built AOL's first sales training and leadership organization. "Figure out who your target customer is and go talk to them," he says. "Understand what their needs are, build a product to fit their needs, give them incredible service, be available to them, listen, and try to come up with a flexible approach that works and makes sense. The type of business will dictate the sales solution you need to put in place."

He advises entrepreneurs and sales professionals, "You should be able to tell your story in a couple of sentences. People should be able to understand quickly what you do, what it is you sell, and how it can benefit them. Customers listen to that. Tell a story about why you're in business, why you're doing what you're doing, how it solves problems for people. And practice telling that story so it becomes something that you're good at telling."

What is your unique selling proposition, the thing business schools call a *USP*? Maybe you're the market leader in innovation—if you are, you can command any kind of price; or maybe you sell for less; or maybe you're solving somebody's unique problem. Your USP should set your business apart. You can differentiate on all kinds of levels— sometimes it's on service. These days, you must make sure that your USP is tailored to each individual customer. So follow through, do your research, and understand your customer's needs. Success comes when you bring solutions that can help customers accomplish their goals.

After you have the pitch down, build revenue through constant activity. Stay up to date with the news, read press releases, go to networking events, and learn about the market and its players. Vince also suggests "discovery meetings" that may occur before the pitch. "I try to understand their business problem, what they're trying solve, where they're spending money—do they need new sales, need to reposition their brand, need to prop their company up for a sale? Then I come up with a solution that does the most for them, if they're willing to buy. This is called a *needs assessment*. Have a list of questions and try to answer most of them before the meeting, so the valuable meeting time will focus on the things that matter most. Follow up with a sales proposal. The prospect may need to build consensus and work with other people prior to buying, so you write to that." Vince helps companies sell the proposal internally, understanding there may be a number of decision makers.

When building a sales organization, "You can't manage the market or market conditions—but you can manage behaviors and set expectations," Vince advises sales managers. "If you have a history with the sales organization, you can begin to take numbers and figure out baselines—knowing the sales per quarter, the close ratio, the number of calls you have to make. You can use a sales management tool like Salesforce or Upshot. You can analyze the hell out of it, but what matters is that you're focusing on the right things."

"To develop the best practices for your industry, make a spreadsheet. In each column, put a problem—like 'I need customers,' 'Getting referrals,' 'Making presentations,' 'Following through'—all the things you're thinking about. Then go out and interview the people in the industry. Maybe they aren't direct competitors, but people who have similar types of businesses. Ask them, 'What is the best way you have found to get to customers?' Then build your own best practices document, based on people you respect. Keep on filling in all the best practices you hear. When you're done, you're going to have a roadmap of the best practices and best ideas."[27]

One of the biggest mistakes that entrepreneurs make is not making their sales numbers because they fall in love with their product or service and stop living by the spreadsheet. So make sure your sales goals are on your desktop and refer back to them every two or three days. It doesn't matter if you are a nonprofit, a for-profit, or a venture-backed company. Strong and creative sales forecasting, great sales teams, good knowledge about what the client needs and wants, and a strong product or service are all critical.

One of the most effective aspects of a sales strategy is to build a community of customers and share knowledge with them. ThirdAge was at the nexus of two trends, the wired boomer/senior and the mature consumer, so our customers appreciated sharing information with each other. Bring your customers together for annual events. Private client meetings can also be extremely effective. These events help build and reinforce your brand. And if they are insightful and fun, the sponsors will return.

Endnotes

1. comScore Media Metrix, 2006.
2. Safa Rashtchy, "The Future of Internet and Boomers" (Keynote presentation, Silicon Valley Boomer Venture Summit, Santa Clara, CA, June 20, 2006).
3. Debra Aho Williamson, "Seniors Online: How Aging Boomers Will Shake up the Market," eMarketer.com, 2005.
4. Pew Internet and American Life Project, "Demographics of Internet Users," 2004, http://www.pewinternet.org/trends/DemographicsofInternetUsers.htm.

5. Internet Retailer, "Number of broadband users explodes, NetRatings reports," www.internetretailer.com.

6. Susannah Fox, "Older Americans and the Internet," Pew Internet and American Life Project, March 8, 2004, 13, http://www.pewinternet.org/PPF/r/117/report_display.asp.

7. Internet Retailer, "Baby Boomers Spend More than Other Age Groups, Jupiter Says," August 1, 2005, http://internetretailer.com/dailyNews.asp?id=15661.

8. Anne Holland, interview by Marty Silberstein, August 1, 2005.

9. Forrester's Consumer Technographics, North American Devices, Media, and Marketing Online Study, August 2004.

10. "Double Digit Growth in Search Seen by AOL and Ask Jeeves from Q1 to Q2, While Top Search Players Google and Yahoo! Maintain Consistent Growth, According to Nielsen/Net Ratings," Net Ratings, Inc., July 21, 2005, http://www.nielsen-netratings.com/pr/pr_050721.pdf.

11. Anne Holland, interview by Marty Silberstein, August 1, 2005.

12. *Ibid.*

13. *Ibid.*

14. *Ibid.*

15. "Make Your Web Site Senior Friendly: A Checklist," National Institute on Aging and the National Library of Medicine, http://www.nlm.nih.gov/pubs/checklist.pdf.

16. WebXACT, http://webxact.watchfire.com/; "Web Content Accessibility Guidelines," The World Wide Web Consortium (W3C), http://www.w3.org/WAI/.

17. Technorati, http://www.technorati.com.

18. Anne Holland, interview by Marty Silberstein, August 1, 2005.

19. B. Eric Rhoads, email message to Marty Silberstein, August 3, 2005.

20. Arbitron, Inc., *2001 Radio Today: How America Listens to Radio* (Arbitron, Inc., 2002), http://www.arbitron.com/downloads/radiotoday01.pdf.

21. Arbitron, Inc., *Radio Today: How American Listens to Radio, 2005 Edition* (Arbitron, Inc., 2005). See Arbitron.com for data on listenership, format, stations and ratings, and geographic breakdown.

22. B. Eric Rhoads, email message to Marty Silberstein, August 3, 2005.

23. *Ibid.*

24. Arbitron, Inc., "November 2005 comScore Arbitron Online Radio Ratings," http://www.arbitron.com/onlineradio/nov_ratings_2005.htm.

25. Susan Hoffman, interview by Marty Silberstein, August 2, 2005. Susan's website is www.cel.sfsu.edu/olli.

26. Mike Pfister, interview by Marty Silberstein, August 1, 2005.

27. Vince Thompson, interview by Marty Silberstein, August 12, 2005.

13

THE CLASS ACT: GOLD AT THE END OF THE RAINBOW

The third act of life is like a birthing process: Sooner or later, a person surrenders to the forces of aging and prepares to create something new and better, something that endures. Older adults tend to be more in tune with the spiritual nature of their lives; they want their final act of life to have meaning and purpose beyond accumulating and spending. As Jesuit scientist Pierre Teilhard de Chardin once said, "We are not human beings having a spiritual experience. We are spiritual beings having a human experience."

Boomers are learning that every moment is precious. They dream of a better world. They want to know that their lives have mattered and that they will leave behind something of value and beauty.

Businesses that understand dream fulfillment, lifestage marketing, and the desire of baby boomers to make a difference will lead the pack. They understand this generation's compelling urge to redefine and invigorate the entire aging process. Baby boomers reject the negative stereotypes of aging and the marginalization of silver-haired people. They are bringing their 1960s idealism into their 60s. They want to build a new society where life experience is respected, where older people fully contribute to the dynamics of healthy communities. They want to bring awareness to the social issues that have plagued the aging process, and find real solutions that add to quality of life all around.

Three characteristics make the boomer generation different. First is the "bonus round," an extra decade or more of active life that will come to millions of boomers who have treated their bodies right. Second is their greater educational attainment and subsequently stronger financial resources that follow a college degree. Third is their passion to give back to society. This is the spiritual component of life. It is what the baby boom generation started in the 1970s with the human potential movement, and it is what they have the potential to realize today.

In his closing remarks at the 2005 Boomer Venture Summit, ABC News columnist Michael S. Malone spoke about the restlessness many boomers feel at midlife. He remembered hearing John Kennedy's call to arms in 1961—"ask not what your country can do for you, ask what you can do for your country." "It still haunts us, as if we haven't fulfilled that quest," he said. "It is as if we haven't answered it the way our parents, the so-called Greatest Generation, did. We still have a great crusade ahead of us, maybe one last chance to change the world. It appears that our great crusade will be discovering how to grow old gracefully and teaching that to the generations that follow us."[1]

When psychologist Erik Erikson defined the life cycle, he saw the final stage, which usually begins in the 60s, as retrospective. He urged people in their 50s to plan for the challenge of integrating elders into community life. That is the overarching theme of *Turning Silver into Gold*, answering that challenge and finding what gerontologists call "spiritual efficacy," or spiritual presence. Integrating older adults into society along the lines of traditional Japanese and Native American cultures exemplifies this mandate. It means a society where the role of older people expands: They mentor the young, heal the sick, mete out justice, declare war or peace, and tell stories that reveal the meaning of life. In sum, elders in these cultures ensure the spiritual well-being of the community.

Businesses that target boomers will need to ask deeper questions. What energizes boomers' spirits? Which causes inspire them? Which products and services will help them realize their dreams? Where can we build communities that will help elders retain their role as contributing members of society? And how can we help boomers fill the third act of life with the riches of family, creativity, and lifelong learning?

The businesses and organizations profiled in this book, and the ones yet to be created, are helping to create a new cultural sensitivity to midlife transitions. Loss is real at this stage of life and loneliness is a heartbeat away. It's up to boomers to set a new course. Whether it is restoring intimacy in a marriage, or building sustainable relationships, the most important job for businesses targeting this market is to serve these deep-felt human needs.

This period in history is "a moment of call," according to gerontologist Harry R. Moody of AARP. Balancing spirit with the bottom lines means that "people will pay a lot of money to fulfill their dreams."[2] By connecting with your customers in a much deeper way, you can do well and do good at the same time.

One of the areas that will be especially ripe for innovative business is civic engagement.

Even if boomers have not yet volunteered to the degree their parents' generation did, studies show that they want to give back during the third act of their lives. As boomers begin reaching age 65 in 2011, they will enjoy an average additional life expectancy of 18 years.[3] They will want to stay engaged, and volunteerism is a key opportunity after retirement.

"Boomers are certainly capable of amazing self-involvement," says Steve Slon, editor of *AARP The Magazine*. "But when something captures our interest, we will band together and make a difference." Tufts University has started a program to steer their 80,000 alumni between the ages of 40 and 70 toward civic engagement both locally and worldwide. The university hopes to establish a career center to help baby boomers with their next calling.[4]

Half of people in their 50s and 60s want to do work that helps others, according to a landmark survey of 1,000 Americans age 50 to 70. This "New Face of Work" survey, which was co-sponsored by the MetLife Foundation and the nonprofit Civic Ventures, found that leading-edge boomers (ages 51-59) are the most passionate about wanting to serve their communities.[5]

- Many support public policy changes to encourage social service work by elders.
- [2002] 59% see retirement "as a time to be active and to set new goals."
- 56% say civic engagement will be at least a fairly important part of retirement.
- 57% volunteered within the past 3 years; another 21% would commit at least 5 hours a week to volunteering if they received a small fee, doubling the current older adult volunteer workforce from 25 to 45%.
- Working with children was the most appealing volunteer activity.

Civic Ventures, based in San Francisco, describes the baby boomers as "an extraordinary pool of social and human capital . . . . They want to share their experience while acquiring new experiences. They are inventors, organizers, leaders, activists, teachers, and entrepreneurs who attach deep meaning to the notion of giving back."[6] Marc Freedman, president and founder of Civic Ventures, says, "We must create an aging America that swaps the old leisure ideal for one that balances the joys and responsibilities of engagement across the life span. And that could produce a society that works better for all generations."[7]

Another organization that is helping boomers give back is the Social Venture Network.

The Social Venture Network was founded in 1987 by leaders in the fields of socially responsible entrepreneurship and investment. It is a global nonprofit network of business leaders who are committed to building a sustainable world through the private sector. Its vision is of a new bottom line for business—one that respects the biosphere and considers the health of future generations.[8]

Many boomers who have made their fortunes now invest in global initiatives. Exhibit A is the Bill and Melinda Gates Foundation, which is committed to promoting education, public libraries, greater equity in global health, and support for at-risk families. The foundation, based in Seattle, has an endowment of around $29 billion, making it the world's largest philanthropic organization. And the foundation's assets could more than double over the next few years, thanks to Warren Buffet's enormous contribution announced in June 2006. Bill Gates, a co-founder of Microsoft, and his wife Melinda have touched the lives of people in need in all 50 states and in more than 100 countries. In so doing, they have followed the advice shared by Bill's mother, philanthropist Mary Gates: "Of those to whom much is given, much is expected." Melinda and Bill brilliantly follow this advice and no one has done a better job of shining a light on people and causes that matter.

Another role model and one of the top boomer philanthropists is Oprah Winfrey. Through her talk show, her magazine, her foundation, and her speaking, she emphasizes the importance of fulfilling your dreams and giving back. It's the deep midlife question of who we are and what we are here to do that informs her philanthropy and her mission.

"You've got to be in touch with your mind, body, and spirit to live the life you were meant to claim," says Oprah. "When all three are completely engaged, you're able to fulfill your potential on earth. To own the abundant life that's waiting for you, you've got to be willing to do the real work. Not your job. Not your career profile. But heeding your spirit, which is whispering its greatest desires for you. You've got to get silent sometimes to hear it. And check in regularly. You must feed your mind with reading material, thoughts and ideas that open you to new possibilities. When you stop learning, you cease to grow, and subconsciously tell the universe you've done it all—nothing new for you. So why are you here?"[9]

And British business mogul Richard Branson, founder of the multi-platform Virgin brand, has committed about $3 billion to combat global warming over the next decade. He announced his investment last fall at the Clinton Global Initiative conference in New York. Former President Bill Clinton started this annual conference in 2005 to bring together thought leaders to brainstorm on solutions to global issues. Clinton and other former heads of state, including his former Vice President Al Gore, are among the brightest of boomers who are using their power to influence change for the better.

One of the biggest lessons in business is about giving back to your own staff. We have seen this example with JetBlue and many other businesses profiled in this book. Another boomer business that has seen extraordinary success by combining a social mission with good business practices is Tom's of Maine, a manufacturer of toothpaste and personal care products. The company's environmental and social strategies are good for the planet, but they are also good for making money—Tom's has a consistent record of expanding market share, increasing profits, and building customer loyalty.[10]

Tom's has grown to about $50 million in annual revenues and commands 4% of the U.S. toothpaste market, which is dominated by goliaths Procter and Gamble and Colgate-Palmolive.[11] Founders Tom and Kate Chappell offer all 160 employees a one-month maternity or paternity leave, partial childcare reimbursement for employees earning less than $32,000 annually, flexible work schedules, and a childcare referral service. "Show your employees respect and concern," says Tom. "Demonstrate that you care about the quality of their lives, and you'll get loyalty and hard work in return."[12]

Other entrepreneurs who have used their networking skills to create an effective philanthropic network are Pierre and Pam Omidyar, founders of eBay. They created the Omidyar Network, which funds for-profit and nonprofit initiatives to make the world a better place.

Pierre says he founded eBay to help people discover their own power to make good things happen. Their giving includes both private entrepreneurs and social entrepreneurs, in keeping with their vision of creating a balance between private pursuits and public service. Now the couple is using eBay-like tools and systems to inspire creative entrepreneurs who seek to make a positive impact.

The market for socially motivated capital is growing because it blends the rational investor mind with philanthropic motivations. Kevin Jones sold his online business-to-business e-commerce site, Net Market Makers, to a public company 10 days before the NASDAQ peaked in 2000. Then he attended a conference for businesses that made a profit while accomplishing a social purpose. Some of the projects were nonprofits, such as thrift shops and places that employ the homeless. He was thunderstruck.

"There were new investors in the room," says Kevin. "There was new money being put into areas like microfinance, which gives tiny loans to groups of village women in developing countries. You'll get $100 for a breeding goat that can be the start of a profitable small business, or $75 for a sewing machine to start a clothes mending business. Other areas like fair trade businesses, social enterprise businesses, and low-income housing were all attracting new funds and new intermediaries to raise money for the funds. It had all the signs of a market ready to emerge. More deals were happening more easily and more quickly. It was what I'd been hoping for for five years."

Kevin recently formed Good Capital, a merchant bank created to accelerate the flow of capital to socially responsible endeavors. "I can finally use the business skills I've acquired in 30 years of successful entrepreneurship to make a difference in the world," he says. "The satisfaction and contentment I feel around this startup is not like anything I have experienced before. Finally, at 55, it all seems to be coming together. I can have the kind of impact I want to have in the world, using the experience of a lifetime of being in business."[13]

Author Ted Roszak has placed his faith in the baby boom generation since his landmark bestseller about the boomers, *The Making of a Counter Culture*, was first published in 1969. Today he still believes that this generation of boomers has a huge destiny. He outlined those beliefs in a 2001 book called *The Longevity Revolution*. "Every society that moves into the modern era will be an aging one," he says. "This is not something to be thought of only in terms of how many people are reaching the age of 60 and will they reach the age of 70. It's the total social pattern of industrial society. Industrial societies have a big destiny, which is to age. And for that reason, their values will change because nothing changes values more than a serious demographic shift."

Baby boomers "once played the role of reinterpreting youth," says Ted, "but their destiny is to play that same important role in reinterpreting age. The industrial revolution was the opening phase of something more, and that's the Longevity Revolution. But it's not going to be a bump that moves through the society so we eventually go back to what's normal. Once the marketing people got into what they called the Conquest of the Cool, we got the impression that from here on out the essence of modernity is youth. They're wrong—the essence of modernity is aging."

As boomers surrender to aging and acknowledge what is real at this lifestage—whether it is a medical crisis or the richness of grandchildren—they will arrive at a different set of values. Great possibilities will arise from this shift, including a culture of service, accompanying loved ones on their death journey, staying connected, and leaving a sustainable legacy. "It's going to happen with the boomer generation," Ted says. "It couldn't happen when they were young. It's going to happen when they're old. The values of their youth will be reborn in their old age."[14]

Businesses have an opportunity to help boomers create a new social legacy of profound importance. Greater longevity gives boomers the chance; their life experiences give them the capability.

And the need for integrity gives them the psychological incentive. You don't need a billion-dollar philanthropic organization to make a difference; everyone needs to be included. A few women in SeniorNet who belonged to a book club shifted their focus to organizing a book drive for women in prison.

Maya Angelou once challenged a conference of 7,000 Texas business women to "become the rainbow" in someone else's cloud. When Rosa Parks refused to give up her bus seat, she changed the world with one seemingly small act. Each boomer has the same opportunity to make a difference, large or small. The third act of the boomers' lives will be their defining one. They have the opportunity to see their spirits flourish and find their generational voice again—with their time, their experience, their sense of adventure, and their desire to leave the world a better place.

Endnotes

1. Michael S. Malone (panel discussion, Silicon Valley Boomer Venture Summit, Santa Clara, CA, June 21, 2005).
2. Rick Moody, interview by author, 2005.
3. Will Lester, "Retirement? 'No Way,' Many Say," *CBS News*, March 9, 2005, http://www.cbsnews.com/stories/2005/03/09/national/main679160.shtml.
4. Angelica Medaglia, "For Retirees, a Journey of Many Returns," *Boston Globe*, February 3, 2005.
5. Carolyn Said, "Boomers Want to Aid Others; Survey Finds They Envision Retirement Jobs that Do Good," *San Francisco Chronicle*, June 17, 2005. Among the findings: Only 2.6% of the funds going into AmeriCorps are for older Americans, while 75% of those for Senior Corps are restricted to low-income seniors. *Ibid.*
6. Civic Ventures, *Civic Ventures Brochure*, 2005.
7. Marc Freedman, "The Selling of Retirement, and How We Bought It," *Washington Post*, February 6, 2005.
8. Social Venture Network, http://www.svn.org/.
9. "This Month's Mission," *O*, April 2005.
10. Jacquelyn A. Ottman, "Two Companies That Do Everything Right," in *Green Marketing: Opportunity for Innovation* (NTC-McGraw-Hill, 1998), http://www.greenmarketing.com/Green_Marketing_Book/Chapter10.html.
11. Al Lewis, "When Moral Opposites Attract," *The Denver Post*, September 27, 2005, C-01.

12. Jacquelyn A. Ottman, "Two Companies That Do Everything Right," in *Green Marketing: Opportunity for Innovation* (NTC-McGraw-Hill, 1998), http://www.greenmarketing.com/Green_Marketing_Book/Chapter10.html.

13. Kevin Jones, interview by author, 2005.

14. Theodore Roszak, interview by author, October 17, 2005.

Appendix A

THE CONNECTED
BOOMER

Unlike their predecessors, boomers are relatively comfortable with technology and the Internet. They've experienced the online revolution at work and, like other working-age groups, they have taken the technology home with them. Today, in the United States, 66% of people between the ages of 50 and 64 are online—that's 33.2 million people. Boomers online in the U.K., Germany, and Japan are also growing in numbers.[1] These numbers are expected to grow steadily as the younger boomers who are even more plugged in turn 50; by 2008 it is estimated that 40.7 million boomers—73.7%—will be officially wired.

TABLE A.1 INTERNET USAGE IN THE U.S., 50–64-YEAR-OLDS

Year	Million	% of Total Age Group Online
2003	28.6	61%
2004	30.7	63.2%
2005	33.2	65.9%
2006	35.6	68.3%
2007	38.1	70.9%
2008	40.1	73.7%

Source: Internet Usage in the U.S., 50–64-year-olds (by millions) and (by percentage), eMarketer, Seniors Online, p. 5.

In fact, those born between 1946 and 1964 represent the largest age group online today, making up almost one-third of the total online population.[2] The younger boomers are increasingly more wired than the older, with nearly 70% of those age 40 to 44 online, compared to 55% of the first-wave boomers, who make up the 55–59 age group. As the younger population ages, it will stay connected; while the percent of total Internet users grows by 2–3% per year, it grows by 7–8% for people age 50 and older.[3]

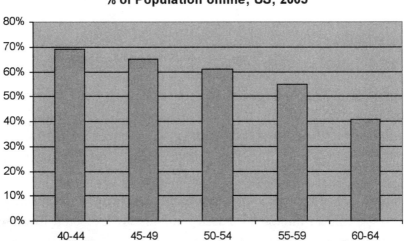

FIGURE A.1 PERCENTAGE OF THE POPULATION ONLINE IN THE U.S. IN 2005
Source: Pew Internet & American Life Project, America's Online Pursuits, 22 December 2003

How Boomers Spend Their Time Online

Boomers take advantage of all the Internet has to offer, from news to email to online purchases.

- Connecting with others through email stands first on the list.
- Gathering information about everything from the weather to health concerns rates high as well.

- Online shopping also tops the list, as boomers, who feel relatively secure with the Internet and have shopping in their blood, hit the virtual malls. Boomers have more money to spend and are willing to spend it online.

TABLE A.2 ONLINE ACTIVITIES OF WIRED 40–58-YEAR-OLDS (U.S.) 2004 (AS A PERCENTAGE OF RESPONDENTS)

Email	98%
Search engines	93%
News	80%
Checking weather	80%
Travel arrangements or getting directions	74%
Shopping	66%
Banking	51%
Instant messaging	44%
Playing games	45%
Listening to or downloading music	23%
Trading or checking investments	23%

Source: eMarketer, Seniors Online, p. 12.

Gathering Information

Finding information is one of the boomers' favorite online activities. With 75% of wired boomers getting their news online and 79% visiting search engines regularly,[4] boomers are looking more and more to the Internet as their prime source of information. The hot topics? According to eMarketer, an online marketing firm, health, real estate, and financial information will be the hot buttons in the information category for wired boomers.

Here's to Your Health

In an age of declining trust in the healthcare system, the abundance of health information online has allowed online populations to take more control of their healthcare. Boomers lead the charge in researching everything from prescription drugs to weight loss and illnesses.

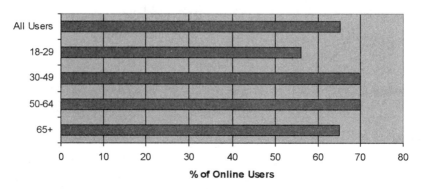

FIGURE A.2 RESEARCHING HEALTH INFORMATION ONLINE
Source: Pew, "Online Pursuits," p. 25

The Virtual Home

Researching real estate options online is another popular activity among boomers. Searching for second homes becomes a popular activity for newly retired boomers and the Internet is often the first place they go for preliminary information.

- According to the National Association of Realtors, more than half of homebuyers overall use the Internet frequently as part of their research.

- Twenty-eight percent of Internet users age 50 and older hit the Internet as their first means of real estate research.[5]

Financial Services

"Financial and transaction activities such as online banking, investing, and online auctions have grown more than any other genre of activity," reports the Pew Internet and American Life Project.[6] This holds true for boomers as well, as they flock to the Net for financial information and transactions. Of the 50–58 age group, fully 49% say they use the Internet to find financial information.

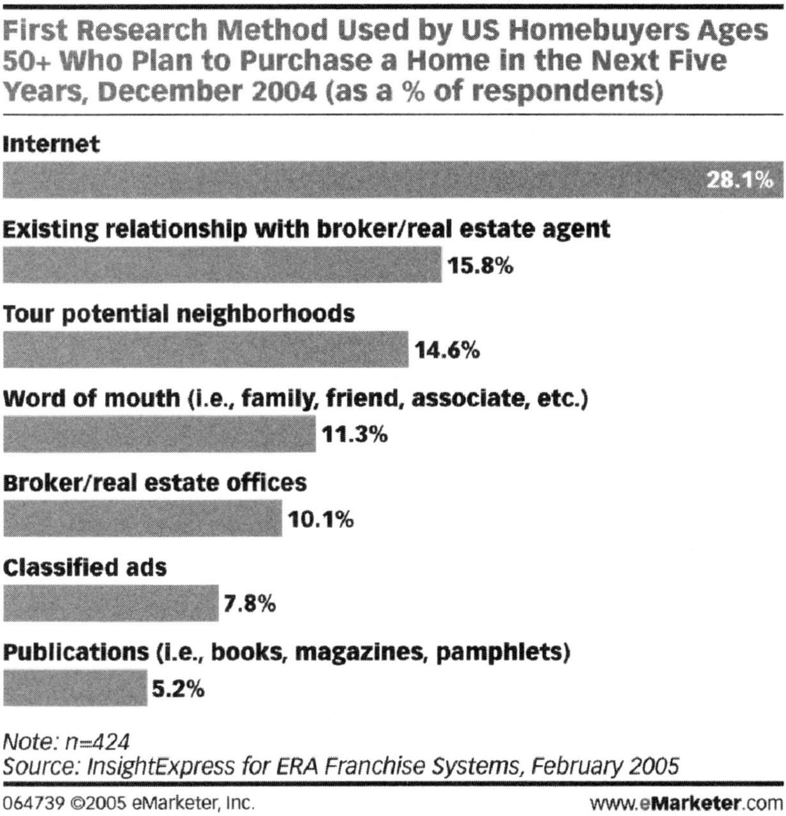

First Research Method Used by US Homebuyers Ages 50+ Who Plan to Purchase a Home in the Next Five Years, December 2004 (as a % of respondents)

Internet

28.1%

Existing relationship with broker/real estate agent

15.8%

Tour potential neighborhoods

14.6%

Word of mouth (i.e., family, friend, associate, etc.)

11.3%

Broker/real estate offices

10.1%

Classified ads

7.8%

Publications (i.e., books, magazines, pamphlets)

5.2%

Note: n=424
Source: InsightExpress for ERA Franchise Systems, February 2005

064739 ©2005 eMarketer, Inc.   www.e**Marketer**.com

FIGURE A.3 FIRST RESEARCH METHOD USED BY U.S. HOMEBUYERS AGE 50 AND OLDER WHO PLAN TO PURCHASE A HOME IN THE NEXT FIVE YEARS
Source: InsightExpress for ERA Franchise Systems, February 2005

TABLE A.3 GROWTH IN ONLINE BANKING 2002–2004

The percentage of those in each group with Internet connections who have tried online banking.

	Oct. 2002	Nov. 2004
All Internet users	30%	44%
Generation Y (ages 18–27)	29%	38%
Generation X (ages 28–39)	34%	60%
Younger baby boomers (40–49)	**33%**	**42%**
Older baby boomers (50–58)	**26%**	**49%**

Making Connections

Even as the world grows smaller, we often feel farther away from one another. Children live thousands of miles away, old friends move, and those who retire often lose many of their social networks. More boomers are turning to the Internet to maintain old connections and to make new ones. Email remains by far the most popular communication tool for all Internet users, and boomers are no exception; 98% of wired boomers in the 40–58 age group report using email regularly to connect with family and friends, while instant messaging, normally considered a "younger" pursuit, reaches 44% of this population.[7]

Who Needs the Mall? Boomers and Online Purchasing

Boomers were born to shop and Internet purchasing has helped them in this practice. With 76% of wired boomers making online purchases,[8] the 45–64 age group makes up 33% of all online buyers.[9] And they're spending more money than younger populations as well, with 37% of those age 45 to 64, but only 32% of other users who have made purchases online, spending more than $250.[10] Travel services, such as purchasing airline tickets and making hotel reservations, are the most popular purchases. Although the majority of boomers feel comfortable with such online transactions, credit card fraud does raise the alarm among some shoppers, especially women.[11]

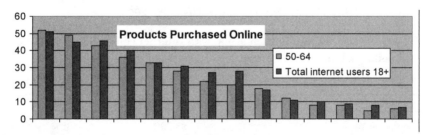

FIGURE A.4 PRODUCTS PURCHASED ONLINE
Source: *Vertis, January 2005*, 064751 ©2005 eMarketer, Inc.
www.eMarketer.com

Silver Technology

As the first generation to grow up in the technology revolution, boomers remain active users of gadgets and doodads; in addition to the obvious home computer, Internet users in the 45–64 age group own more fax and copy machines, large-screen TVs, and satellite dishes than other age groups,[12] and more than 50% of older online boomers use broadband.[13]

TABLE A.4 TECHNOLOGY PRODUCTS USED AT HOME BY WORKING AND RETIRED U.S. ADULTS OCTOBER–NOVEMBER 2004 (AS A PERCENTAGE OF RESPONDENTS)

	Mobile Phone	Personal Computer	DVD Player	Direct Internet Access	Digital Camera	Video Camera
Working						
45–54	84%	88%	88%	82%	55%	52%
55+	79%	73%	71%	73%	43%	47%
Retired						
45–64	69%	76%	66%	68%	45%	44%
65–75	64%	64%	59%	58%	35%	29%

Source: eMarketer, Online Seniors, p. 15 (ACNielsen for AXA Group, January 2005)

Aging Related Technologies

New tech companies aimed specifically at the aging population are emerging in the marketplace. With "smart" products that improve connectivity and allow 24/7 access, millions of people over age 50 who care for their elderly parents worldwide can breathe easier. Products such as talking-pill bottles, teapots that alert loved ones if not used, and computers that give advice for more than 45 health conditions are now available from a handful of companies.[14] (Refer to Chapter 10, "Financing Your Dream," for more details.) As the boomer population ages, the demand for these products will grow.

More Applications That Boomers Will Buy

- Smart, quick connectivity—connecting with the kids, friends, and family

- Smart home—*Not just the big TV and my Tunes*—residential wireless sensors, security, maintenance issues, fire/theft plus taking care of Mom's and Dad's home and/or your second home

- Smarter mobile devices—wireless with voice recognition, location based services, everyday micro commerce

- Smart auto—dashboard technology, aware driving, and illumination

- Smart aids—RFID and GPS—finding lost items

- Consumer assistive technologies—for easy travel, shopping, staying socially connected, financial management, lifelong learning, and lots more . . .

Source: SmartSilvers Alliance power point

Marketing to Boomers Online

Simplicity is the golden rule for creating websites for older audiences. Companies looking to attract aging boomers will need to consider the "age friendliness" of their sites: the look, the information, and the language. Here are the top four things your company can do to attract (and keep) older audiences to your site:

1. *Simplify the look.* The older you get, the less impressed you are by flashing lights and animated images. In fact, research shows that flashing pictures disrupt older people's concentration and make it difficult for them to make decisions.[15]

2. *Simplify the message.* Don't try to cram a library of information onto your website. Rather, highlight the core of your message using clear, everyday language. Steer clear of tech or industry

jargon that older users may not be familiar with.[16] Some experts also suggest couching your message in positive terms.[17]

Most Common Grumbles of Older Website Users (40+)

- I cannot find what I am looking for.
- I find it difficult to read the text.
- I don't understand what they are talking about.
- I keep forgetting where I am on the site.
- It keeps stopping me from doing what I want to do.

Source: Dick Stroud, "Digital Marketing for the 'Charmed Generation,'" Henry Stewart Publications 1746-0166 (2005) VOL .7 NO.1 PP 36–46. *Journal of Direct, Data and Digital Marketing Practice*

---

3. *Offer information rather than making the user search for it.* "The navigation should anticipate the user's questions and provide a simple way for them to get answers," says Dick Stroud, an expert in online marketing to aging boomers. "Provide the information to aid in making the decision, and clearly label it (for example, Which Product May Be Right for You?)."[18]

4. *Market to their lifestage.* Focusing on lifestages, such as grandparent, parent, or empty nester, allows the marketer to connect with boomers without focusing directly on age.[19]

Endnotes

1. Dick Stroud, "Digital Marketing for the 'Charmed Generation,'" *Journal of Direct Data and Digital Marketing Practice*, (2005) V7 NO.1 pp. 36–46. Figure 2, p. 40.

2. "Baby Boomers Spend More Online than Other Age Groups, Jupiter Says," InternetRetailer.com, August 1, 2005, http://Internetretailer.com/dailyNews.asp?id=15661.

3. eMarketer, *Seniors Online: How Aging Boomers Will Shake up the Market*, June 21, 2005. PowerPoint presentation.

4. Pew Internet and American Life Project, http://www.pewInternet.org/.

5. eMarketer, "*Seniors Online: How Aging Boomers Will Shake up the Market,*" June 21, 2005. PowerPoint presentation.

6. Pew Internet and American Life Project, *America's Online Pursuits*, December 22, 2003, p. ii.

7. eMarketer, *Seniors Online: How Aging Boomers Will Shake Up the Market*, p. 12.

8. "Baby Boomers Spend More Online than Other Age Groups, Jupiter Says," InternetRetailer.com, August 1, 2005, http://Internetretailer.com/dailyNews.asp?id=15661.

9. eMarketer, *Seniors Online: How Aging Boomers Will Shake Up the Market*, p. 19.

10. "Baby Boomers Spend More Online than Other Age Groups, Jupiter Says, InternetRetailer.com, August 1, 2005, http://Internetretailer.com/dailyNews.asp?id=15661.

11. eMarketer, *Seniors Online: How Aging Boomers Will Shake Up the Market*, p. 19.

12. "Baby Boomers," Euromonitor International, June 2003, http://www.researchandmarkets.com/reportinfo.asp?cat_id=0&report_id=65184&q=niche percent20baby percent20boomers percent202002&p=1.

13. eMarketer, *Seniors Online: How Aging Boomers Will Shake Up the Market*, p. 10.

14. "Home Alone," *Economist*, June 9, 2005.

15. Dick Stroud, "Digital Marketing for the 'Charmed Generation,'" *Journal of Direct Data and Digital Marketing Practice*, (2005) v7 NO.1 pp. 36–46.

16. Dick Stroud, "Digital Marketing for the 'Charmed Generation,'" *Journal of Direct Data and Digital Marketing Practice*, (2005) v7 NO.1 pp. 36–46.

17. James Maguire, "Seniors and E-Commerce: Selling to the Older Shopper," *E-Commerce Guide*, September 12, 2005, http://www.ecommerce-guide.com/news/trends/article.php/3547886.

18. Chuck Nyren, *Advertising to Baby Boomers*, p. 33.

19. James Maguire, "Seniors and E-Commerce: Selling to the Older Shopper," *E-Commerce Guide*, September 12, 2005, http://www.ecommerce-guide.com/news/trends/article.php/3547886.

Appendix B

BOOMERS AND MONEY

Introduction

Entrepreneurs, corporations, and investors are interested in the financial situation of the baby boomers. Boomers are in, or about to enter, their peak earning years, and they are about to experience the biggest wealth transfer in history. There are life changes (such as a health crisis, a long-term care situation, a job loss, a divorce, adult children or siblings with financial needs) and world events that may impact their financial security. In this appendix we will share data about the financial picture of the boomers through a menu of information sources, charts, and graphs. These include entrepreneurial ventures (Motley Fool, CBS MarketWatch, BankRate.com, and Financial Engines) and corporate initiatives (Metropolitan Life and Intuit) that are tracking research and providing products and services to this marketplace.

The financial needs of boomers will continue to change over the next three decades. Boomers have consumed and they will continue to consume—and they will also need money to finance their passions, dreams, and retirement.

"Financial issues are family issues," says the American Institute of Financial Gerontology.[1] As boomers become retirees, caretakers, grandparents raising grandchildren, or empty nesters, money issues will be key. Today *retirement*, *inheritance*, and *health care* have different meanings—and raise different concerns—for boomers than for previous generations. With demographics predicting average life spans of almost 100,[2] many boomers will find themselves needing another 35 years of income after retirement.

The material in this appendix gives a snapshot of key boomer issues regarding financial security so as to inspire entrepreneurial ventures. Larry Kramer created value when he came up with the concept for MarketWatch. Now CBS MarketWatch is a valuable tool. Some seniors and increasing numbers of boomers will power up their computers and spend the first three hours of the day working through their money. As the most well-educated and wired generation, boomers will increasingly use the Internet to answer financial questions. Financial products and services is an area that continues to be ripe for innovation and creative development as financial assessment and planning are an anchor application. Websites that tap into the need to stay on top of your money will continue to be useful to boomers.

The New Retirement

"If you look at *Webster's* definition of retirement, it says 'to go away. To Disappear.' Do you think that's how the baby boomer generation is going to view retirement?" asks Ken Dychtwald, President and CEO of Age Wave.[3]

"The game has changed," says the Motley Fool, an entrepreneurial venture that provides a friendly environment in which to manage money. "The old rules don't apply." Social Security and company pensions, both controlled by somebody else, are the old paradigm. Today it's about financial independence, saving beyond pensions, and Social Security.[4]

You're a New Century Retiree

We all are.

The old rules **don't apply to you**. For better or for worse—*mostly for better*—the game has changed. It's time to start **playing the new game**.

It's time to start winning!

Old Rules:

- Counting on Social Security
- Lifelong company pensions
- Kicking back on the porch
- Letting others dictate *your* future

New Rules:

- Investing for *your* future
- 401(k)s, 403(b)s, IRAs
- Staying engaged in life—for life
- Taking control *of your destiny*

—Motley Fool

A retirement study by MetLife identified good health and financial security as being the most important elements of a satisfying retirement.[5] A newer MetLife study shows that baby boomers are increasingly anxious about retirement. Conducted in 2005 with Zogby International, this recent study reports that the number of boomers worried about retirement has doubled, with younger members, ages 41 to 49, more likely to voice concern. Only 66% of those surveyed believe they are saving at the rate needed to maintain their lifestyle, a decline from 77% in 2001.

To take advantage of "the best years of your life," do-it-yourself financial stability is a must.

Are boomers saving enough for retirement? The answer has been a resounding "no" for some time. A full 65% of non-retired people age 50 and older say they are worried about having enough money for retirement.[6] And many of them have good reason. After all, nearly 33% of boomers in the United States, or 25 million people, have saved "virtually nothing" for retirement[7] and nearly 66% of U.S. boomers spend

TABLE B.1 ARE BOOMERS SAVING ENOUGH FOR RETIREMENT?

How Much Have You Saved Toward Retirement?	Have Typically Saved Toward Retirement	Contribute Each Month to Retirement	Have Not Yet Started Saving for Retirement
Working households of younger adults (ages 25–40)	$9,000	$92	21%
Working households of mid-life adults (ages 41–54)	$30,000	$187	14%
Working households of pre-retirees (ages 55 and older)	$60,000	$229	11%

Source: Fidelity Retirement Index

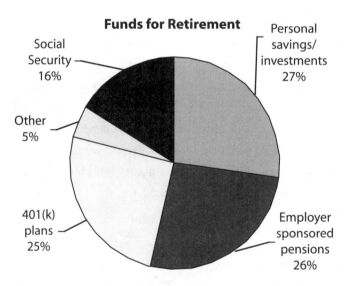

FIGURE B.1 FUNDS FOR RETIREMENT

Source: The MetLife Survey of American Attitudes towards Retirement, Conducted by Zogby International, 2001, Mature Market Institute, p. 5

only one hour or less on retirement planning per month; the other 33% say they don't spend any time at all.[8]

So, how much is enough? Experts say you should aim to maintain your current standard of living, which basically means you need to have as much income in retirement as you did before retirement. It used to be thought that retirees' spending decreased after retirement, but boomers' active lifestyles will change that rule, keeping post-retirement expenses close to those of pre-retirement.

TABLE B.2 WHERE'S THE MONEY?

The Percentage Workers Covered Primarily by Either DBs or DCs[9]

	1978	1997
Defined Benefit Plans (DBs)	38%	25%
Defined Contribution Plans (DCs)	7%	25%

The traditional pension is fading as workers change jobs constantly throughout their careers and companies switch their retirement benefits to employee-managed funds. Americans say they are counting on personal savings/investments, pensions, and 401(k) plans as their primary sources for funding their retirement.[10] Younger boomers who are in their early and mid-40s will depend even less on employer pensions as their main funding source during retirement.

Social Security, once a major safety net for retirement, remains important for lower-income households, with 53% of those earning $15,000 or less relying on Social Security as a primary income source for retirement. There is an inverse relationship between household income and dependence on Social Security: as income increases, dependence on Social Security decreases. Only 2% of households with annual incomes of $75,000 or more rely heavily on Social Security as a primary source of income for retirement.[11] Still, overall, Americans today continue to rely heavily on pensions and Social Security, a reliance that will force many to take significant pay cuts upon retirement, causing financial problems as health care costs rise and life spans increase.[12]

Working During Retirement

Unlike the traditional retirement model, 76% of boomers plan to continue some type of job during retirement. But while only 6% of boomers plan on working full-time, most imagine creating a better balance between work and leisure by working flexible work hours, working part-time, or starting their own business.[13]

Working into retirement serves two general purposes: First, for those who must continue working past age 65 because of inadequate saving or poor investing—a significant number of Americans—working maintains a revenue stream, allowing them to conserve their retirement savings for later.[14] Robert Reby, a financial planner, believes

**WHICH REPRESENTS THE IDEAL PLAN FOR HOW YOU WILL
LIVE IN THE NEXT STAGE OF YOUR LIFE?**

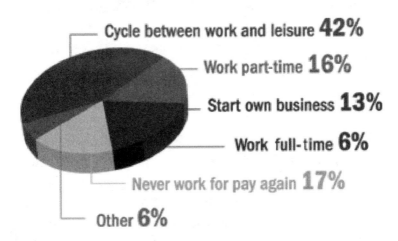

Cycle between work and leisure **42%**

Work part-time **16%**

Start own business **13%**

Work full-time **6%**

Never work for pay again **17%**

Other **6%**

**FIGURE B.2 WHICH REPRESENTS THE IDEAL PLAN FOR HOW YOU
WILL LIVE IN THE NEXT STAGE OF YOUR LIFE?**

many boomers will need to keep working to some degree during retirement. "Baby boomers have demonstrated they're among the greatest consumers in history," he says. "As a result, many of their retirements are going to be underfunded because they lack savings."[15]

Second, many active boomers want to continue working to stay active, maintain social contacts, or try something new, such as lifelong learning. A full 56% of boomers plan to start a new career during "retirement."[16]

TABLE B.3 FINANCIAL PLANNING FOR MEN AND WOMEN

	Men	**Women**
Are you comfortable with your retirement planning?	58%	43%
How much time per month do you spend planning your finances?	4 hrs.	2.5 hrs.
Yes, I will be worse off in retirement than I am now.	10%	25%

Source: ING, Boomers Still on the Brink.

Surveys show that, on average, men spend more time planning their finances than do women and are more optimistic about their financial future than women. In a Gallup poll on retirement, men scored between 10 and 12 percentage points higher than women in the same age group when asked whether they will have sufficient funds for retirement.[17]

Helping women with their finances, therefore, can require a slightly different approach than working with men. When Judy Goldman switched careers from registered nurse to financial planner at age 43, she found a niche in the financial planning business that had previously been ignored. She began focusing on mentoring women to become strong and independent thinkers as they transitioned from married life after either death or divorce. As men typically spend more time on financial planning than women, newly single-again women too often find themselves with little financial knowledge. Using the listening skills she learned as a nurse and her desire to help people, Judy worked to help others "organize their thoughts, goals, and dreams, with a constant eye to reality. The needs, wishes, and dreams of people are the same," she says. "I just used financial knowledge rather than medical knowledge to assist them in their quest."

Long-Term Care

Good health is one of the top requirements for enjoying retirement. Therefore, good health care must be factored into retirement planning. But planning for long-term care—a broad range of supportive medical, personal, and social services needed by people who are unable to cover the costs of their basic living needs for an extended period of time—is something relatively new.[18] The majority of boomers still plan to rely on their families to care for them if they are not able to care for themselves; 85% understand the government will not foot the bill, whereas 63% say their savings will not cover long-term care costs.[19] Formal long-term care, such as nursing home residency, costs between

How do you plan to finance your long-term care?

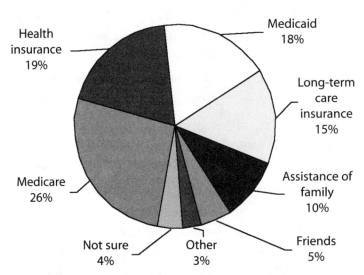

FIGURE B.3 HOW DO YOU PLAN TO FINANCE YOUR LONG-TERM CARE?

Source: MetLife Survey of American Attitudes towards Retirement

$30,000 and $80,000 per year, while home care costs between $12,000 and $50,000 per year. These expenses often drain financial reserves; after only one year of such care, 72% of elderly Americans have lost most of their savings.[20]

Although 25% of boomers plan to use Medicare and another 19% plan to rely on their health insurance to cover costs, neither of these sources can be relied upon to cover the full cost of extended care.[21]

Suze Orman, a leading financial consultant and author, urges boomers to purchase long-term care health insurance. "Long-term care coverage can be costly, but with nursing home residency pushing $50,000 or more a year in many areas, the insurance is well worth it," she says. "I recommend buying a policy when you are between 50 and 60 years old. Wait any longer and you will face much higher premiums, as well as run the risk of being denied coverage if you have a preexisting condition."[22]

Legacy Planning

Rather than considering only the inheritance of material wealth, boomers pay attention to moral wealth, such as values and life lessons. In fact, while 39% of people age 65 and older feel that financial assets are very important to pass on to their children, only 10% of boomers feel it is important to receive money from their parents or pass it on to their own kids.[23]

To support this view of inheritance, new industries are sprouting up to help people create snapshots of their lives as legacies. For example, to compose an ethical will—a written documentation of your life's stories, memories, and beliefs—you can hire a writer to record the story, a videographer to tape you reading it, and even a therapist to help you work through any rough spots. Some financial advisors and lawyers have begun incorporating ethical wills into traditional legacy planning.[24] Bringing the idea of ethical wills to the home computer is Seth Socolow, CEO of Telling Stories, Inc., a software company that makes it easy for "casual PC users" to create digital scrapbooks of their lives (see Chapter 8, "A Family of Our Own Choosing").[25] "It's quite a powerful thing to see people watch their whole life flash before them," says Seth. "There is truly an emotional impact being made by our software."[26]

Helping Adult Children with Their Money

Many boomers complain that their adult children are more child than adult when it comes to money—bad investments, not saving enough, overspending, or just not making enough to cover today's high cost of living. Whichever it is, tough love is the answer, say experts. Parents facing financial requests from adult children must consider not only their own financial situation, but also the possible strains that lending money could put on the relationship.

As boomers, we rejected the materialism of the '50s and hoped to set on a more idealistic course. Then, we went out and embraced every consumer's dream during the '80s and '90s and sent our children off to school with designer T-shirts as we bought multiple cars. Our children learned from us to go out to dinner, take trips and adventures, and use credit cards. Then, as they became college students and adults, they had to take on financial responsibility. It didn't always take.

Suze Orman was the first to figure out the problem, and she talks about the issue on her TV show and in her book *How to Teach Your Kids about Money*. Now boomers choose between bailing out their adult children from credit card overindulgence and saving for their own retirement. The boomers are learning how to set boundaries and, as Suze says, to be "money-wise."

Suze advises boomers to talk to their kids when they are as young as 5 or 6 years old about where money comes from, maintaining a positive yet responsible learning atmosphere for children as they grow up. "Financially coddling your kids when you can't afford to is not a way to show love," she says.[27] "You need to build your financial security before building a college fund. There are plenty of financial aid options for a college student. But there is absolutely no program I know of that will float you a loan or give you a grant so you can pay your own bills when you retire."[28] So the kids need to pitch in.

Internet Resources

eTrade (http://www.etrade.com)

The original online trading site remains strong by offering a myriad of services ranging from stock trading to solid financial information on everything from retirement planning to banking and credit cards. eTrade is also a financier, offering eTrade-branded bank accounts, credit cards, IRAs, and mortgages.

Financial Engines (https://www.financialengines.com)

Managed finances have always been popular for those of us who can't tell the difference between a 401(k) and a DB. Financial Engines uses its personalized financial technology to help individual investors, corporate clients, and financial institutions manage their investments, plan for retirement, and forecast employee stock options. It offers advice and information online, by phone, or in person.

Intuit (http://www.intuit.com/)

Scott Cook created Intuit and it has grown from a startup to one of the world's most influential suppliers of personal finance and small business software and services. It provides a platform of tools that make money management easier. Quicken and QuickBooks are world-leading brands and the first-step place for an entrepreneur to start.

Three software products can help organize business or personal finances:

- Turbo Tax allows you to do your taxes on your computer and submit them online.

- QuickBooks helps small businesses start and manage payroll services, credit cards, and financial management. The class on QuickBooks is often the most oversubscribed class at senior computer centers and local entrepreneurship programs.

- Quicken, which manages personal finances, includes various applications that help with paying bills, managing credit cards, and keeping track of medical expenses.

Motley Fool (http://www.fool.com)

Motley Fool's mission is "to educate, enrich, and amuse individual investors around the world." As one of the first Internet sources for the average investor, Motley Fool has gained a wide audience of those who want basic yet complete information on all things financial—from retirement to credit management. Its Fool's School gives a complete rundown of finance basics while subscription services such as the Stock Advisor and the Money Advisor provide objective advice on making the best investments.

Certified Financial Planners (http://www.cfp.net/)

Working to "help people benefit from competent, professional, and ethical financial planning," the Certified Financial Planner organization is mostly for financial planners but can also help you find a good planner in your area. The organization's free financial planning kit also has solid information about selecting a good financial planner.

Yahoo! Finance (http://finance.yahoo.com/)

The famous Yahoo! website is more than just a search engine. Its financial section connects you to an abundance of information about managing your finances, from planning and taxes to banking and loans. Yahoo! also provides useful tools such as Bill Pay, which allows you to pay all your bills online at one time and in one place. Tools for managing your finances, such as Savings Finder, ask questions about your individual financial habits such as credit card use and then help you find a card that is best for you. The money management tips are complemented with regular columns by finance guru Suze Orman. Yahoo! Finance also offers several international sites, from Argentina to Singapore.

CBS MarketWatch (http://www.marketwatch.com)

Merging television with the Internet, CBS's MarketWatch offers short video segments, online articles, and personalized stock watches. While the personal finance section covers basic investments, retirement, and real estate, the Investor Tools section goes into greater depth with resource centers for personal finance and small business, market advisors, and travel planning. *Retirement Weekly*, an electronic newsletter, sends regular information about all things retirement.

Bank Rate Monitor (http://www.bankrate.com/)

Bank Rate Monitor is a one-stop shop to find U.S. national interest rate averages for home mortgages to auto loans to CDs and investments. Perhaps the most exciting part of the site, though, is the calculator section: more than 80 different calculators can help you figure out how much you'll need to retire, assess whether you should refinance your home, and calculate your net worth.

Institute for Financial Gerontology (http://www.asaging.org/aifg/foundations.cfm)

Financials for boomers and their parents have become so big that the Institute for Financial Gerontology has created a subcategory of financial management specifically for older clients that considers active lifestyle and expanded life spans. Financial Gerontology is a multidisciplinary approach to financial management that examines how money issues relate to middle-age lifestages. The Institute offers courses for financial, social, or legal professionals who work with mature adults and seniors, focusing on the connections between financial planning and issues such as long-term health care, wills, and general financial planning for the new model of retirees.

Lower My Bills (http://www.lowermybills.com/)

Tired of spending hours on hold on the phone with 10 different long-distance phone companies, trying to secure the lowest rate? For anyone who ever felt this frustration, Lower My Bills is a one-stop comparison shop for everything from home mortgages to credit cards to cell phones. Just specify what you're looking for, and the site gives you a list of available plans to compare side by side. You can even sign up for the plan you select directly from the site.

@Prime! (http://www.atprime.com)

AtPrime's website provides financial advice, pension advise, and pension calculators.

Endnotes

1. The American Institute of Financial Gerontology (AIFG), http://www.asaging. org/ aifg/foundations.cfm.
2. Andrea Coombes, "The Game of Life Expectancy," *MarketWatch*, September 18, 2005.
3. Merrill Lynch, http://askmerrill.ml.com/html/mlrr_learn/.
4. Motley Fool, http://www.fool.com.
5. *MetLife Retirement Crossroads Study: Paving the Way to a Secure Future*, February 2002, p.8.
6. David W. Moore, "Retirement Income Is Biggest Financial Worry in U.S.," Gallup News Service.
7. USNews.com, "Today's Retirement Journey," June 14, 2004.
8. ING, "Baby Boomers Not Getting the Retirement Message," Boomers Still on the Brink, http://www.ing.com/us/newsroom/pr/news_090803_1.html.
9. Metlife, *Crossroads*, p. 10.
10. MetLife, *Zogby*, p. 5.

11. MetLife, *Zogby*, p. 5.

12. Fidelity Retirement Index, http://personal.fidelity.com/myfidelity/InsideFidelity/index_NewsCenter.shtml?refhp=pr.

13. The Merrill Lynch New Retirement Survey, http://askmerrill.ml.com/html/mlrr_learn_create/.

14. Kathie O'Donnell, "Some Americans Delaying Retirement: Fidelity Says a Third of Workers Cite Financial Reasons," *MarketWatch*, http://www.marketwatch.com/news/story.asp?guid={3450bfe5-1a03-4cd4-b157-4cb4a3d1ecaf}&siteid=mktw&dist=SignInArchive&archive=true&param=archive&garden=&minisite=, August 24, 2005.

15. Eileen Alt Powell, "Baby Boomers Getting Finances in Order," The Associated Press, February 3, 2004.

16. *The Merrill Lynch New Retirement Survey*, http://askmerrill.ml.com/html/mlrr_learn_create/.

17. David W. Moore, "Retirement Income Is Biggest Financial Worry in U.S.," Gallup News Service.

18. Long Term Care, http://www.longtermcarelink.net/about_longtermcare.html.

19. *The MetLife Survey of American Attitudes towards Retirement*, p. 21–22.

20. Long Term Care, http://www.longtermcarelink.net/about_longtermcare.html.

21. *The MetLife Survey of American Attitudes Towards Retirement*, p. 21–22; MetLife, The Future of Retirement Living; Long Term Care, http://www.longtermcarelink.net/about_longtermcare.html.

22. Suze Orman, "Long-Term Care Insurance," http://biz.yahoo.com/pfg/e41insurance/art051.html.

23. The Allianz American Legacies Study.

24. Karen Cheney, AARP, "Gift of a Lifetime," September–October 2004, pp. 34–35.

25. Tellingstories.com.

26. Venture Momentum, http://www.venturemomentum.com/ezine/may2005issue.htm#hdr3.

27. Suze Orman, "Respect Your Kids Even If You Don't Respect Yourself," http://biz.yahoo.com/pfg/e11college/art031.html.

28. Suze Orman, "Putting Your Children First by Putting You First," http://biz.yahoo.com/pfg/e33college/index.html;Suze Orman, "Retirement or College Savings," http://biz.yahoo.com/pfg/e11college/.

INDEX

singles travel, 59
special interest travel, 58
women-only travel, 57-58
case studies
Elderhostel, 53-55
Generations Touring
Company, 51
JetBlue, 47-49
Level Travel, 55-57
TLC, Inc. (Travel Learning
Connections, Inc.), 49-50
cruise travel, 53
cultural travel, 53-54
intergenerational/family travel,
51-52
market analysis, 44-46
NTA (National Tour
Association), 45
overview of, 41-43
voluntourism, 46
Travel Learning Connections, Inc.
(TLC, Inc.), 49-50
Turbo Tax, 263

U

universal home design, 126-127
Untouched World, 105
urban housing market
luxury condominiums, 133-135
New Urbanism movement,
135-136

V

venture capitalists, 187-192
expectations of, 191
finding, 192
overview of, 186-187
presenting to, 190-191
Venture Wire, 192
verbal marketing cues, 226-227
Viagra, 92
visual marketing cues, 226-227
Vitez, Michael, 203
Voices of Civil Rights case study,
156-157
volunteerism, 235-237
voluntourism, 46

W

The Wall Street Journal's "Encore:
A Guide to Retirement
Planning and Living,"
208-209
Warren, Neil Clark, 90
Watson, Tom, 77
WebMD, 28-30
websites
common complaints of older
website users, 251
as marketing tools, 221-222
weight-loss industry, 4
Wells Fargo Private Client Elder
Services, 172
Weyner, David, 71
widows, 87-88
wikis, 215
Williamson, Debra, 29
wine, 78
Winfrey, Oprah, 237
Wolfe, David, 111
women homeowners, 123
women-only travel market, 57-58
WomenSage, 152-153
working during retirement, 258-260

X-Y-Z

Yahoo! Finance website, 264
Yarnell, David, 188-191
younger men, older women, 95

Zimman, Jeff, 32-34, 200

MANAGING CUSTOMERS AS INVESTMENTS
The Strategic Value of Customers in the Long Run

Sunil Gupta and Donald R. Lehmann

What's a customer really worth? Can you find out, without endlessly complex modeling? And once you know, what should you do with that knowledge? *Managing Your Customers as Investments* has the answers. You'll learn simple ways to get reliable customer value information—in a form you can use. You'll discover how to use it to measure marketing effectiveness, generate improvements throughout the entire customer relationship lifecycle, and improve decision-making. Everyone tells you to manage your business around customers. This book gives you the tools to do it.

ISBN 9780131428959 ■ ©2005 ■ 224 pp. ■ $29.95 USA ■ $36.95 CAN

SELLING BLUE ELEPHANTS
How to make great products that people want BEFORE they even know they want them

Howard Moskowitz and Alex Gofman

Can you remember the world before the iPod? How about the world before chunky tomato sauce or brown mustard? Many of these products came about not through focus groups and polling, but rather through research and development labs and marketers developing the products they knew customers would want, before customers knew they wanted them. Today your customers can actually help you create your next product. Rule Developing Experimentation (RDE) is a solution-oriented learning experience. RDE is the systematized process of designing, testing, and modifying alternative ideas, packages, products, or services in a disciplined way so that the developer and marketer discover what appeals to the customer, even if the customer can't articulate the need, much less the solution. *Selling Blue Elephants* delivers exactly what you're looking for. Discover Rule Developing Experimentation (RDE): the disciplined experimentation process that points you to breakthrough product opportunities in just days. Using this simple, automated, seven-step process, you'll discover what your customers really want, and what they'll really respond to... even if they can't tell you!

ISBN 9780136136682 ■ ©2007 ■ 272 pp. ■ $27.99 USA ■ $34.99 CAN